Acclaim for
HAROLD SCHECHTER,
"America's principal chronicler of its greatest psychopathic killers"
(The Boston Book Review)

BESTIAL
The Savage Trail of a True American Monster

"Yet another essential addition to Schechter's canon of serial murder history.... Deserves to be read and pored over by the hard crime enthusiast as well as devotees of social history."

—*The Boston Book Review*

"*Bestial* spare[s] no graphic detail.... Reads like fast-paced fiction, complete with action, plot twists, suspense, and eerie foreshadowing.... Provides chilling insights into the motivations of a man who killed for killing's sake."

—Amazon.com

"[A] deftly written, unflinching account."

—*Journal Star* (Peoria, IL)

DEPRAVED
The Shocking True Story of America's First Serial Killer

"Must reading for crime buffs. Gruesome, awesome, compelling reporting."

—Ann Rule, bestselling author of ... *And Never Let Her Go*

"A meticulously researched, brilliantly detailed and above all riveting account of Dr. H. H. Holmes, a nineteenth-century serial killer.... Schechter has done his usual sterling job in resurrecting this amazing tale."

—Caleb Carr, bestselling author of *The Alienist*

DERANGED
The Shocking True Story of America's Most Fiendish Killer

"Reads like fiction but it's chillingly real....What Albert Fish did...
would chill the bones of Edgar Allan Poe."

—The Philadelphia Inquirer

DEVIANT
The Shocking True Story of Ed Gein, the Original "Psycho"

"[A] grisly, wonderful book.... A scrupulously researched and complexly sympathetic biography of the craziest killer in American history."

—Film Quarterly

THE A TO Z ENCYCLOPEDIA
OF SERIAL KILLERS
by Harold Schechter and David Everitt

"[A] grisly tome.... Schechter knows his subject matter."

—Denver Rocky Mountain News

**Praise for Harold Schechter's masterful historical novel
featuring Edgar Allan Poe**

NEVERMORE

"Caleb Carr and Tom Holland are going to have some competition
for turf in the land of historical literary crime fiction."

—The Boston Book Review

"Authentic...engaging.... Schechter manages at once to be faithful
to Poe's voice, and to poke gentle fun at it—to swing breezily between parody and homage."

—The Sun (Baltimore)

Pocket Books by Harold Schechter

The A to Z Encyclopedia of Serial Killers
  (with David Everitt)
Bestial
Depraved
Deranged
Deviant
Outcry
Nevermore
Fiend

For orders other than by individual consumers, Pocket Books grants a discount on the purchase of **10 or more** copies of single titles for special markets or premium use. For further details, please write to the Vice President of Special Markets, Pocket Books, 1230 Avenue of the Americas, 9th Floor, New York, NY 10020-1586.

For information on how individual consumers can place orders, please write to Mail Order Department, Simon & Schuster, Inc., 100 Front Street, Riverside, NJ 08075.

FIEND

The Shocking True Story of America's Youngest Serial Killer

Harold Schechter

POCKET BOOKS

New York   London   Toronto   Sydney   Singapore

1951484

An *Original* Publication of POCKET BOOKS

POCKET BOOKS, a division of Simon & Schuster, Inc.
1230 Avenue of the Americas, New York, NY 10020

ISBN: 0-671-01448-X

First Pocket Books trade paperback printing October 2000

10 9 8 7 6 5 4 3

POCKET and colophon are registered trademarks of Simon & Schuster, Inc.

Cover design by Brigid Pearson
Front cover photo courtesy of the author

Printed in the U.S.A.

For my friends
Miklos, Lisa, Andrei, and Alex

The imagination of man's heart is
evil from his youth.

—Genesis 8:21

PROLOGUE

The level of actual violence as measured by homicide . . . has never been lower. . . . It may seem that we live in violent times, but even the famously gentle Bushmen of the Kalahari have a homicide rate that eclipses those of the most notorious American cities. All appearances to the contrary, we who live in today's industrial societies stand a better chance of dying peacefully in our beds than any of our predecessors anywhere.

—Lyall Watson, *Dark Nature*

The longing for a bygone age—for a time when life was slower, sweeter, simpler—is such a basic human impulse that it often blinds us to the fact that the "good old days" were a lot worse than we imagine.

Living at a time of pervasive pollution, we yearn for those delightful preautomotive days when the air was free of car exhaust—forgetting that the streets of every major nineteenth-century city reeked of horse piss, manure, and the decomposing carcasses of worked-to-death nags. Reading about the pathetic state of public education, we grow teary-eyed for the age of the "Little Red Schoolhouse"—completely unaware of the deplorable conditions of nineteenth-century classrooms (according to one authoritative source, "a survey of Brooklyn schools in 1893 listed eighteen classes with 80 to 100 students; one class had 158"). Affronted by the nonstop barrage of media violence, we pine for a return to a more civilized time—conveniently forgetting that, a hundred years ago, public hangings were a popular form of family entertainment, and that turn-of-the-century "penny papers" routinely ran illustrated, front-page stories about axe-murders, sex-killings, child-torture, and other ghastly crimes.

Clearly, there is some abiding human need to imagine the past as a paradise—a golden age of innocence from which we have been tragically expelled. But a dispassionate look at the historical facts suggests that there are few, if any, contemporary problems—from gang violence to drug use to tabloid sensationalism—that didn't plague the past. And often, in more dire and insidious forms.

For those Miniver Cheevys among us who are convinced that they inhabit the worst of times, one irrefutable sign of present-day degeneracy is the terrifying rise in vicious juvenile crime. And in truth, the past few years have witnessed a string of particularly savage murders committed by children. The whole world was aghast in 1993 when two ten-year-old British boys named Jon Venables and Robert Thompson abducted three-year-old James Bulger from a Liverpool shopping center, then led him to a remote stretch of railroad line, where they tortured him to death before placing his mangled remains on the tracks to be cut in half by the next passing train.

More recently, our own country has been shaken by a rash of staggeringly brutal teen homicides. In the span of just a few months during 1997, two adolescent thrill-killers lured a pair of pizza delivery men to an abandoned house in rural New Jersey and gunned them down for fun; an ex-altar boy and his fifteen-year-old girlfriend butchered a middle-aged man in Central Park; an eleven-year-old schoolboy selling door-to-door candy for his P.T.A. fund-raiser was raped and strangled by a fifteen-year-old neighbor; seven Mississippi high-schoolers were gunned down by a rampaging classmate (who began his murder spree by knifing his mother to death); and a fourteen-year-old Kentucky boy mowed down eight members of his high school prayer group with a .22-caliber Luger handgun. In March 1998, just three months after the Kentucky massacre, a pair of schoolboy snipers—ages eleven and thirteen—ambushed their classmates in Jonesboro, Arkansas, killing four female students and a teacher and wounding nine other children.

But even the Jonesboro massacre paled beside the bloodbath that took place the following year at a Colorado high school whose name has become synonymous with the nightmare of juvenile gun-violence: Columbine.

This spate of atrocities by underage killers provoked the inevitable reaction, from a *People* magazine cover story on "Children Without Conscience" to the outcries of assorted pundits, who pointed accusatory fingers at the usual sociological suspects: family disintegration, loss of religious values, ultraviolent videogames, etc. In attempting to come to grips with any cultural phenomenon, however, it helps to place it in a larger context. And even a cursory glance at the annals of crime makes it clear that "killer kids" have always been with us.

Journalist David James Smith, for example, begins his study of the Bulger killing with a survey of British juvenile murder cases, the earliest of which—that of ten-year-old William York, who was convicted of stabbing a four-year-old girl to death— took place in 1748. In our own country, homicidal children have been a subject of psychiatric and criminological concern for decades. In an article called "Youthful Killers," published in *Outlook and Independent* magazine in January 1929, journalist Milton Mackaye cited the histories of the top ten "notorious boy killers" of the preceding five years, whose ranks included "Gordon Pirie, the fifteen-year-old New York City lad who killed his chum with an axe to see what it was like" and seventeen-year-old Frank McDowell, who "burned his two sisters to death and exactly a year later shot and killed his father."

In the December 1959 issue of *The American Journal of Psychiatry,* Dr. Loretta Bender of Creedmore State Hospital published an essay, "Children and Adolescents Who Have Killed," in which she declared that, since 1935, she had "personally known *thirty-three* boys and girls who, before they were sixteen years of age, had been associated with the death of another person." A few years later, in the January 1962 issue of *Social Work,* another mental health professional, Dr. Douglas Sergeant of the Detroit Child Study Clinic, flatly asserted that "homicide committed by children is not rare" and noted that no fewer than "nine child homicide cases" had been referred to the Wayne County Juvenile Court in the previous year.

The redoubtable crime historian John Marr has dug up dozens of U.S. cases involving murderous minors, dating from the pre-Civil War period to the Great Depression. And during the winter season of 1998, Manhattan's cultural offerings included both Paul Simon's Broadway musical *The Capeman*— about a notorious double-slaying committed by a sixteen-year-old gang member in 1959—and a major exhibit of photographs by the legendary cameraman "Weegee," which featured a precinct-house portrait of a sixteen-year-old named Frank Pape, who confessed to strangling a four-year-old boy in

November 1944, "for no motive" (according to the *New York Times*) "other than to try out something he had seen in a motion picture." Other examples abound.

It seems evident that—far from being the product of any particular cultural moment—juvenile violence is a manifestation of something inherent in human nature, of that instinct for primordial cruelty English novelist William Golding portrays so powerfully in his classic parable, *Lord of the Flies*. Shakespeare, too, obviously knew all about children's potential for evil, as Gloucester's bitter observation in *King Lear* reveals:

> As flies to wanton boys, are we to the gods;
> They kill us for their sport.

What Shakespeare doesn't say, but what criminal history makes frighteningly clear, is that the wanton boys who begin by torturing insects sometimes progress to higher life forms: lizards and frogs, kittens and puppies—and eventually to other children.

If examples of juvenile murder can be found throughout American history, so can instances of public alarm—even hysteria—over the phenomenon. Besides our own time, there have been two periods in particular when worries about "killer kids" have been especially intense—the 1920s, the era of Leopold and Loeb, when (at least according to assorted Jazz Age pundits) the whole country was being engulfed by a tidal wave of youthful crime; and the 1950s, when concern over juvenile delinquency reached a fever pitch, and it was impossible to open a magazine or newspaper without encountering a scare-piece like Gerald Walker's "Why Children Kill" in the October 1957 issue of *Cosmopolitan:*

> During the next twelve months, what are the chances that your son or daughter will kill someone? Will the victim be a classmate, a brother or sister, or you, yourself?
>
> Like most parents, you may feel these are unlikely and unnecessarily morbid questions. However, during the year just past, the heartsick families of perhaps a thousand American youngsters had the tragic knowledge forced on them that the unthinkable can happen: Their children had committed murder!

It was during this period—in the spring of 1956—that a man named George Woodbury, a resident of Bedford, New Hampshire, wrote to the Massachusetts Department of Correction in Boston. His letter (which has been preserved in the files of the Massachusetts State Archives) began with a straightforward statement of purpose: "As a professional writer, I am working on an article on Jesse Harding Pomeroy, longtime (1874–1932) prisoner." Woodbury acknowledged that "few prisoners have been more written about" than Pomeroy. Still, he believed that the story was worth retelling, in light of contemporary concerns over youthful crime. "My interest in writing about Jesse Pomeroy," he explained to the officials, "relates to the present-day excitement about juvenile delinquency—as though it was something new."

For fully half a century, Pomeroy had proudly held the status of Boston's most infamous murderer—a figure of such monstrous proportions that several generations of recalcitrant children were kept in line with the same parental warning: "If you don't behave yourself, Jesse Pomeroy will come and get you!" At the time of Woodbury's letter, however, this legendary bogeyman had been dead for nearly twenty-five years and largely forgotten by the public. He remains obscure today—despite a brief but memorable appearance in Caleb Carr's bestselling 1994 novel, *The Alienist*.

Pomeroy's cameo occurs about halfway through the book, when the titular hero, Dr. Laszlo Kreizler, travels to Sing Sing with his reporter-companion, John Moore, to interview the infamous killer. They find him locked in a dank, windowless room at the far end of a forbidding cell block—his wrists shackled, his head encased in a heavy, cagelike "collar cap." In spite of these impediments, the prisoner is deeply engrossed in a book:

> "Pretty hard to get an education in this place," Jesse said after the door had closed. "But I'm trying. I figure that's maybe where I went wrong—no education. I taught myself Spanish, you know." He continued to sound very much like the young man he'd been twenty years ago.
>
> Laszlo nodded. "Admirable. I see you're wearing a collar cap."
>
> Jesse laughed. "Ahh—they *claim* I burned a guy's face with a cigarette while he was sleeping. They say I stayed up all night, making an arm out of wire just so's I could reach him

with the butt through the bars. But I ask you—" He turned my way, the milky eye floating aimlessly in his head. "Does that sound like me?" A small laugh escaped him, pleased and mischievous—again just like a young boy's.

"I gather, then, that you've grown tired of skinning rats alive," Kreizler said. "When I was here several years ago, I heard that you'd been asking other prisoners to catch them for you."

Still another chuckle, this one almost embarrassed. "Rats. They do squirm and squeal. . . ."

Availing himself of artistic license, Carr deviates in this episode from strict historical accuracy. For one thing, Pomeroy was never imprisoned in Sing Sing (he spent nearly all the years of his long incarceration in the Massachusetts State Prison at Charlestown). Moreover, Carr turns Jesse into a figure of almost superhuman evil, a character that owes more to the overwrought fantasies of psycho movies and horror novels than to the facts of real life.

Still, Pomeroy was frightening enough: if not an adolescent Hannibal Lecter then certainly a junior John Wayne Gacy—an incipient serial killer who tortured over half-a-dozen children and butchered two more by the time he was fourteen. At a time when juvenile misbehavior was epitomized in the popular mind by the shenanigans of Tom Sawyer—conning his chums into whitewashing a fence—and the comical hijinks of Peck's Bad Boy, the atrocities of young Jesse Harding Pomeroy seemed almost unimaginably monstrous.

And even today, they remain uniquely appalling. As any chronicle of U.S. crime proves, there have been plenty of bad seeds scattered throughout our history. But beyond doubt, the most heinous of all was the barely pubescent child-torturer and killer who came to be known as the "Boston Boy Fiend," and whose crimes—committed just a few years after the Civil War ended—would continue to haunt America for the next half century.

PART 1

Dead Eye

1

He had now entered the skirts of the village. A troop of strange children ran at his heels, hooting after him, and pointing at his gray beard. . . . The very village was altered; it was larger and more populous. There were rows of houses which he had never seen before, and those which had been his familiar haunts had disappeared. Strange names were over the doors—strange faces at the windows—everything was strange.

—Washington Irving, "Rip Van Winkle"

AUGUST 1, 1929

Dressed in the street clothes they had given him—a shabby gray suit, its baggy pants supported by galluses; a rumpled white shirt, its collar too small to button; an old silk tie that dangled halfway down his chest; and a grotesque, checkered cap that sat on his head like an enormous mushroom—he emerged into the sun-drenched prison yard. In his right hand, he clutched a paper-wrapped bundle about the size of a shoebox. His entire fund of worldly possessions was inside: a Bible, two or three poetry books, a few legal documents, some old, dog-eared letters.

Above him—patrolling the walls and stationed in the armored cupola of the gray, stone rotunda—the rifle-wielding guards peered down curiously at the spectacle below.

A crowd of journalists—reporters, photographers, representatives of international wire services—had assembled in the yard. At the first glimpse of the shambling old man—his face half-hidden by the brim of his comically oversized cap—they began calling his name, snapping pictures, shouting questions.

He pulled the brim lower over his eyes, tightened his mouth into a deep frown, and allowed the attendants to hurry him past the crowd and toward the rotunda.

The clamor of the mob was deeply unnerving. Still, their presence was a source of some satisfaction—a confirmation of his celebrity. He had always taken pride in his status as "America's most famous lifer," in the awed looks he drew from new inmates when they caught their first glimpse of him. Lately, however, a whole generation of fresh fish had begun to filter inside—young punks who neither knew nor cared anything about the old man everyone called "Grandpa." And when somebody told them who he was, they just shrugged, sneered, or looked utterly blank. His name—once so notorious that its mere mention could induce shudders in impressionable children—meant nothing to them.

Now—sullen-tempered as ever—he cursed under his breath as he waited for the attendants to unlock the double-barred doors and usher him into the reception room. Inside, Warden Hogsett and a few other officials were waiting. Ignoring the warden, he grumbled a few words of farewell to the chaplain.

Then—at precisely 11:35 A.M.—Hogsett nodded to the attendants, the screen door was thrown open, and—flanked by two officers, Joseph O'Brien and William Robinson—he stepped out into the world.

It was the first time in more than fifty years that he had breathed the air beyond the dark walls of the state prison. Everyone involved in sending him there was long gone—the judge who had tried him, the attorney general and D.A. who had prosecuted him, the governor who had spared his life and sentenced him to a living death instead. He had survived them all. That was another source of satisfaction. The thought of it nearly brought a smile to his face. If it had, the sight would almost certainly have caused his captors to take notice. No one in all the years of his incarceration had ever seen him smile.

A small sedan was waiting in the cobblestoned square outside the main iron gate. So was an enormous crowd of curiosity-seekers—more than one thousand people in all. They had been there since daybreak. At various points throughout the morning, policemen from Station Fifteen in City Square, Charlestown, had tried to disperse them. But the milling crowd would only wander a short distance away, then gather again in front of the prison as soon as the officers had left.

Even *he* was taken aback by the size of the crowd. Evidently, the public had not forgotten his name after all.

"Get in, Jesse," said Officer Robinson, motioning him toward the open door.

He knew all about motorcars, of course. During the past dozen years—ever since the granite door of his tiny cell had been opened and he had been allowed to emerge, Lazarus-like, from his tomb—he had seen one or two official automobiles in the prison yard. Still, he had never actually ridden in one. So unfamiliar was he with the procedure that, as he stepped onto the running board, his foot slipped, he smacked his head against the top of the doorframe, and his cap tumbled onto the cobblestones. He stooped to retrieve it, mashed it back down onto his head, and—ducking into the car—sank into the rear right seat.

Several squealing children ran up to the sedan, pointing up at the rear window as they capered and laughed. He put his face to the glass and glared down at them. Their laughter died instantly, and they scurried away. His face always had the power to frighten little children and, if anything, it had grown even more unsettling over the years—the heavy jaw jutting grotesquely; the down-turned mouth made even more baleful-looking by the drooping walrus moustache; the left eye now filmed by a cataract; and the right one—its pupil a dead, milky white—as profoundly disconcerting as ever.

Officer Robinson slammed the rear door closed and climbed into the passenger seat. The engine roared. An escort of three motorcycle officers cleared a path. The convoy was on its way.

Measured in space, the trip to his new home was relatively short—a distance of around forty miles. But the leap through time was almost inconceivably vast—every bit as staggering as Rip Van Winkle's supernatural experience in the ghost-haunted Kaatskills, or the fantastic voyage of H. G. Wells's imaginary time-traveler. When he had last set eyes on the outside world, Ulysses S. Grant was president and Victoria queen. The whole country was in an uproar over the Custer massacre. The telephone hadn't been invented. And the neighborhoods of Charlestown, as one commentator described them, offered unbroken vistas of "muddy streets, horse-cars, oil-lamps, and two-story frame shacks."

Now, fifty-three years and one global war later, he was traveling through a world of telecommunication and transatlantic flight, neon signs and subways, radio stars and racing cars, motion pictures and jazz music, Cubist painting and quantum physics. For the nearly two hours of his trip, he gazed wordlessly at the marvels of modern civilization. He saw steam shovels, airplanes, elevated trains, and thoroughfares clogged with motorized traffic.

The whole world had changed. Except for one thing. The sidewalks were still full of frolicking children. And as the car came to a halt in front of a drugstore—where Jesse would be treated to his first-ever taste of ginger ale and vanilla ice cream in a sugary cone—it was hard for him not to remember those days, more than fifty years back, when he roamed this world freely. A time when the streets were his stalking-ground, and the little children his prey.

2

Pity is not natural to man. Children always are cruel. Savages are always cruel.

—James Boswell, *Life of Samuel Johnson*

Everything about the two men has been lost to history: who they were, where they lived, what they were doing upon that lonely hill. The newspapers report that a bitter wind was blowing on that frigid afternoon in 1871, the day after Christmas. So it is possible that, at first, they could not distinguish the sound—or that, hearing it, they mistook it for the wailing of the wind. Only gradually would they have recognized the noise for what it was: the thin, keening cry of a very young child.

It was coming from the only structure in the vicinity: a tumbledown privy perched atop Powder Horn Hill, lying on the outskirts of Chelsea. Exchanging a look, the men hurried toward the little outbuilding and threw open the door. The sight that struck them caused them to gape in confusion.

It was the half-naked body of a very young boy—three, maybe four years old—dangling limply from a roof beam by a rope lashed around his wrists. His eyes were closed and he might have been dead, except for the piteous sounds that issued from his lips. The frigid air that whistled through the cracks in the deserted outhouse had turned his mouth a ghastly purple-blue. His exposed torso was equally discolored and covered with gooseflesh. As the suspended body spun slowly in the air, one of the thunderstruck men let out a gasp at the huge, ugly welts that covered the child's back.

Pulling out a pocket knife, he rushed toward the little victim and cut him down from the beam, while his companion stripped off his coat and wrapped it around the brutalized, half-frozen child. Gradually, the boy's quaking subsided and he opened his eyes. But the terror he had suffered had left him too traumatized to speak. All the information they could get from him was his name—Billy Paine. By evening, his rescuers had located his home and returned the little boy to his overwrought parents, who wasted no time in alerting the Chelsea police.

With no solid information to go on, however, the authorities were helpless. They could only hope that the abduction and torture of little Billy Paine was an isolated incident.

They had no way of knowing that it was only the first, and by no means the worst, of a whole series of related atrocities—that a reign of terror had just begun.

3

Some months ago, a big boy decoyed a smaller one to an old house in the rear of Powder Horn Hill, where he stripped and tied and beat him in a most cruel manner without any provocation or apparent motive whatever. This fiendish brute has appeared again, for it can hardly be possible that the same villain should have an imitator.
—*Chelsea Pioneer and Telegraph*, February 22, 1872

Two months later, on February 21, 1872, officers from the same Chelsea station were summoned to a weatherbeaten little house occupied by a family named Hayden. In spite of the cold, a small group of neighbors—their faces taut with dismay—had gathered out front. They parted in silence as the two policemen strode up to the door.

The officers found Mr. Hayden inside the dimly lit parlor, surrounded by five of his six children, none older than twelve. Except for the sobbing infant cradled in its older sister's arms, all the children had the same half-frightened, half-bewildered expression on their pale faces. Hayden himself—a stoop-shouldered, twenty-eight-year-old workingman with a sallow face and thin, yellow moustache—wore a look in which anxiety and rage seemed equally commingled.

At his first sight of the officers, he began pouring out a story about his little son, Tracy, who had been lured to an abandoned outhouse by an older boy and savagely attacked.

"Where is he now?" asked one of the policemen, an officer named McNeil.

Hayden nodded toward the rear of the house. "My wife is tending to him until the doctor arrives," he said grimly. "The boy is in a bad way. Come. See for yourself." Leading the way, he ushered them toward the bedroom he shared with his wife.

The officers could hear the sounds even before they crossed the threshold: the ragged whimpering of the child, the soothing words of the mother. Her gaunt, prematurely aged face illuminated by an oil lamp, Mrs. Hayden stood by the bedside, applying compresses to the back of the brutalized boy, who lay face downward on the mattress. After welcoming the officers with a nod, she removed the damp cloths, revealing a row of ugly raised welts across the child's back.

"Let the policemen see what the bad boy did to your face," she said softly, helping little Tracy to sit up on the edge of the mattress.

The sight of the seven-year-old's face made the two officers wince. He looked like a fighter who had just suffered a terrible beating in the ring: eyes swollen and badly discolored, nose broken, upper lip split. Two of his front teeth had been knocked out.

It took a while for the officers to extract a coherent statement from the terrorized boy—and even then, important details were lacking, most crucially a precise description of the assailant. According to Tracy, he had been playing in the street when he was approached by a "big boy with brown hair" who had asked if he "wanted to go to Powder Horn Hill to see the soldiers." When Tracy agreed, the big boy had led him to an abandoned outhouse on top of the hill and set upon him.

Officer McNeil asked him to describe exactly what the other boy had done.

"He stripped me and put a handkerchief in my mouth," Tracy answered in a tremulous voice. "Then he tied up my feet and hands and tied me to a beam. Then he whipped me with a hard stick and said"—here, the boy's voice dropped so low that his listeners couldn't make out the rest of the sentence.

"*What* did he say, lad?" McNeil coaxed.

Tracy cleared his throat and, lisping through his missing front teeth, replied:

"He said he would cut my penis off."

Like Tracy Hayden, Robert Maier was enticed from the safety of his Chelsea neighborhood by an offer that no eight-year-old boy could possibly resist. On May 20, 1872—three months after the Hayden incident—Maier was approached by an older, brown-haired boy, who—after striking up a conversation with Robert—asked if he would like to go to see Barnum's circus.

When Maier eagerly agreed, the older boy led him toward Powder Horn Hill. On the way, they passed a pond, its surface clotted with scum. All of a sudden, the stranger grabbed Robert by the arm and tried to push him into the pond. Struggling wildy, the little boy managed to break free of the stranger's grasp.

"Why'd you do that?" Robert cried.

In response, the big boy cuffed him on the side of the head, then dragged the stunned and sobbing victim to an isolated outhouse, where he stripped off Maier's clothing, shoved a milk cork in his mouth, and tied him to a post with a length of clothesline. Laughing and jumping, he whipped the helpless boy with a stick. Then he pulled the cork from his mouth and forced him to say bad things—"prick," "shit," "kiss my ass."

Hearing these profanities seemed to make the boy even more excited. He began to breathe very hard and fiddle with himself through his coveralls. After a few minutes he gave a great shuddering moan and leaned against the privy wall, eyes tightly closed, mouth agape.

He seemed to be calmer after that. Freeing Robert from his bonds, he told the terrified boy to put on his clothes. Then he let him go.

By the following morning, word of the most recent assault had spread throughout Chelsea. Over the next few weeks, hundreds of boys were questioned by the police. At some point, a rumor sprang up that the attacker was a young man with fiery red hair, pale skin, arched eyebrows, and a pointy chin adorned with a wispy, red beard. Parents began to warn their children to watch out for this red-haired stranger—never realizing that this Mephistophelean figure was a figment of communal fears: a description, not of the actual perpetrator, but of a devil.

length of rope from his pants pocket, lashed together the little boy's wrists, tossed the opposite end of the rope over an exposed roofbeam, and hauled Johhny into the air of the stinking little outbuilding.

"Now I will flog you!" cried the older boy, his voice quivering with a terrible excitement.

Pulling off his belt, he began to beat the dangling boy all over the body, beginning with his back, then his chest and belly, his thighs, his buttocks. He saved the child's genitals for last. The torture lasted for nearly ten minutes.

All at once, the older boy let out a long, tremulous moan. His frenzy subsided. He stood in the murk of the outhouse, panting heavily, as though he had just run a great distance. Then he lowered the sobbing boy to the ground, undid the rope from his wrists, and hissed: "If you leave this place, I will come back and slit your throat."

Coiling up the rope, he slipped it back into his pocket, threw open the outhouse door, and vanished.

For the next two hours, Johnny Balch—his body mottled with black-and-blue welts—lay naked on the floor of the outhouse. It wasn't until nearly five o'clock that a passerby named Frank Kane heard his muffled cries and—after helping the half-conscious boy back into his clothes—carried him all the way to the City Marshal's office. A physician was called, a statement taken, and an officer sent to notify Johnny's parents, who—fearing that some terrible mishap had befallen their missing son—had begun their own frantic search of the neighborhood.

The story of the savage attack on little Johnny Balch was carried by newspapers throughout the area. Under the headline, "Unaccountable Depravity," the *Boston Evening Transfer* of July 23, 1872, reported that "In the Common Council last night, Mr. Rogers of Ward 4, alluding to the diabolical outrage committed upon the Balch boy and to the nearly similar case of two or three months ago involving young Robert Meier, offered an order appropriating $500 as a reward for the arrest and conviction of the miscreant or miscreants. The order was unanimously adopted."

The so-called "Boy Torturer" now had a bounty on his head. And there were plenty of people eager to collect it. Within the week, armed vigilance committees had formed throughout Chelsea.

As the *Boston Globe* reported in a July 28 story headlined "A Fiendish Boy": "The public are considerably excited—and it is a good thing for the inhuman scamp that his identity is unknown just now."

5

†

My mother groaned! my father wept.
Into the dangerous world I leapt,
Helpless, naked, piping loud;
Like a fiend hid in a cloud.
—William Blake, "Infant Sorrow"

On the morning after the attack on the Balch boy, a woman named Ruth Ann Pomeroy sat at the kitchen table of the run-down little house she rented in Charlestown, reading about the incident in the local newspaper. When she looked up from the page, her face was deeply creased with concern.

The most generous of observers would have been hard-pressed to find anything complimentary to say about that face. The features—heavy jaw, jutting brow, narrow eyes, sullen mouth—had been exceptionally coarse even in her youth. Now, at the age of thirty-three, she could have easily passed for a man. A particularly dour and evil-tempered man.

Part of the harshness that suffused her face could have been traced to the tribulations of her life. She was a shrewd and industrious woman—but even so, she had always struggled bitterly to make ends meet. Now that she and her husband, Thomas, had split up, she would have to work even harder.

She had finally gotten rid of the drunken brute just a few days earlier. It happened after their younger son, Jesse, ran away from home again following a savage argument with the old man. Thomas had tracked the boy down, dragged him home, then—after ordering him upstairs—stripped off all his clothes and flogged him unmercifully with a belt. It was almost as bad as the beating he had given Jesse a few years earlier, when he had horsewhipped his son in the woodshed for playing truant.

When Ruth came home from her errands and saw her son's back, she flew into a rage and—shrieking wildly at Thomas—went for him with a kitchen knife. Her husband had fled the house, cursing. Now she was on her own, the sole caretaker of her two young boys.

Not that Ruth herself hadn't punished Jesse on occasion. From his earliest childhood, he had always been . . . difficult. It wasn't that he was dim-witted. Quite the contrary. The boy had a solid head on his shoulders and always seemed to have his nose buried in a book. Still, he was constantly getting into trouble. She remembered the time, about six years back, when he was sent home from primary school for supposedly tormenting the younger children by sneaking up on them and making scary faces. And then there was that time, after they moved to Bunker Hill Street, when he'd made his teacher at the Winthrop Grammar School so angry by tossing a firecracker into a group of little boys gathered outside during recess.

And then, of course, there was the incident with the neighbor's kitten.

For the most part, Ruth had dismissed these accusations as malicious lies. Even as a toddler, Jesse had always made an easy target for people because of his unfortunate appearance. He was a natural scapegoat, that was all.

Still, even she had to admit that he was a handful. She knew he sometimes stole small sums of money from her—money she could ill afford to spare. And he was always running away from home or playing hooky. And then there was the business with the canaries.

Ruth would have liked to brighten up their home with a songbird. But she didn't feel easy about bringing pets into the house. Not since she had come home that afternoon a few years earlier and found the two canaries she had recently purchased on the bottom of their cage, their heads twisted completely off their bodies.

Still, she could not help feeling protective of Jesse. She was a ferociously loyal mother. And he was, after all, her baby boy.

Now, as she sat at her kitchen table, she thought about the article she had just read—about the third dreadful assault committed right across the river by the juvenile reprobate that the papers had started calling the "boy torturer." She was worried about Jesse—and not because she was afraid that he might become another victim.

Not that she *seriously* believed he could be the culprit. Still . . . with Thomas gone and all of Chelsea in an uproar over the "boy torturer," it might be a good time to move.

One week later, on August 2, 1872, she packed up her meager belongings and, with her two sons in tow, found a new place to live—a small frame house at 312 Broadway in South Boston.

6

†

These repeated cruelties on these babyish victims created a tremendous excitement all over Chelsea and South Boston. . . . Of course, the parents were half crazed, and search was made by the most skilled detectives for the ghoul-like monster who seemed to be preying on human blood. The little victims were so terrified that they could hardly give an intelligible description of the vampire who had tortured them; and for this reason, the police had very poor clues upon which to work.

—Anonymous, *The Life of Jesse H. Pomeroy, the Boy Fiend* (1875)

On August 17, 1872, a child named George Pratt became the fifth known victim of the "boy torturer." This time, however, the outrage did not take place in Chelsea. It happened in South Boston—not far from the neighborhood that Ruth Ann Pomeroy and her two young sons had moved into a few weeks earlier.

Shortly before ten on that sultry Saturday morning, the Pratt boy—a frail, pallid seven-year-old who had recently recovered from a bout of the German measles—was walking on the beach along South Boston bay, searching for any treasures that might have washed up onto the sand. All at once, he became aware that he was no longer alone—someone had come up beside him.

It was an older boy, who told George that he needed help with an errand and would reward him with the impressive sum of twenty-five cents. When George agreed, the stranger led him to an abandoned boathouse. Once inside, the older boy struck George a powerful blow on the side of the head, then—after forcing a filthy handkerchief into the stunned child's mouth—stripped him naked and tightly bound his wrists and ankles with two pieces of cord.

"You have told three lies," the older boy said cryptically, his voice trembling with a strange excitation. "And I am going to lick you three times."

In spite of the stifling air inside the little building, the seven-year-old was shivering with terror. But his fear only seemed to make his attacker more aroused. In the dimness, George could not make out the older boy's features. But he could hear him panting with excitement.

Very suddenly, the older boy tore off his leather belt and—dancing about in a kind of frenzy—began flogging George with the buckle. After a while, he started to kick the boy savagely—in the head, in the stomach, between the legs. He dug his dirt-caked fingernails into the boy's upper body and raked deep, ragged furrows across his abdomen and chest. At one point, he bent his head to the seven-year-old's face and—like a scavenger battening on fresh kill—bit a chunk of flesh from his cheek.

When the little boy began to lose consciousness, his tormentor slapped him awake. The child's eyes fluttered open and—through his tears—he saw the big boy's hand only inches away, holding something slender and shiny.

"Know what I'm going to do now?" the big boy said.

George made a high-pitched, imploring sound deep in his throat. The thing in the big boy's hand was a long sewing needle.

"Little bastard," the big boy hissed and jabbed George in the arm with the needle. The seven-year-old shrieked, but his cry was muffled by the gag.

The big boy jabbed George in the chest. Then in his wounded cheek. Then he pulled the writhing boy's legs apart and thrust the needle into his groin.

George's eyes were squeezed tight with the pain. The older boy started fumbling with George's right eyelids, trying to pry them apart. Finally, he managed to expose the white of the eye-ball. But the little boy's face was so slippery—with tears, blood, and perspiration—that his tormentor's fingers lost their purchase on his skin, and George was able to clamp his lids shut again. He twisted his head and pressed his face against the floor of the outhouse so that his tormentor couldn't get at his eyes.

Suddenly he felt a sharp, tearing pain in the right cheek of his buttocks and realized that the other boy had bitten off another piece of his flesh.

* * *

The outrage committed against little George Pratt (who was discovered several hours after the attack by a local fisherman and immediately rushed to the City Marshal's office) caused a panic among the parents of Boston and its environs. "The public began to lose patience with the upholders of law and order," wrote one contemporary journalist. "There were many grumblings. People favored the creation of a vigilance committee in Boston. Mothers hardly allowed their children off their doorsteps. An atmosphere of terrified suspense settled down over the neighborhoods."

Assuming that only a child suffering from a severe mental deficiency could commit such dreadful crimes, the police rounded up "every half-witted boy in Greater Boston" (in the words of one newspaper story) and brought him in for questioning. But the actual perpetrator was far from "half-witted." On the contrary, he had an unusually cunning mind. It was precisely this quality that made him so dangerous—that and the deeply malevolent passions which, at the age of twelve, already had possession of his soul.

7

My prayer is,
"UTINAM DEUS AUX ILIRIAT BOSTONIAM."
Oh that God would come to the rescue of Boston!
—Rev. Henry Morgan, *Boston Turned Inside Out!* (1880)

Three months had elapsed between the assault on Tracy Hayden and the attack on Robert Maier. Between the latter incident and the torture of Johnny Balch less than two months had gone by. And it was only three weeks later that the "boy torturer" brutalized George Pratt.

This kind of pattern is characteristic of sociopathic behavior. For example, a hiatus of several months separated the first two killings committed by Earle Leonard Nelson—the so-called "Gorilla Murderer" who strangled more than two dozen women during a cross-country spree in the mid-1920s. By contrast, his last two victims were killed within twenty-four hours of each other. The same was true of Ted Bundy, who began his unspeakable career by murdering four young women in the course of four months, and ended it by savagely attacking a quartet of coeds in the span of a few hours.

The "boy torturer" who terrorized Chelsea and South Boston in 1872 was not a serial killer—not yet, at any rate. But he was already a budding sexual psychopath with the sadistic drives (if not yet the physical capabilities) of a classic lust-murderer. Criminals of this ilk typically possess an appetite that (to paraphrase Hamlet) grows by what it feeds on, becoming more urgent—even frenzied—with each new atrocity. And this would prove to be the case with the Boston "boy torturer," whose attacks on little children would grow increasingly frequent—and increasingly savage.

It was during his next attack—committed on Thursday, September 5, 1872—that the "boy torturer" first used a knife.

His victim was a six-year-old child named Harry Austin, who was taken to a spot beneath a railroad bridge in South Boston. There, his tormentor stripped off his clothes, beat him black-and-blue, then pulled out a pocket knife and stabbed the shrieking child under each arm and between the shoulder blades. Raising the bloody knife high in the air, the older boy capered about his victim, laughing and cursing.

Then, squatting on his haunches, he forced the Austin boy's legs apart, took hold of his penis, and tried to cut it off.

The seventh attack occured less than one week later, on Wednesday, September 11. This time, the "boy torturer" lured a seven-year-old named Joseph Kennedy to a vacant boat-house near the salt marshes of South Boston bay. Once inside the building, he slammed his victim's head against the wall, stripped him naked, and administered a ferocious beating, breaking the little's boy's nose and knocking out several of his teeth. Then, pulling out his pocketknife, he forced the seven-year-old to kneel and ordered him to recite a profane travesty of the Lord's Prayer, in which obscenities were substituted for Scripture.

When young Joseph refused to commit this blasphemy, his tormentor slashed him on his face, his back, his thighs. Then he dragged the bleeding child down to the marsh and—laughing delightedly at the little boy's suffering—doused his wounds with salt water.

Just six days later, on the afternoon of Tuesday, September 17, three railroad workers, walking along a remote stretch of the Hartford and Erie line in South Boston, found the limp and naked body of a five-year-old boy, lashed to a telegraph pole beside the tracks. The boy's scalp had been slashed and his face was drenched in blood. He was carried to Police Station Six, where a physician was called. Eventually, the boy—whose name was Robert Gould—was able to give a coherent account of what had befallen him.

He had been playing near his house when a bigger boy approached and asked Robert if he wanted to go see some soldiers marching in a parade. Robert, who had never seen a parade before, eagerly agreed.

Leading Robert to the railroad line, the bigger boy had marched him along the tracks a considerable distance. Eventually, Robert began to grow tired and confused. He couldn't see any soldiers. In fact, he couldn't see anybody else at all; he seemed to be in the middle of nowhere. He was just about to ask his companion how much farther they had to go, when—with a startling cry—the big boy set upon Robert, stripping off all his clothes and tying him to a pole.

Pulling out two knives, one much larger than the other, the older boy had danced gleefully around the boy, spouting filthy words and slashing his victim on the head, under the eyes, and behind each ear. Then he had placed the blade of the bigger knife against Robert's throat and said, "You will never see your mother and father anymore, you stinking little bastard, for I am going to kill you."

Robert could feel the sharp edge of the blade pressing against his windpipe. All at once, however, his tormentor cursed, dropped his knife, and ran—evidently scared away by the approaching railroad workers, who came upon the bound and bleeding child just a few moments later.

That Robert Gould had become the eighth victim of the diabolical "boy torturer" seemed indisputable. Everything about the crime paralleled the previous outrages. There was, however, a single and very significant difference between this case and the others. Unlike all the preceding victims—who had been too terrorized, traumatized, or simply unobservant to recall any distinguishing features of the culprit—Robert had noticed a peculiar physical detail. Questioned by an officer named Bragdon, the five-year-old described his assailant as a "big bad boy with a funny eye."

"Funny in what way?" Officer Bragdon asked gently.

Robert—who, like other children, loved to play marbles—explained that his attacker had an eye like a "milkie."

"A milkie?" asked Bragdon.

A marble that was all white, the little boy explained, like the color of milk.

Robert Gould's observation would prove to be a breakthrough. For the first time, the authorities possessed a critical clue to the identity of the bloodthirsty juvenile who had been terrorizing Boston for the better part of a year. By the following day, some newspapers were already referring to this shadowy figure by a new and unsettling nickname. He was no longer the "boy torturer. He was the "boy with the marble eye."

8

If thine eye be evil, thy whole body shall be full of darkness.
—Matthew 6:23

The precise cause of Jesse Pomeroy's disfigurement is hard to determine, since contemporary accounts differ. According to one source, he developed cataracts soon after his birth. Another states that he suffered from a severe childhood illness that left him with corneal scars. A third insists that his eye became ulcerated from a virulent facial infection. And several claim that a violent reaction to a smallpox vaccination left him half-blind.

All that can be said with certainty is that, from a very young age, his right pupil was covered with a pale, lustreless film, as though (in the words of one boyhood acquaintance) there was "a white lace curtain" pulled over it. It is also the case that this albino eye rarely failed to have a powerful effect on others. Many people (including, according to certain accounts, his own father) could barely look at it without a shudder. To others—primarily the bigger, crueler boys in the neighborhood—his "marble eye" made him an object of ridicule and contempt.

Of course, it was not only Jesse's unsettling appearance that made him seem so peculiar to his peers. It was his eccentric behavior, too. Years later—after Jesse had achieved such notoriety that the newspapers never tired of running stories about his life and crimes—one of his former schoolmates would recall the days, shortly after the Pomeroy family moved to South Boston, when the neighborhood boys would gather to play. The schoolmate's name was George Thompson, and his reminiscences appeared in a *Boston Globe* article headlined "Pomeroy's Evil Eye."

"He would never kick football with the other boys," Thompson wrote. "When it came to 'choosing up sides' for a game of baseball, Jesse would never consent to be on either side—nor would he consent to umpire." Instead he would sit on the grass "with his eyes cast down, sticking his knife into the sod, absently."

He was equally indifferent to the other kinds of recreation available to young boys growing up around South Boston bay. "When it came to swimming and jumping off cross-trees of schooners and coal stagings into the bay," Thompson went on, "Jesse wasn't interested. He would sit on the wharf, or on the side of the schooner, legs dangling over, quiet and furtive. . . . Sometimes, we wouldn't see him for days and days. Then, suddenly, he would slope onto our playground and get away by himself to resume his old occupation of sticking his knife into the greensward."

The only time Jesse came alive "was when we played 'Scouts and Indians.' " Of course, there was nothing unusual about that—all the boys loved to run around the neighborhood, engaging in raucous games of frontier make-believe. What distinguished Jesse from the others was his preference for villainous roles. While the rest of the boys pretended to be Western heroes, Jesse liked to imagine he was the infamous eighteenth-century renegade, Simon Girty, leading Shawnee Indians on the warpath against white settlers. What seemed especially appealing to him was all "the fun he'd have with the prisoners of war. The running of the gauntlet, and the different modes of putting captives to death"—skinning them alive, roasting them at the stake, slicing off bits of their flesh and making them eat their own bodies.

Not that the other boys were uninterested in bloodshed and gore (Thompson's own personal favorite was Wild Bill Hickock "because he had killed thirty-nine men"). Still, all Jesse's talk about Indian torture seemed slightly excessive, even by the violence-crazed standards of preadolescent boys. Even so, no one imagined that Jesse Pomeroy had any connection to the series of outrages that had churned all of Boston into "a sea of excitement."

Thompson recalled one occasion in September 1872 when he and his chums were talking excitedly about the latest atrocity committed by the "boy torturer," who had already assumed the status of a local bogeyman, a being of almost supernatural evil. Supposed sightings of this diabolical figure had grown so common that, according to Thompson, "the number of boys who had been chased and escaped by the enamel of their teeth at this time was legion."

One of the boys in their group, a strapping fifteen-year-old named Ollie Whitman, claimed that, a few days earlier, he had fallen into the clutches of the fiend and managed to escape only because he had "fought like a tiger and run like a comet." Listening to his tale, the other boys stared at him in awe. Jesse alone had a big smirk on his face.

Noticing this expression, Whitman took a threatening step toward Jesse. "What are you smilin' about, you white-eyed freak," he demanded.

Jesse flushed but said nothing. He was a big boy for his age but still puny compared to the hulking fifteen-year-old. When Whitman, his hands balled into fists, repeated his question, Jesse wordlessly slunk away, while the other boys hooted and shouted catcalls at his receding back.

For as long as Jesse could remember, people had made fun of his appearance—not just his pallid eye but his massive head, his heavy jaw, and the oversized mouth that seemed fixed in a permanent scowl. Even his own father had often muttered comments about Jesse's looks, cursing his son as a "goddamn jack-o'-lantern." That was one reason Jesse was glad the old bastard wasn't around anymore. The beatings, of course, were another.

It was a funny thing. Though the floggings he had gotten from his father hurt worse than anything he had ever felt in his life, Jesse couldn't stop thinking about them. He kept replaying them in his mind, almost as if he took some kind of pleasure from recollecting them. He often wondered if other boys were beaten in the same way. Sometimes, he got so absorbed in his daydreams—about the whippings and the Indian tortures and the look on the little boys' faces when he showed them how it felt to be stripped naked and flogged without mercy—that he wasn't even sure where he was. That happened frequently at school, particularly when the teacher, Mrs. Yeaton, started yapping about some boring subject like geography.

Given his propensity for sadomasochistic daydreaming, it is possible that Jesse was lost in one of his perverse reveries on the morning of September 21. Or it may be that he was simply trying to hide his identity. In any case, he kept his head bent low and his gaze fixed on the desktop when the headmaster, Mr. Barnes, entered the classroom early that Friday morning, accompanied by a burly policeman and a frail, visibly nervous little boy.

The policeman was Officer Bragdon of Station Six in South Boston; the little boy was Joseph Kennedy—the seven-year-old who, less than two weeks earlier, had been attacked on the marshes, where his assailant had flogged and cut him, commanded him to spout obscenities, then drenched his wounds with salt water. With the police under intense pressure to apprehend the "boy torturer," Bragdon had decided to conduct a school-to-school search. Little Joseph was there to identify the suspect. Bragdon would have preferred Robert Gould, the torturer's most recent—and observant—victim. But five-year-old Robert—whose gashed scalp had required dozens of stitches—was still recuperating from the attack, and his parents would not allow him out of bed.

Standing in front of the classroom, Joseph was asked to take a careful look at the other boys. He surveyed the seated students, then shook his head and said: "He isn't here."

All of a sudden, the teacher noticed that Jesse Pomeroy appeared to be staring at his desk. "Hold your head up, Jesse," she commanded.

Jesse did as he was told. But he kept his eyes downcast, so that his pale, lifeless pupil was concealed by his half-shuttered lid. The Kennedy boy took another look at Pomeroy, then shook his head again.

Apologizing to Mrs. Yeaton for disrupting the class, Officer Bragdon and the little boy departed.

It had been a close call for Jesse, but he had managed to escape detection. And then, on the way home from school that afternoon—for reasons that will forever remain unknown—he decided to stop off at the police station and take a look inside.

Perhaps it was his guilty conscience that impelled him to commit such a self-destructive act, though—given every known fact of Jesse Pomeroy's long, utterly incorrigible life—that explanation seems very unlikely. Another possibility is that he was playing a kind of cat-and-mouse game with the police. Certainly, that sort of behavior is consistent with the actions of many sociopathic criminals, who—driven by a desperate need to prove their power and superiority—frequently engage in taunting, "catch-me-if-you-can" gambits with their pursuers.

Whatever his motives, it is doubtful that Jesse himself understood them. He was often at a loss to explain his behavior. His usual response, when asked why he had committed his dreadful crimes, was to shrug and say, "Something *made* me," or "I *had* to," or "A *feeling* came over me."

So it is probable that even Jesse would have been hardpressed to say why—just hours after his young victim had looked him in the face and failed to identify him—he paused on his way home from school, strolled into Police Station Six, and contrived to get himself arrested.

9

†

"What was you and your Ma down at the police station for so late last night?" asked the grocery man of the bad boy, as he kicked a dog away from a basket of peaches standing on the sidewalk. "Your Ma seemed to be much affected."

—George W. Peck, *Peck's Bad Boy and His Pa*

The depredations of the Boston boy torturer were by no means the only crimes involving young children in the fall of 1872, as even a cursory look at contemporary newspapers makes clear. In early September, a seven-year-old boy named William Loftus lured a five-year-old neighbor—a little girl named Jenny Chandler—into a stable. There, according to an account in the *New-Albany Ledger*, "he tried to get her to put her arm under the blade of a cutting machine, in order that he might cut it off." When the little girl resisted and ran away, the Loftus boy grabbed a shotgun, pursued her into her backyard, and discharged the weapon into her body, "filling the poor little girl's stomach with slugs." She died at sunrise the next morning, after clinging to life for more than sixteen agonizing hours.

Just a few days later, Boston papers reported the shooting death of a four-year-old named William Hill at the hands of a sixteen-year-old neighbor, James Duffy, who—while showing off his father's new Colt revolver—accidentally discharged the loaded pistol into his little neighbor's head. On the same day in New York City, another four-year-old boy, Stephen Quail of East Fourteenth Street, was slain when an elderly woman—irritated at the noise coming from the alleyway, where little Stephen and several raucous friends were playing ring-a-levio—threw a brick at the child from the roof of their tenement and fractured his skull.

And then there was the case of the Newark, New Jersey, girl

named Becky Holloway—also four years of age—whose parents were arrested after punishing her "by holding her mouth to the spout of a tea-kettle which was filled with boiling water" (as the *New York Times* reported). "The steam rushed into the child's mouth, scalding her so severely as to threaten fatal consequences."

Even among these assorted tragedies and atrocities, however, the arrest of Jesse Pomeroy drew special attention in the press. For, as the *New York Times* proclaimed—in a piece that ran on Sunday, September 22, under the headline "A Fiendish Boy"—the case of this "mere child" who "delighted in torturing and mutilating other children" was "one of the most remarkable on record."

When Jesse—impelled by whatever unknown motive— peered into Police Station Six that Friday afternoon, September 20, 1872, his eyes immediately lit upon the two individuals who had visited his school a few hours earlier: Officer Bragdon and little Joseph Kennedy. Without a moment's hesitation, he turned on his heels and headed out the door. Back on the street, he bent his steps toward home—a small rented flat at 312 Broadway.

He hadn't gone more than a block, however, when a strong hand gripped him by the arm and pulled him to a halt. Startled, he turned and found himself staring up into the face of Officer Bragdon, who had spotted Jesse hastening from the station house.

Keeping a tight grip on the boy's arm, Bragdon led him back inside the station and brought him face to face with Joseph Kennedy. This time, there was no way for Jesse to keep his most conspicuous feature concealed. "That's him!" Kennedy cried. "I know him by his eye!"

Tearfully protesting his innocence, Jesse was locked in a cell, where Bragdon and a colleague, William Martin, subjected him to a harsh, protracted grilling. But in spite of their threats, curses, and cajolements, Jesse would not be budged. He had never hurt anyone, he insisted. After several relentless hours of questioning, Jesse lost control. "Go away!" he shrieked, his face reddening with fury. He would not talk to them anymore.

Leaving him alone in his cell, the two officers proceeded to 312 Broadway, where they informed Jesse's mother that her younger son was under arrest as a suspect in the Chelsea and South Boston child-assaults. Ruth Pomeroy was stricken. Her son could not possibly be the culprit, she cried. He was a good boy—dutiful, obedient, hardworking at school. Besides, he was only twelve years old—far too young to be guilty of such atrocities. When she asked if she could see him in his cell, the officers shook their heads and returned to the station house.

By then, Jesse had dozed off on his cot. They let him sleep until midnight, when Bragdon shook him awake and began to curse and threaten him again. Jesse burst into tears. At that point, Martin came into the cell, took the sobbing boy onto his lap, and gently explained that unless Jesse confessed, he would end up in prison "for a hundred years."

Jesse finally broke down. At approximately half past midnight on Saturday, September 21, he admitted that he was the "boy torturer."

Early the following morning, he was transferred to the Tombs, where five of his victims were paraded before him. First in line was Johnny Balch, who took one look at Jesse's pallid eye and began to shout, "That's the boy who cut me!" The other little victims—Tracy Hayden, Harry Austin, George Pratt, Robert Gould—rapidly confirmed the identification.

That same afternoon—Saturday, September 21, 1872—Jesse was arraigned in a room crammed with people: spectators, witnesses, newsmen, and family members of both the defendant and his accusers. Five of Jesse's victims—Johnny Balch, Harry Austin, George Pratt, Joseph Kennedy, and Robert Gould—testified against him. Called upon to speak on her son's behalf, Ruth Pomeroy repeated the same story she had told the police—that her son was a good boy who had never demonstrated the slightest tendency toward cruel behavior, etc., etc. Jesse himself—when asked why he had done such awful things—only bowed his head and said that "he could not help himself."

After a brief consultation with Officer Bragdon and City Marshal W. P. Drury of Chelsea, the judge—William G. Forsaith, recently appointed to handle cases involving juvenile offenders—handed down his sentence. Jesse was to be confined to the House of Reformation at Westborough "for the term of his minority"—a period of six years. Hearing the verdict, all three members of the Pomeroy family—Jesse, his brother, Charles, and their heartbroken mother—broke into bitter tears.

As Jesse was led from the courtroom, the mothers of several

of his victims approached Ruth Pomeroy to express their sympathy—a remarkable act of Christian compassion, considering the
horrors that Mrs. Pomeroy's boy had inflicted on their own sons.
As the *New York Times* reported, several of the victims present at
the arraignment had suffered permanent mutilation at the hands
of their attacker, who had deliberately "cut small holes under
each of their eyes, so as to leave them disfigured for life."

10

I hope you will behave up there, for if you do you will get out soon. If you don't you will get a good flogging every time you don't do right.
                            —Letter from Jesse Pomeroy to a friend

Established in the town of Westborough in 1847, the Massachusetts House of Reformation—like other institutions of its kind—combined the features of a prison, sweatshop, and vocational school. Overseen by a board of trustees appointed by the governor, it was designed to turn incorrigible boys into industrious ones through a regimen of forced labor, firm discipline, and practical education—to achieve (in the words of its official charter) "reform through instruction and employment, so that when discharged the boys could enter a normal relationship with society."

Any boy between the ages of ten and sixteen convicted of a crime against the Commonwealth could be sentenced to a term at Westborough. It was also possible for the parents of particularly unmanageable boys to have their sons committed, in the hope that a stint at reform school would straighten them out before it was too late. (One typical industrial school of the era urged the parents of "bad boys" to "send them to us at eight. Then maybe we can reform them in time.") An inmate could be discharged, according to the charter, for only three reasons: "if his term had expired, or he had reached the age of twenty-one, or he was reformed."

Daily life in the school consisted of a stringent routine. The boys arose at 5:00 A.M., made their beds, washed up in the communal washroom. They then trudged off to their morning classes, remaining in school until 7:30, when they proceeded to the dining room for their unvarying breakfast of bread and coffee.

At 8:00, the work-whistle blew, and the boys marched off to their various jobs: in the chair shop, shoe shop, sewing room, laundry, kitchen, or farmhouse. They worked until noon, with a fifteen-minute break at 10:30, then broke for their dinner: mush on Monday, hash on Tuesday, beans on Wednesday, fish chowder on Thursday, meat soup on Friday, beans again on Saturday, and leftovers on Sunday.

The boys were given a half hour to eat and another half hour to play. Then it was back to their jobs until 4:30 P.M., when it was time for their afternoon classes. School was dismissed at 5:30. At 6:30, dinner was served—more bread and coffee. After their meal, the boys were allowed to play for about forty-five minutes until bedtime. The lights were doused at 7:45. Altogether, the average day at Westborough consisted of nearly eight hours of work, three hours of school, and about an hour and a half for "amusement," which—according to accounts of former inmates—more than one boy devoted to intense, yearning daydreams of escape.

Of course, there were other features of reform school life not specified in any official charter: The floggings for even the smallest infractions. The "dungeons" where the most intractable inmates were locked for prolonged stretches of solitary confinement. The brutal persecutions that smaller boys suffered at the hands of bigger ones. And the frantic, furtive, and often coercive sex.

Every time a new boy was admitted to the reform school, the salient facts of his case were recorded in a massive, leatherbound volume titled *History of Boys.* This volume—still preserved in the vaults of the Massachusetts State Archives—offers striking confirmation of the claim made by the *New York Times:* that the case of the Boston "boy torturer" was "one of the most remarkable on record."

On the day Jesse Pomeroy arrived at Westborough—September 21, 1872—there were slightly more than 250 boys at the reform school. Most of them had been sent there for crimes ranging from shoplifting to breaking-and-entering. A significant number had been committed by their own fed-up parents for what the official registry calls "stubbornness." The *History of Boys* is full of cases like that of "William Fitzgerald, 13 yrs., admitted Sept. 13, 1872, because he will not attend school and plays with bad boys against his parents' wishes." Another typical entry reads: "John O'Neill, 14 yrs., admitted Sept. 2, 1872, because he stole two boxes of cigars from a store on Hanover Street." Only one inmate in the entire population—an eighteen-year-old named Richard Moore—had been sentenced to the school for a violent assault on another person.

All of these cases, even Moore's, appear positively trivial in comparison to that of Jesse Pomeroy, whose crimes were of a shockingly different order from those of any other boy in the history of the institution. His official entry in the reform school register—recorded on the day of his admission, when Jesse was still two months shy of his thirteenth birthday—reads as follows:

> The boy pleaded guilty to the several assaults. . . . The statement given at the hearing by the Austin boy was that the Def. met him on a street in South Boston and induced him by offering a small sum of money to go with him under a Rail Road bridge in So. Boston, and when they arrived there the Def. stripped all the clothing off the Austin boy, and with the blade of a pocketknife stabbed him several times between the shoulder blades, under each arm, and in other places. The Dr. stated that "he examined the Austin boy Sept. 5—the day the assault was alleged to have been committed—and found wounds like stabs made by some sharp instrument between the Austin boy's shoulders, under each arm, and penis nearly half cut off."
>
> The statement given by the Pratt boy was that the Def. induced him by the offer of money to go with him to a beach and boathouse in So. Boston, that Def. took all the Pratt boy's clothing off, and then tortured him by sticking pins into his flesh.
>
> The statements made by the other two boys [Kennedy and Gould] were that they were induced by Def. to go with him to some out of the way place, that he took their clothing all off and then cut them with a knife and beat them.
>
> Another complaint was made at the same time by Mr. Drury, City Marshal of Chelsea, against this Def. alleging assaults of a similar character on two small boys [Hayden and Balch] in Chelsea in the months of Feb. and July last. Johnny Balch (about nine years old), one of the boys assaulted in Chelsea, stated that in July last, he met the Def. in the street

and was induced by Def.'s offering a small sum of money to go with him to a locality in Chelsea known as Powder Horn Hill. When they arrived there, Def. stripped all the clothing from the Balch boy, tied him to a post by the hands, and beat him with a rope. All the boys were very much younger and smaller than the Def.

In a population of 254 "bad boys," Jesse Harding Pomeroy was easily the worst—a sexual sadist of remarkable precocity. But he was no fool. It didn't take him long to figure out that the sooner he could prove he was "reformed," the sooner he'd be back on the street. Or that—in Westborough as in other institutions of its kind—severe corporal punishment was swiftly meted out to the misbehaved.

Not that Jesse wasn't intrigued to the point of raptness by the idea of corporal punishment—as long as it happened to someone else. He loved nothing better than to hear all about a flogging, particularly from the lips of a boy who had just received a good one. He would often seek out a recent victim and urge him to describe the experience in detail—exactly how many lashes had been administered, how hard they'd been applied, how much the scourging hurt. At night, Jesse would sometimes lie awake in his cot for hours and bring himself to climax over and over while picturing the torture in his mind.

During the days, he kept out of trouble. When the bigger boys taunted him because of his looks, he did his best to ignore them. The younger inmates tended to give him a wide berth, partly because of his creepy appearance, partly because of the stories they'd heard about Jesse—about the things he had done to all the little boys outside.

At first, Jesse was put to work in the chair shop, caning seats at the rate of one and a half per day. His eyes, however, proved too weak for the task, and after several months at the reform school, he was made into a kind of dormitory monitor, responsible for maintaining order in the sleeping halls. For a temperament like Jesse's—one that derived profound satisfaction from the exercise of power—it was an ideal job. He thrived in this position of authority.

As far as his teachers and supervisors were concerned, he was a model inmate, applying himself to his studies, performing his work with efficiency and zeal. Not that they didn't notice a few peculiarities about Jesse. He seemed to take unusual—if not un-settling—pleasure in the sight of blood: when two boys engaged in a savage fistfight, for example, or someone punctured a finger in the shoe shop, or a child got his hand slashed in the barn. And—at least on one occasion—his teacher witnessed a degree of cruelty in Jesse that left her deeply appalled.

This latter incident occured during the fall of 1873, when his teacher, Laura Clarke, came hurrying around to the front of the school, where Jesse was enjoying a few moments of quiet. She had been tending her garden, she breathlessly explained, and had encountered a big black snake among the flowers. Would Jesse please come and kill it.

Eager to oblige, Jesse had followed her back to the garden, snatching up a stick along the way. After a brief search, he un-covered the snake and immediately began to strike it again and again, working himself up into a kind of frenzy as he reduced the writhing creature to an awful, oozing pulp. In the end, his shrieking teacher could only get him to stop by grabbing his shoulders and shaking him. At last, panting and vacant-eyed, he dropped the bloody stick and stood staring at her sightlessly, as though his mind had drifted somewhere far away. It was a look she would never forget.

Still, even Mrs. Clark had to admit that, on the whole, Jesse was a reliable, hardworking boy, who not only followed all the rules but could be counted on to make sure that others stuck to them as well. Once—when two particularly incorrigible boys en-gineered a breakout—it was Jesse who discovered the escape and alerted the authorities. And good luck seemed to conspire with him. On the morning of May 5, 1873, nearly one hundred boys—fully a third of the population—managed to abscond when the main gates of the reform school were accidentally left unlocked. Nearly all of the fugitives were recaptured by nightfall and subjected to severe penalties. As Jesse later admitted, he might have gone along with the escape himself, but was saved from this catastrophe—which would have left an ineradicable blot on his record—by a fortuitous illness, which had him con-fined to the infirmary at the time of the episode.

Altogether, his exemplary behavior made a deep and favor-able impression on his superiors. As the months went by, Jesse was given free run of the institution, and even allowed to go on several field trips—to a cattle show in Westborough village, a military parade in Framingham.

As the superintendent of the reform school noted in the register about a year after Jesse's admission: "The boy's conduct here has been excellent."

11

No wonder that the workmen at the gas-house at Cambridge shrank back aghast when they found the headless trunk of a murdered man. It was a treasure trove that does not often float on tidal waters.

—From the trial of Leavitt Alley (1873)

With the perpetrator safely consigned to reform school—presumably for the term of his minority—the case of the notorious "boy torturer" quickly faded from the papers. But Bostonians who craved sensational crime stories didn't have to wait long for a new one.

On the afternoon of Wednesday, November 6, 1872—less than two months after Jesse Pomeroy was sent away to Westborough—an employee of the Cambridge Gas Works named Stephen McFadden spotted a pair of barrels bobbing along the Charles River. As they floated toward shore, McFadden noticed something strange sticking out of the larger one. Making his way down to the river's edge, he took a closer look—then let out a startled cry.

The thing protruding from the barrel was a human hand.

With the help of several coworkers, McFadden retrieved the barrels, then summoned the police, who took one look at the contents and immediately sent for the coroner, Dr. W. W. Wellington. By the time Wellington arrived, a large, excited crowd had gathered around the barrels, whose staves enclosed a ghastly trove.

Inside the larger one, packed among a load of horse manure and sawdust, was a man's decapitated trunk, both legs chopped off at the thighs. Whoever had butchered and disposed of the body had taken few precautions to conceal the victim's identity. The torso was still clothed in a suit, the pockets of which were full of personal items—keys, pieces of scrip, an engraved pocket

47

watch. The smaller barrel contained the missing head, its features perfectly recognizable. The murdered man—who had died from an axe-blow to the back of his skull—turned out to be a prosperous merchant and landlord named Abijah Ellis, missing since the previous night.

A more thorough search of the barrels turned up a vital clue— a piece of brown paper with the words *P. Schouller, No. 1049 Washington Street* printed on it. Questioned by the police, Schouller—a reputable manufacturer of billiard tables—revealed that the sweepings from his factory were generally carted away by a local teamster named Leavitt Alley, who used the sawdust to carpet the floor of his stable.

Alley, it turned out, had a direct link to the murdered man. Not only was he one of Ellis's tenants; he was in arrears to Ellis for one hundred dollars—two months' rent.

An investigation of Alley's home and stable on Hunneman Street turned up a spate of evidence. The boards of one horse-stall were spattered with blood, concealed by a pile of dry manure, which—from the looks of it—had been hastily shoveled into the compartment sometime within the last twenty-four hours. Inside Alley's bedroom, police found several articles of bloodstained clothing. Alley's own son would later testify that, on the morning after the murder, he had noticed a large patch of dried blood on his father's shirtfront. When he asked where it came from, Alley had mumbled something about a horse's nosebleed.

And there was other damning evidence, too: A witness who had seen the two men arguing on the night of the murder. A neighbor who had heard Alley cursing at someone in his barn. A merchant who swore that he had sold an axe to Alley shortly before the killing. A man who spotted Alley's wagon carting the two barrels toward the mill-dam bridge. When he passed the wagon again a little while later, the barrels were missing.

Alley was immediately indicted for the crime.

For Bostonians, the slaying of Abijah Ellis became a major front-page story—the most sensational murder case in a quarter-century. Not since 1849—when Professor John Webster of Harvard killed his colleague, George Parkman, and incinerated the corpse in a lab furnace—had the public been so riveted by a crime. The story dominated the front pages for days, until it was supplanted by another, far more calamitous event—a huge conflagration that erupted in the wholesale district on Saturday evening, November 9, and raged unabated until the following noon, laying waste to more than sixty-five city acres.

When Alley was brought to trial in February 1873, however, the case exploded back into the headlines. His case seemed so hopeless that his own attorney, Gustavus Somerby, appeared visibly dispirited at the start of the proceedings. But as the trial progressed, Somerby grew increasingly confident, summoning expert witnesses who seriously undermined the prosecution's case. A particular blow was struck by Dr. Charles Jackson, a graduate of Harvard, who testified that—contrary to the assertions of the prosecution's "expert" (a self-styled physician who had never formally studied medicine)—it was scientifically impossible to determine whether dried blood came from humans or horses.

In the end, Somerby managed to sow enough reasonable doubt to reap a victory. In spite of the overwhelming circumstantial evidence against the defendant—and a closing argument by Attorney General Charles Train characterized by observers as "one of the ablest ever made in a capital case in Massachusetts"—Alley was acquitted.

On February 12, 1872—the day the trial ended—Jesse Pomeroy had been locked away for five months, long enough to be forgotten by everyone except those most directly involved in his case: his victims, their parents, and his own brother and mother. (As for Jesse's father—estranged from the family and working as a meat porter in Quincey Market—there is no way of telling what he thought of his son's notoriety, history having left no record of his reactions.)

Ruth Ann Pomeroy was a familiar type: the mother of a frighteningly dangerous criminal who maintains to her dying day that her darling boy is a victim of false charges—a good, dutiful son who, whatever his flaws, couldn't possibly have done the terrible things he's been accused of. Virtually from the moment of Jesse's incarceration, she had begun petitioning for his release. In letter after letter to the board of trustees at Westborough, she insisted that her son was innocent. "He could not be the one who whipped the boys in Chelsea, for he was far too young at that time," she declared in one letter. The police had picked on Jesse because he had drawn attention to himself by impulsively taking a look inside the station house on his way home from school.

He made a suitable scapegoat, moreover, because the Pomeroys were strangers in the neighborhood, having moved to South Boston only a few months earlier. Sequestered in a cheerless cell—terrified and alone—her twelve-year-old child had been browbeaten into confessing. If he had been allowed to see a lawyer, he "would not have been sent to the reform school." Her son, she insisted, was a "bright and happy" boy who had never given her cause for complaint.

"I have never believed him guilty of these crimes," she proclaimed. "NEVER!"

As the months progressed and Jesse continued to be a model of upright behavior, the board began to heed his mother's pleas. Finally, in January 1874, an investigator named Gardiner Tufts— an agent of the State Board of Charities—was dispatched to 312 Broadway to evaluate the condition of the Pomeroy household. He came away favorably impressed. Mrs. Pomeroy struck him as an honest, hardworking woman, who had opened a little dressmaking business at 327 Broadway, directly across the street from her residence. Jesse's older brother, Charles, seemed equally commendable—a thrifty and diligent young man who ran a little newsstand in the front of the shop and had his own paper route.

True, there were some troubling aspects of the situation. Mrs. Pomeroy was bitterly separated from her husband, who had nothing to do with the family. As the product of a broken home, Jesse had clearly been without adequate parental control—"left to drift pretty much at his own will," as Tufts reported. On the whole, however, the investigator was impressed by Mrs. Pomeroy's obvious devotion and reassured by her promise to keep her son under close supervision.

As part of his final report, Tufts also interviewed Police Captain Dyer of Station Six in South Boston, who—expressing his belief that "it isn't best to be down on a boy too hard or too long"—suggested that Jesse be set free on probation. "Give him a chance to redeem himself," he urged.

On January 24, 1874, the trustees received Tufts's report and forwarded their recommendation to the superintendent of the reform school. Two weeks later—on February 6—Jesse Harding Pomeroy was sent home.

His release went unnoted by the newspapers. As far as the people of Boston knew, their city's most notorious juvenile offender was safely locked away for the rest of his adolescence. Eventually—and much to its outrage—the public would discover the truth: less than seventeen months after his arrest, "the boy torturer" had been turned loose on the streets.

PART 2

The
Boy-Killer

12

A simple child
That lightly draws its breath,
And feels its life in every limb,
What should it know of death?
                    —William Wordsworth, "We Are Seven"

To secure her son's release, Mrs. Pomeroy had promised that Jesse would be put to work right away, assisting his older brother, Charles—a strapping sixteen-year-old who earned a small but steady income by selling newspapers. More than a half-dozen papers were published in Boston during the 1870s—the *Globe,* the *Post,* the *Journal,* the *Herald,* the *Daily Advertiser,* the *Evening Traveller,* the *Evening Transcript,* and others. Charles sold them all from the little newsstand he ran in the front part of his mother's dressmaking shop at 327 Broadway. He also had a delivery route, with more than two-hundred-and-fifty subscribers.

True to his mother's word, Jesse was given a job as soon as he got home. Two days after his return, he was put in charge of Charles's afternoon route. Setting off from the shop at around 3:00 P.M.—a big canvas pouch slung over his shoulder—Jesse would deliver papers to approximately one hundred homes in the city. At other times, he helped out in the store.

Jesse approached his new responsibilities in a methodical fashion, keeping a little notebook in which he neatly listed the names and addresses of his customers and the papers they took. This notebook is still preserved in the archives of the Massachusetts Historical Society, and anyone examining it today is bound to be struck by how exceptionally ordinary—how entirely nondescript—it seems. Written in an almost compulsively tidy hand, it could be the ledger of any earnest, hardworking adolescent—the type of boy who, in the old days, might have tried to earn a pair of roller skates by joining the Junior Sales Club of America and peddling door-to-door greeting cards after school. The notebook stands as concrete evidence of Ruth Pomeroy's contention that her younger son was a bright, studious, industrious boy.

Of course, Jesse's energy and aptitude were in no way inconsistent with his extreme psychopathology. Homicidal maniacs of the type that we now call "serial killers" have often been effective, highly organized businessmen and professionals. John Wayne Gacy, for example—whose suburban crawl space contained the rotted remains of twenty-seven victims—ran a thriving contracting business. Ted Bundy distinguished himself in law school and was regarded as a rising young star of the Republican party. Other serial killers have been successful military officers, stock market speculators—even physicians.

Indeed, the disparity between the seeming normality of sociopathic sex-killers and their hidden pathology is one of the most fascinating—and frightening—things about them. In this regard, Jesse Pomeroy was typical of the breed. His rational faculties were fundamentally intact. But his human qualities—empathy, conscience, a capacity for remorse—were completely missing from his makeup. In their place, concealed beneath his "mask of sanity," was a second, utterly ungovernable self—a being of ferocious appetite that would erupt at the right provocation: a suitable victim, an importunate need, an unforeseen opportunity.

Given Jesse's predatory nature, it was only a matter of time before the creature he contained showed its face.

Early on the morning of Wednesday, March 18, 1874—just six weeks after Jesse was released from reform school—a ten-year-old girl named Katie Curran remembered that she needed a new notebook for school. Her mother—who was busy dressing Katie's younger sister, Celia Abby—told the girl to take some coins from her purse and hurry over to Tobin's, a neighborhood store not far from the Currans' South Boston home.

Katie, who was wearing a black-and-green-plaid dress, threw on an old jacket, tied a scarf about her neck, and made for the front door. Just before she stepped outside, she turned back to her mother and called: "Have Celia Abby ready when I get back. We've got a new teacher, and I don't want to be late."

As Katie disappeared down the front steps, Mrs. Curran glanced at the mantelpiece clock. The time was precisely 8:05 A.M.

On Wednesday, March 18, it was Jesse's turn to open the shop, a chore he and Charles performed on alternating days. The shop—located on the street-level floor of a little two-story house owned by a family named Margerson—stood directly across from the Pomeroys' flat. Arriving at approximately 7:30 A.M., Jesse—still groggy with sleep—unlocked the door, stripped off his jacket, grabbed a broom, and began to tidy up the place.

He had just finished sweeping the floor when a neighborhood boy named Rudolph Kohr—who earned a little pocket change by running errands for the Pomeroys and assisting with the newspaper deliveries—showed up. The time was a few minutes past 8:00.

As Kohr stood chatting with Jesse, a little girl—wearing a threadbare jacket over a black-and-green-plaid dress—entered the shop. She needed a notebook for school, she explained. She had been to Tobin's, but hadn't found the kind she was looking for. Did Jesse have any for sale?

Jesse nodded. He had one notebook left, though it was slightly damaged. "There's an ink spot on the cover," he explained. If she wanted it, he'd let her have it at a discount—three cents instead of the customary nickel.

Katie Curran eagerly agreed.

Just then, the Pomeroys' old tabby emerged from the cellar, mewing for food. Jesse asked Rudolph if he would mind running over to the butcher's for a few scraps of meat. The Kohr boy left at once.

He came back about ten minutes later. When he entered the store, the little girl was gone.

When her daughter wasn't back by 8:35, Mary Curran grew anxious. By 9:00 A.M., she was almost beside herself with worry. Mrs. Curran had always kept a watchful eye on her children. Except during school hours—or when Katie and her friends were skipping rope or playing hopscotch on the block—her ten-year-old girl had never been out of her sight for more than half an hour.

Throwing on her shawl, she rushed to Tobin's. The proprietor, Thomas Tobin, confirmed that a little girl had come in earlier. He had shown her a few notebooks, but none of them had been been to her liking. The last he'd seen of her, she was headed up Broadway, looking for another store that carried stationer's goods.

Thanking Mr. Tobin, Mrs. Curran hurried away. She asked at another neighborhood shop called Gill's, but no one there had seen her daughter. As the frantic woman made her way through the neighborhood, she encountered a girl named Lee, who said she had spotted Katie entering the Pomeroys' shop at 327 Broadway earlier that morning.

The news sent a pang of alarm through Mrs. Curran's breast. Like everyone else in the neighborhood, she had heard the stories about Jesse Pomeroy. She went immediately to Police Station Six.

Both Captain Dyer and an officer named Adams listened to her story and did their best to reassure her. They doubted that Jesse Pomeroy had anything to do with her daughter's disappearance. By all accounts, the boy had undergone a complete rehabilitation in reform school. And even at his worst, Jesse had never been known to attack little girls. Katie had probably gotten lost in her search for a notebook. Captain Dyer told Mrs. Curran to go back home and wait. His men would bring her daughter back safe and sound.

Twenty-four hours later, however, there was still no sign of the ten-year-old child.

By then the whole neighborhood was abuzz with news of the missing girl. Sometime that afternoon, Mrs. Curran received a message from the Kohr boy, who said that he had some information about Katie. Mrs. Curran immediately proceeded to the Kohr home, where Rudolph informed her that he had seen her daughter with Jesse in the Pomeroys' shop early the previous morning.

Mrs. Curran lost no time in conveying this intelligence to the police. Once again, however, Dyer and Adams pooh-poohed her suspicions. The Kohr boy was a known liar, they said. But if it would make Mrs. Curran feel better, Detective Adams himself would pay a visit to the Pomeroys' shop.

When Mary Curran returned to the station the following day, Adams assured her that he had made a thorough search of the premises and—as expected—turned up nothing. He had also interviewed Rudolph Kohr and come away more convinced than ever that the boy was lying.

The disappearance of Katie Curran caused a considerable stir in South Boston. Over the next few weeks, the police continued to investigate every lead. Newspapers ran regular stories head-lined "Where Is Katie Curran?" The mayor offered a reward of five hundred dollars for information about the missing child.

Eventually, an ostensible witness came forward, who claimed that he had seen the weeping child being lured into a covered carriage on the morning of her disappearance. The police con-cluded that she had been kidnapped.

Because Katie's father was Catholic (a fact the newspapers never failed to point out), others chose to believe that he had ab-ducted his own daughter and shipped her off to a convent—a rumor that struck a responsive chord in a Puritan city during an anti-Catholic age, when lurid tracts like *Secrets of the Black Nunnery, Slaves of the Priestcraft, Confessions of a Nun,* and *America's Menace, or the Politics of Popery* were popular sellers.

13

A violent man enticeth his neighbour, and leadeth him into the way that is not good.

—Proverbs 16:29

In the weeks immediately following the disappearance of Katie Curran, a number of children were accosted by an adolescent boy who tried to entice them away from their South Boston neighborhoods. Several of the young ones were tempted to accompany the stranger, who promised to treat them to the circus, take them to a parade, or give them small sums of money to help with an errand. In the end, however, nearly all the little boys resisted.

One who didn't was named Harry Field. During the first week of April, the five-year-old was standing at the gate of his parents' house at No. 1027 Shawmut Avenue, when a big boy with a funny-looking eye approached, an old broom handle clutched in one hand. Harry assumed that he was on his way to play stickball.

"Know where Vernon Street is?" asked the big boy.

When Harry nodded, the stranger said, "I'll give you five cents if you will take me there."

The little boy readily agreed and the two set off side by side. As soon as they reached their destination, Harry asked for his nickel—but instead of paying up, the stranger grabbed the younger boy by the collar, dragged him into a doorway, and threatened to beat him with the stick unless he obeyed.

"What do you want?" whimpered Harry.

"Come with me," snarled the older boy. "And keep your flytrap shut."

Grabbing Harry by one hand, the big boy began to lead him rapidly through the streets, every step carrying the terrified child farther from his home.

All at once, as they rounded the corner of Eustis Street, they passed another older boy, who recognized Harry's captor and called out angrily to him. As the two adolescents stopped to exchange words, Harry yanked his hand free, spun on his heels, and fled. Halfway down the block, he paused to cast one quick look over his shoulder and saw the two adolescents engaged in a violent altercation. Harry didn't slow down again until he burst through the front door of his house and threw himself into his mother's arms. Through his sobs, he explained what had happened.

Her son was so upset that Mrs. Field didn't have the heart to scold him too harshly for going off with a stranger—something she had warned him against many times. Still, she could not entirely refrain from admonishing him.

"Who knows what might have happened to you if that other lad hadn't happened along," she declared. "You were a very lucky boy."

It wasn't until two weeks later—after the Horace Millen story broke—that Mary Field realized just *how* lucky her child had been.

14

The wicked flee when no man pursueth.
—Proverbs 28:1

The Panic of 1873 began on Thursday, September 18, with the failure of two of New York's leading banking houses—those of Jay Cooke and George Opdyke. Stock prices fell so precipitously on the following day—"Black Friday," September 19—that the Stock Exchange was closed for the rest of the month. The resulting depression was the worst since 1837 and did not abate for five years. Bankruptcies increased by the month, hitting their peak in 1878 when nearly 11,000 businesses failed.

One melancholy sign of the depression was the sharp rise in the number of paupers. There were no homeless shelters *per se* in the 1870s. In New York and other big cities, people without a roof over their heads sought shelter in police stations. The accommodations were rudimentary: a rough wooden plank to sleep on (generally in an unventilated cellar) and, occasionally, a meager breakfast in the morning. But for many vagrants—particularly women—even this bare-bones hospitality was preferable to an unprotected night on the streets.

According to statistics maintained by the New York City Police Department, there were just over 136,000 of these so-called "station-house lodgers" in 1871. By 1875, that number had risen to nearly a quarter-million.

Though the depression hadn't reduced him to beggary, John Anderson Millen—a thirty-one-year-old cabinetmaker with a dusty little shop in Charlestown—had been hit hard by the crisis. His business had fallen off so drastically that he could no longer afford the rent on his house. And so, during the second week of April, 1874, he and his family—his wife, Leonora, and their two small boys, Sidney and Horace—packed their scant belongings and moved to cheaper lodgings, a rundown frame house on Dorchester Street in South Boston.

As it happened, their new dwelling was located almost directly across the street from the home of John and Katherine Curran, whose ten-year-old girl, Katie, had vanished without a trace just a few weeks earlier. Every now and then, Mrs. Millen would glance out her kitchen window and see one or the other of the missing girl's parents emerge from their front door, shoulders bowed, faces haggard with grief.

The sight of her care-ravaged neighbors never failed to fill Mrs. Millen's heart with pity and make her count her own blessings. Her own family may have fallen on hard times. But nothing could possibly be harder than the ordeal of the Currans, whose little child had left home on a simple errand one morning and was never seen again.

Mrs. Millen's own younger child, four-year-old Horace, had features of such extreme delicacy—porcelain skin, large dark eyes, rosebud mouth, silky blond hair—that he was frequently mistaken for a girl. Mrs. Millen did her best to emphasize his beauty by dressing him in the prettiest clothes the family could afford. On the morning of April 22, 1874—a raw, overcast Wednesday, precisely five weeks after Katie Curran's disappearance—his outfit consisted of knee breeches with a checkered waist; a red-and-white-checked shirt trimmed with black velvet; a white and black jacket; white woolen socks and high-laced boots; and a black velvet cap trimmed with gold braid and a tassel.

Slender as Horace was, there was nothing especially dainty about his appetite, particularly his craving for sweets. Shortly before 10:00 A.M.—just a few hours after he had polished off a substantial breakfast—he began nagging his mother for money to visit the bakery. Though the family was hard-pressed for cash, Mrs. Millen—whose husband regularly accused her of spoiling their sons—could not resist Horace's demands and finally handed him a few pennies.

"Come back by lunchtime," she called as he hurried out the front door.

Though her children were newcomers to the neighborhood,

Mrs. Millen allowed them to go off unaccompanied, so long as she knew exactly where they were headed and when they would be home. Before returning to her housework, she made sure to check the clock. The time was 10:20 A.M.

About fifteen minutes later, a neighbor of the Millens—a woman named Sarah Hunting—encountered little Horace near the lamppost on Dorchester Street. He was in the company of a bigger boy. Mrs. Hunting didn't take a close look at the latter, though he struck her as "lop-shouldered."

When she asked Horace where he was off to, he exclaimed, "The bakery!" Holding up his right hand, he uncurled his fingers and showed her the coins he had clutched in his palm. Then Horace and the older boy headed down the street.

Mrs. Eleanor Fosdick was sitting by her bedroom window at around eleven o'clock when a slender boy, four or five years old, rounded the corner of Dorchester Street. He caught her attention because of his black-velvet, gold-braided cap. Her own five-year-old son had been hankering after just such a cap for weeks.

All at once, Mrs. Fosdick became aware of something else: a second, older boy following the younger one around the corner.

As the little boy in the velvet cap headed for the bakery down the block, the older boy retreated to a nearby doorway and took a quick look around him. From her vantage point across the street, Mrs. Fosdick could clearly see his expression. It struck her as so odd—so strangely *excited*—that she went to fetch her spectacles.

When she returned to her window seat, she saw the little boy emerge from the bakery with a drop cake in his hand. At that moment, the older boy emerged from the doorway and—after speaking briefly to the younger one—took away the drop cake, broke it in two, gave one part back to the little boy, and devoured the rest himself.

Then, taking the little boy by the hand, he led him away along Dorchester Street, in the direction of the bay.

About forty minutes later, a man named Elias Ashcroft spotted two boys walking along the Old Colony Railroad tracks toward McCay's Wharf. The older of the two was leading the smaller one by the hand. He assumed that they were brothers out for some fun.

Fifteen-year-old Robert Benson had been digging clams in the bay for several hours. He was returning home with his haul at around noon when he encountered a couple of boys, who were heading toward a strip of marshland locally known as the "cow pasture." As the older of the two boys helped his little companion across a ditch, gunfire resounded in the distance.

"What're they shooting?" the older boy asked Benson.

"Wild ducks," he replied.

Without another word, the older boy led the smaller one away. Benson continued in the opposite direction, wondering idly about the little boy's outfit. The fancy clothing—knee breeches with a checkered waist, velvet-trimmed shirt, black velvet cap—seemed totally inappropriate for an outing to the marsh.

About twenty minutes later, a man named Edward Harrington, who had also spent the morning clamming, was washing his haul in a little creek when, glancing up, he spotted a teenaged boy sprinting toward the railroad tracks, away from the marsh. As he ran, the boy kept casting nervous looks over his shoulder.

Curious, Benson paused and looked back in the direction of the marsh to see if someone was chasing the boy. But no one was there.

15

It's like a lion at the door;
And when the door begins to crack,
It's like a stick across your back;
And when your back begins to smart,
It's like a penknife in your heart;
And when your heart begins to bleed,
You're dead, and dead, and dead, indeed.
—Nursery rhyme

By the time they arrived at Savin Hill Beach at around 3:45 P.M., the tide was in and the water too high for clamming, so the two Power brothers—eleven-year-old George and his older brother, James—decided to do a little beachcombing instead. George, as he always did, quickly took the lead. Striding along the shoreline, he kept his gaze fixed on the sand for any treasures that might have washed up with the tide. He had gone about a hundred yards when he stopped and let out a piercing yell.

Deaf since birth, thirteen-year-old James didn't hear his brother's cry. But when he glanced up, he saw George waving to him frantically and took off at a run. The sight that struck him when he reached his brother's side made him gape in confusion.

A few feet away in the sand, surrounded by a circle of charred stones, lay a little clambake pit, empty shells scattered all around. Something resembling a doll was stretched out inside the pit. Looking closer, James saw that it was the half-naked body of a little boy. He lay stiffly on his back, britches and drawers pulled down around his ankles. There was caked blood all over his face, hands, and upper thighs. His shirtfront was covered with gore.

Glancing around for help, George spotted two men about fifty yards away. They were moving cautiously through the tall grass, rifles cradled in their arms. Leaving his older brother with the body, George ran across the marshland and alerted the pair—a couple of duck-hunters named Obed Goodspeed and Patrick Wise—who hurried back to the little stone-ringed pit. A few moments later, they were joined by another man, a fellow named H. F. Harrington, who had noticed the commotion and come over to investigate.

Kneeling by the body, Goodspeed took note of its condition— the blood issuing from the mouth and right eye, the stab wounds on the hands, the punctured shirt, the mutilated groin. Then— leaving the others to stand watch over the dead child— Goodspeed headed toward Washington Village in search of a policeman, while the thirteen-year-old deaf-mute, James, took off in the opposite direction.

At around 5:15 P.M., Officer Roswell M. Lyons of the Ninth Police Station was patrolling his beat near the Old Colony Railroad line when a breathless young boy came running up to him and began motioning frantically in the direction of the bay.

"What's the matter, lad?" asked Lyons. The boy—who looked to be about thirteen—was so deeply agitated that he seemed incapable of intelligible speech. It took Lyons a moment to realize that he was a deaf-mute.

Raising his chin, the boy ran a hand across his windpipe in a throat-slitting gesture. Lyons interpreted this pantomime to mean that someone was dead. Pulling out a notebook and pencil, he flipped to an empty page and printed the words,"Is anyone drowned?" The boy quickly scanned the query, then snatched the pencil from the policeman's hand and, on the bottom of the same page, wrote: "One murdered."

Frowning, Lyons gestured for the boy to lead the way. They had gone about half a mile in the direction of Savin Hill Beach when Lyons saw three men and another, smaller boy huddled around a circle of stone just a few yards from the shoreline. As he drew closer to this solemn little group, he noticed the stricken look on the faces of the men. Then he glanced down into the pit, and felt his own features grow taut with dismay.

Lyons would later testify that, in all his years of police work, he had never confronted a more appalling sight. It was clear at a glance that the little victim in the pit—who looked barely older than a toddler—had been subjected to an agonizing ordeal. The writhing of his limbs had caused his heels to gouge deep furrows in the sand, and his fists were so tightly clenched in pain that his fingernails were embedded in his palms. There were ugly lacerations on the back of his hands that Lyons immediately recognized as defensive wounds, inflicted when the child had tried to ward off his attacker. The boy had been stabbed in the chest at least half-a-dozen times, and his throat was gashed so deeply that his head was nearly severed from the body. Bloody fluid oozed from one punctured eyeball. He had also been partially castrated. Looking down at the child's exposed groin, Lyons saw one testicle hanging loose from the mutilated scrotum.

After rearranging the dead boy's undergarments and pants, Lyons carefully took the little corpse in his arms and—with the help of Wise, Harrington, and Goodspeed (who had returned to the crime scene after his own futile search for a policeman)—carried it to the Crescent Avenue railroad station, where he quickly secured a carriage. Then he conveyed the body to Police Station Nine, where it lay for an hour or so before being transferred to Waterman's undertaking parlor at 1912 Washington Street to await the arrival of Coroner Ira Allen.

At first, Leonora Millen had assumed that her son was simply dawdling. But when Horace still wasn't home by 11:30 A.M., she became worried enough to throw on a shawl and go looking for him.

The bakery owner, a woman named Moulton, confirmed that she had sold a penny drop cake to a four-year-old boy in a black velvet cap about a half-hour earlier. But she had no idea what had become of the child once he left the store.

After searching the neighborhood streets without finding her son, Mrs. Millen felt sufficiently alarmed to seek out her husband. After months of unemployment, John Millen had just secured a job at John Clark's cabinet manufactory on Newman Street, and his wife was reluctant to disturb him. But by then, she had worked herself into a state and did not know where else to turn.

Her husband tried to soothe her fears. Horace had probably encountered some chums on his way home from the bakery and, ignoring his mother's instructions, had decided to go off and have fun. The boy was due for a licking; he was becoming more disobedient by the day. Turning back to his work, John advised Leonora to go straight home. Horace was probably already there, wondering where his mother was.

When John arrived home later that afternoon, however, he found his wife sobbing at the kitchen table. Horace had never come back. Now, it was the father's turn to become alarmed. Turning on his heels, he hurried from the house and scoured the neighborhood.

At approximately 5:30 P.M., after failing to turn up any trace of Horace, he bent his steps toward Police Station Six, to report that his four-year-old son was missing.

It was approximately 7:30 P.M. when Coroner Allen arrived at Waterman's undertaking parlor. By then, word of the gruesome discovery on Savin Hill Beach had spread throughout the neighborhood, and the street outside the funeral home was packed with curiosity-seekers. When a number of people tried to force their way inside the building to get a glimpse of the victim's remains, the undertaker summoned the police, who promptly dispersed the morbid crowd and cordoned off the block.

Allen's examination of the body—conducted in the embalming room with a six-man coroner's jury in attendance—revealed two distinct wounds to the child's throat, inflicted with a sharp, small-bladed implement like a pocketknife. One of the incisions had exposed the boy's windpipe; the other had severed his jugular vein. In Allen's estimation, either of these wounds would have been "necessarily fatal, as there was no one about who could staunch the flow of blood."

The postmortem made it horribly clear that the "poor little victim" (as the newspapers would invariably describe the murdered boy in the coming days) had been subjected to an attack of unspeakable savagery. His right eyeball had been punctured through the lid, his hands had been slashed more than a dozen times, there were no less than eighteen stab wounds in his chest, and—in the words of the coroner's official report—"an attempt had apparently been made to sever the whole of his private parts. The scrotum was opened so much that the left testicle had fallen out and was lying in that condition."

The examination lasted until nearly 9:00 P.M., by which time reporters from every newspaper in Boston were crammed into the outer rooms of the mortuary, waiting to learn the results. At a few minutes after nine, a police sergeant named Hood—who had observed the postmortem along with the coroner's jury—emerged from the embalming room and supplied the clamoring newsmen with a graphic description of the crime. Then, while the reporters hurried off to make their midnight deadlines, Hood proceeded to Police Station Nine to transmit a bulletin to other precincts around the city in the hope of identifying the still-unknown victim.

Police news traveled fast in 1874. Though the telephone would not be invented for another two years, all the station houses in Boston were connected by an ingenious communication system known as a "patent-writing telegraph." Using an electromagnetic pen, an officer would write out a message that, within seconds, was transcribed in facsimile by a matching apparatus on the receiving end.

When Hood's bulletin reached Police Station Six—where John Millen had gone earlier in the day to report his son's disappearance—Captain Dyer immediately wired back for further details. Moments later, the electromagnetic device produced a reply: "He is rather tall for a child four or five years old but is slender with long light hair, light complexion, with dark brown eyes and dressed in knee breeches with a checked waist, attached to which is a red-and-white checked shirt trimmed with black velvet. He wore white woolen socks and high-laced boots. His cap is of black velvet trimmed with a gold lace band."

The captain exchanged a grim look with his subordinates. Every detail of the murder victim's dress and appearance precisely matched the description of John Millen's missing boy. Dyer and an officer named Childs immediately repaired to the Millen home on Dorchester Street, where—as the *Boston Evening Traveller* reported—the "scene that ensued was heartrending." Though both parents had already begun to fear the worst, Dyer's awful tidings left them shattered.

Leaving his prostrate wife in the company of Childs, John Millen accompanied Captain Dyer to Waterman's, where he broke down anew at the sight of his butchered son. Helped into a waiting room, he was observed by a reporter for the *Boston Evening Journal*, who described the father's "terrible bereavement." Arrangements had been made to leave the child's body at the undertaking parlor overnight. Horace would be retrieved by his parents in the morning—though exactly how the Millens would afford a proper funeral for their murdered boy was an agonizing question.

"The family are in indigent circumstances," the reporter wrote, "and amid the father's lamentations came the painful inquiry, 'How shall we bury our dead?' "

16

I continued my daily work of carrying newspapers, as usual, and nothing worthy of record happened until the 22nd day of April. On that day a small boy was murdered on the South Boston marsh. Somehow—I have never been able to find a reason—suspicion fell on me.
—*Autobiography of Jesse H. Pomeroy* (1875)

In the hours immediately following the discovery of Horace Millen's body, the crime produced a chilling sense of *déjà vu* in the people privy to its details. No one familiar with the facts of the case—policemen, reporters, Coroner Allen and his jury—could fail to be reminded of the horrific attacks committed in Chelsea and South Boston less than two years before.

At first, there was some confusion about the name of the "boy torturer" who had terrorized the city in 1872. In their early morning editions, some newspapers would refer to him as "Willie Pomeroy," others as "Eddie." But there was no doubt that the Millen crime shared the same grisly *m.o.* with the earlier outrages: a very small boy slashed, tortured, and sexually mutilated after being lured to an isolated location. As the *Boston Globe* put it when the story first broke: "The similarity of the crimes is so great that it seems almost a logical conclusion that they are the work of one and the same hand."

Among the people whose thoughts immediately turned to Pomeroy was the chief of the Boston police, Edward Hartwell Savage.

Sixty-two years old at the time of the Millen murder, Hartwell was a failed businessman from New Hampshire who had emigrated to Boston in his twenties, reportedly five thousand dollars in debt. After working several years as a handcart-jobber to pay off his creditors, he joined the police force in 1851 and quickly worked his way up the ranks. Within just three years, he was made captain in the North End, the toughest section of the city. By 1861, he had been promoted to Deputy Chief of the entire department. During his tenure as deputy, he instituted a number of important innovations, including an extensive rogues gallery, a modernized system of record-keeping, and a specialized detective corps. In his spare time, he was also an amateur historian, who published a popular chronicle of the city, *Boston Events*, and a bestselling history of the department, *Police Records and Recollections, or Boston by Daylight and Gaslight for Two Hundred and Forty Years*.

In 1870, Savage—then a distinguished, gray-haired widower who lived at home with a spinster daughter—became head of the force. He quickly established himself as the most successful and popular police chief in Boston history. Among the city's business elite, he was known as a stalwart protector of property. During the Great Fire of 1872, he was in direct command of over 1800 men—including members of the military—and remained continuously on duty for nearly ninety-six hours, ensuring that civil order was maintained. It was a particular source of pride to him that, during his nearly decade-long service, no more than $100,000 in property was stolen in any given year (a drop of more than 300 percent from previous years). Not a single bank in Boston was robbed during the entire time he was chief.

Savage also took credit for a dramatic improvement in the department's investigative capabilities. At the time Horace Millen's savaged body was discovered on the marsh, not a single homicide had gone unsolved by his detectives in four years.

At around 9:30 on the evening of the Millen murder, one of Chief Savage's most trusted men—a detective named James R. Wood—arrived at police headquarters in City Hall. Wood (who, fifty years later, would publish a personal reminiscence of the case in *The Master Detective*, a popular true-crime magazine of the 1930s) was immediately directed to the chief's office. There, he found Savage in consultation with three other detectives named Dearborn, Ham, and Quinn.

"A young boy has been murdered in South Boston," Savage

said by way of a greeting. "Brutal business. Some clam diggers found his body on the marshes."

"Any suspects?" asked Wood.

Savage shook his head. "It's the damndest thing," he said, as if musing aloud. "It sounds just like the work of that kid we've got in the reformatory. Remember? The one with the mania for tying up little boys and slashing their faces?"

"You mean the Pomeroy boy?" said Detective Quinn. "He's not in the reformatory. They let him out on probation in February."

Savage cast a sharp look at his subordinate. "Are you sure?"

"Positive," Quinn said. "I heard that he's living with his mother. She keeps a dress shop somewhere in South Boston."

Rising from his chair, Savage crossed the room and, using the patent-writing telegraph device, transmitted a message to Captain Dyer at Station Six: "Is Jesse Pomeroy living in your precinct?"

Several moments elapsed while the chief and his four detectives huddled silently around the apparatus. All at once, the electromagnetic pen stirred to life and printed the reply: "Yes. His mother has a store on Broadway. They live at 312 Broadway."

Savage immediately wired back, instructing Dyer to "send an officer to the house. If he can find young Pomeroy, bring him along to the station house. I'll send some men over without delay." Then—after officially assigning Dearborn, Wood, and Ham to the case—he ordered them to proceed to Station Six at once.

Without a word, the trio hurried outside onto Congress Street, summoned a hack, and headed for South Boston.

In response to Savage's message, Captain Dyer immediately dispatched two of his men—Officers Samuel Lucas and Thomas H. Adams—to the Pomeroy home at 312 Broadway. Arriving at the ramshackle little house shortly after 10:00 P.M., they were admitted by Mrs. Pomeroy, who grudgingly informed them that her younger son was up in his room, getting ready for bed.

Summoned downstairs, Jesse sauntered into the parlor still dressed in his street clothes. As the two officers questioned him about his whereabouts that morning, they studied his appearance, taking special note of several fresh scratch marks on his face and the reddish-brown mud stains on his trouser cuffs and shoes.

After listening to Jesse's rambling account of his day's activities, the two policemen announced that they were taking him down to Station Six for further questioning. Mrs. Pomeroy bitterly protested, but the officers assured her that her son would be back soon.

"Don't fret, Ma," Jesse said breezily as he was led out the door. "I didn't do nothing."

The hack carrying Dearborn, Wood, and Ham pulled up at Police Station Six just as Jesse was being escorted inside. Ushered into Captain Dyer's office, he was seated in the center of the room, while more than half a dozen men—Dyer, Coroner Allen, the three detectives, Lucas, Adams, and a few of their fellow officers—crowded around his chair and began pummeling him with questions.

By this time, Jesse's mood had gone from cocky to peevish. Asked again to describe his day, he sullenly repeated the story he had already told Lucas and Adams. After rising at 6:00 A.M. and eating breakfast, he had gone across the street to help his brother sweep out the store. At around 7:30, he headed off to the city to fetch the weekly papers at the New England News Company, returning with his load about an hour later.

He remained in the store until about half past eleven, when he had strolled home for lunch. Afterward, he had killed a few hours ambling around the city before picking up his afternoon papers at the offices of the *Boston Evening Traveller* and the *Boston Journal.* Then he set off on his 3:00 P.M. route. By 4:30, his supply had run out. Making his way back to the store, he collected another batch of papers, then spent the next hour or so completing his deliveries. He had arrived back home at around half past six, his work day finally over.

It was immediately clear to his interrogators that there were gaping holes in Jesse's story, particularly concerning the hours between 11:30 A.M.—when he'd left the periodical shop and returned home for lunch—and 2:30 P.M., when he had picked up his papers for his afternoon route. He claimed that, after crossing the Federal Street Bridge and making his way to Tremont Street, he had spent most of the time strolling around the Boston Common and Public Garden. But when asked for more precise details, his memory got suspiciously hazy. He could not recall, for example, if there was any construction work taking place on

Tremont Street (a large section of which had, in fact, been torn up for a public works project). Nor could he say whether there was a baseball match or a military display taking place on the parade ground.

As the interrogation proceeded, the detectives scrutinized Jesse with practiced eyes. He was wearing an old, visorless cap, mud-stained pants, and a damp, dirty coat with no vest. His boots, like his trousers, were conspicuously muddy.

"How did your shoes get so dirty?" one detective inquired.

"From walking around so much," Jesse answered coolly.

He was ordered to remove the boots. Upon closer inspection, the left one proved to have several stalks of what appeared to be marsh-grass sticking from a crack between the heel and sole.

Next, Jesse was told to strip off his jacket. Detective Ham carefully went through the pockets but found nothing incriminating. When Jesse was ordered to remove his shirt, however, the detectives noticed a reddish-brown stain about the size of a thumbprint on the front of his flannel undershirt. This garment was immediately confiscated, along with his boots. Jesse's jacket and shirt were returned to him.

Like Lucas and Adams—the two officers who had picked Jesse up at home—Detective Wood and his colleagues were struck by the ugly marks on Jesse's face: a nasty scratch across his left cheek, and three smaller lacerations under his left ear. They found some other scratches at the base of his neck and on the back of his left hand. As Wood would later testify, "they all seemed of recent origin." When Jesse was asked how he'd scratched his face, he shrugged and answered: "Shaving."

Having learned from Coroner Allen that Horace Millen had been stabbed and mutilated with a small-bladed implement, Captain Dyer asked if Jesse owned a knife. After a moment's hesitation, Jesse admitted that he did.

"Do you have it on you?" Dyer asked.

Jesse shook his head. The knife was at home, in the pocket of his vest.

Dyer immediately dispatched a sergeant named Hood to the Pomeroy home. A short while later, he returned with the knife. It was a typical boy's pocketknife, with two slightly rusty blades, the longer of which measured about three inches. When the knife was opened, the investigators noticed that the aperture was clogged with particles of moist dirt. They also found a smudge of what appeared to be dried blood on the mother-of-pearl handle. The weapon was turned over to Coroner Allen, who—eager to learn if the knife matched the stab wounds in the victim's body— promptly left for Waterman's undertaking parlor.

Altogether, the interrogation lasted nearly three hours. At around 2:00 A.M., Jesse was finally led off to a cell, where he curled up on the bunk, closed his eyes, and immediately drifted off into a deep and—to all outward appearances—untroubled sleep.

17

Dorchester may soon be called "the dark and bloody land," for nearly all the great tragedies which have occured in Boston within the past few years have had that location within the limits of that district.

—*Boston Evening Traveller*, April 23, 1874

Early the following morning, Thursday, April 23, a team of investigators—the three detectives from headquarters, along with Sergeants Henry O. Goodwin and Thomas Hood of Station Six—traveled out to Savin Hill Beach. Clutched in Goodwin's hand was a paper-wrapped bundle containing two sets of footwear: the mud-caked boots confiscated from Pomeroy, plus the smaller—though equally bespattered—shoes belonging to Horace Millen.

It was another cheerless morning, with a damp, bitter wind coming off the bay and a sky obscured by leaden clouds. In spite of the dismal weather, however, a crowd had already gathered on the marsh. Anticipating this development, Captain Dyer had posted a detail of men around the murder site. When the five officers arrived at around 9:30 A.M., they found a half-dozen guards at the scene, keeping the curiosity seekers from trampling on the evidence.

Detective Wood and his colleagues began by examining the little clambake pit where the corpse had been found. The soggy mud inside the pit still bore the impression of the child's body. Two small, parallel gouges were visible in the dirt, where the dying boy had ground his heels in agony.

The mud all around the little stone-ringed pit was covered with footprints, left by the people who had discovered the body. But—as Detective Wood would later recall—"two pairs of footprints, always close together, stood out distinctly from the rest."

These prints formed a slightly meandering trail that led to the pit from the direction of the Old Colony Railroad Station.

Tearing open his bundle, Sergeant Goodwin knelt down in the dirt and carefully laid the two sets of shoes inside the prints. Though the match seemed very close, it was impossible to say whether the tracks had been made by Pomeroy and his victim, since other children—like the two Powers brothers, who had first stumbled onto Horace Millen's body—were known to have been on the marsh.

With the curious—and steadily growing—crowd following at a slight distance, the investigators began to follow the parallel tracks back toward the railroad station. Fifty years later, Wood would remember the occasion with perfect clarity. "We followed the trail in silence. Sometimes, when the ground grew hard or became grass-covered, the footprints were almost obliterated. Then we would come upon them again—always close together."

The trail led to a place called McCay's Wharf. From the pattern that their shoes had made in the soft clay, it was clear that the older of the two boys had jumped from the wharf first, then assisted the smaller child, apparently by reaching up, taking him in his arms, and lifting him down.

The officers were about two hundred feet from the railroad station when—as Wood described it—"the trail was lost for good. By then, however, we had seen enough to arrive at the conclusion that the larger footprints, almost the size of a man's, were evidently those of an older person who had led the younger child on." Some of the footprints were virtually effaced. Others, however, "were revealed in such startling clarity that it occurred to me that molds could be made." When Wood voiced this suggestion to his colleagues, Sergeant Hood recalled that a man named Moulton lived nearby. A stonemason by trade, Moulton was sure to have plenty of plaster of Paris on hand.

An officer was immediately dispatched to Moulton's shop. A short while later, he returned with a sackful of the powdery substance, which was quickly mixed and poured into the most distinct of the footprints. Altogether the investigators made fifteen casts. In his published reminiscence of the case, Wood described what happened next:

"As soon as the plaster was sufficiently dry, we lifted the casts out carefully. Then commenced a minute study. There was a peculiar indentation on the plaster sole impression of one of the larger footprints. Further examination satisfied us that those prints could have been made by only one pair of shoes.

"Those were the shoes we had taken from the feet of young Jesse Pomeroy."

The detectives had found what they were looking for: solid evidence of Pomeroy's presence at the crime scene. Now there was just one more thing Wood was determined to get.

He wanted to hear Jesse Pomeroy confess.

It was close to noon when the investigators returned to Station Six. They found Chief Savage waiting for them in Captain Dyer's office. While Wood and his colleagues reviewed their findings for the chief, two officers were sent downstairs to fetch Jesse from his cell. Seeing that the boy was still fast asleep, one of the men began pounding on the door until Jesse stirred and sat up groggily. At that point—according to Jesse's own account—the second policeman put his face close to the bars and jeered: "You are guilty and will be shut up for a hundred years!" Then—laughing and cursing—they took Jesse from the cell and roughly escorted him upstairs.

Inside Dyer's office, Jesse was subjected to another thorough grilling, this one conducted primarily by Savage. The chief began by asking him about the motives for his earlier crimes, the series of slashings that had landed him in Westborough.

Jesse gave his usual, shrugging response: "I don't know. I couldn't help myself."

Next, he was made to repeat his account of the previous day's events. This time, he displayed considerably more confidence about certain details, relating his story with a coolness that struck the observers as nothing less than remarkable in a fourteen-year-old boy in such daunting circumstances. He maintained his composure even when Savage suddenly leaned forward and announced that Jesse was under arrest for the murder of Horace Millen.

"You can't prove anything," Jesse replied offhandedly.

"I wouldn't be so sure," said Captain Dyer. "We found some pretty damaging evidence against you this morning."

Jesse appeared unimpressed.

"Well, then," said Savage, "if you did not kill Horace Millen, then I suppose you won't mind going out to Mr. Waterman's funeral establishment and looking at the body."

The statement had its intended effect. Jesse was visibly rattled. "I don't want to go," he said nervously.

Ignoring his protests, Chief Savage nodded to Dearborn, Ham, and Wood, who immediately hauled the boy outside, bundled him into a hack, and drove him to the undertaking parlor in Roxbury. Jesse—his arms tightly clamped in the grip of Dearborn and Wood—was dragged inside and ushered into the embalming room, where a small, shrouded figure lay stretched upon a table.

"I don't want to see him," Jesse cried, struggling to break free of his captors' hold. "You can't make me."

"Yes, we can," Wood said grimly, then signaled to Waterman, who lifted the sheet from the tiny form. When Jesse tried to turn his head away, one of the detectives grabbed him by the back of the neck and forced him to look squarely at the corpse.

At the sight of the savaged body—the gaping throat, the ruptured eye, the perforated chest—Jesse began to tremble violently.

"Did you do it?" asked Dearborn. "Did you kill him?"

In a tremulous voice, Jesse replied, "I guess I did."

"What did you do it for?" demanded Wood.

"I don't know," Jesse said weakly. "Something made me." For the first time, he appeared genuinely stricken. "Take me out of here. I don't want to stay here."

Seated again in the carriage, Jesse continued to tremble. "I am sorry I did it," he said as the vehicle headed back to the police station. "Please don't tell my mother."

"Where did you wash the blood off your knife?" Wood asked.

"I didn't wash it," Jesse answered. "I stuck the blade into the marsh mud and cleaned it."

"What about your hands? Did you wash *them?*"

There was no need to wash them, Jesse explained. He had been careful not to get any blood on his hands.

When Wood asked Jesse what he thought should be done with him, the boy tearfully replied: "Put me somewhere, so I can't do such things."

Not long afterward, the carriage pulled up at Station Six, where—in order to prevent him from communicating with other prisoners—Jesse was placed in an isolation cell with a heavy wooden door. By that time, Wood and his colleagues had gone without food since just after daybreak and were ravenously hungry. Informing Captain Dyer that they were going out for lunch and would return shortly, they requested that no one be allowed to see Pomeroy on any account during their absence. Dyer gave them his assurance, and the three men departed.

From a purely professional point of view it had been a gratifying morning. The ghastly crime had been solved less than twenty-four hours after its commission. As he and his colleagues looked for a place to eat, Wood could not help feeling pleased. He had gotten exactly he was hoping for: a confession from Jesse Pomeroy's lips.

18

It is a matter of great surprise to those conversant with the facts of the case that the Pomeroy boy, after his conviction of so many heinous offenses, should have been pardoned out of reform school.

—*Boston Evening Journal,* April 24, 1874

Few figures in the annals of American crime have had the ability to generate as much controversy as Jesse Harding Pomeroy. For more than fifty years, he managed to find ways of stirring up intense indignation in the Boston public. And that power to provoke manifested itself from the very beginning of the Millen case, even before Pomeroy was officially named as a suspect.

Nowadays, an accused criminal can count on a fair degree of protection from the excesses of the press. Even when the evidence points overwhelmingly to someone's guilt, the news media must be careful to identify him as a mere *suspect*. A man can be discovered with a dozen corpses in his crawl space, a freezer full of human viscera, and a bedroom decorated with body parts. But until he's been convicted—or has confessed—journalists are legally required to describe him as an "alleged" criminal.

Things were substantially different a hundred years ago, when the press had fewer compunctions about branding someone a criminal. Just hours after the Powers brothers made their awful discovery on Savin Hill Beach—and before he had even been picked up by the police—Jesse Pomeroy was already being trumpeted by some newswriters as the killer. By the following morning, his name was plastered on the front page of every paper in the city, along with a detailed account of his earlier crimes against children. The result was an immediate explosion of public outrage, directed at those who had elected to put "the boy fiend" back on the streets after less than eighteen months in reform school.

Typical of this outcry was an editorial that ran in the *Boston Globe* on Friday morning, April 24, under the headline "The Boy Murderer":

> There must be something wrong in the regulations under which an inmate of the Reform School, sentenced for his minority, can be pardoned out on probation and turned loose in the community without regard to the crimes that he has committed or the propensities which he has displayed. In the case of the young fiend, Jesse Pomeroy, all that was necessary to secure his liberty on probation seems to have been an appeal of his mother, backed by a friend, although he had wantonly tortured no less than seven small boys for no apparent reason but a morbid delight in their sufferings. There is evidently need of a more careful consideration before the decrees of the law in the case of juvenile offenders are thus nullified. The boy Pomeroy seems to be a moral monstrosity. He had no provocation and no rational motive for his atrocious conduct. He did not know the little lad Millen at all, but enticed him away, and cut and hacked him to death with a penknife merely for sport. . . .
>
> While we favor a humane treatment for juvenile delinquents . . . it should not be so easy to obtain a remission of penalties on pleas of good behavior or the interposition of too sympathetic petitioners.

Other papers were even more harsh in their condemnation of the officials who had authorized Pomeroy's probation. "That a pardon should have been granted to such a fiend as Pomeroy shows a culpable lack of judgment somewhere," proclaimed the *Boston Herald*, "and excites high indignation among those familiar with the circumstances which resulted in his committal to reform school."

In the face of such criticism, the people responsible for Jesse's early release from Westborough immediately found themselves on the defensive. Some—like Mr. John Ayers, one of the trustees who had supported the parole—hastened to justify their decision. Interviewed by a reporter from the *Globe*, Ayers declared that "when boys are sent to the Reform School, they are sent for their minority—unless, after a considerable stay, their behavior has been exemplary. If they give promise of reform and of future good behavior, and if they have a good home to which their parents are anxious to have them returned, they are often pardoned on probation. This is an everyday occurrence, and this was the case with Pomeroy."

Others involved in the parole process insisted that they had spoken out against Jesse's release. Mr. D. B. Johnson, for example—an assistant visiting agent of the State Board of Charities—issued a public statement in which he claimed that he had "actively opposed the pardon on the ground that Pomeroy had been in Reform School but seventeen months, and that there had been seven cases of inhuman treatment, by torturing boys, against him at the time of his sentence."

Whether scrambling to defend his decision or presenting himself as a valiant (if hopelessly outmatched) dissenter, everyone connected to Jesse Pomeroy's parole from reform school obviously felt himself to be in imminent professional jeopardy. And with good cause. Already the citizens of Boston—appalled at a penal system that had made their children vulnerable to the depredations of a fiend—were demanding an accounting. There was no way of telling yet where the axe would eventually fall. But sooner or later heads were bound to roll.

One official who quickly came under fire was Police Captain Henry T. Dyer, who had supported Jesse's pardon under the theory that—as he had stated during his interview with Gardiner Tufts of the State Board of Charities—"it isn't best to be down on a boy too hard or too long." In the wake of the Millen murder, stories began to spread throughout South Boston that Dyer had been motivated less by his faith in juvenile redemption than by his friendship with Mrs. Pomeroy, with whom—according to rumor—he was on "intimate" terms.

That Dyer was, for whatever reason, inordinately sympathetic to the Pomeroys appeared to be confirmed on Thursday afternoon, not long after Jesse made his tearful confession to Detective Wood.

Wood, Ham, and Dearborn had permitted themselves less than a half hour for lunch before hurrying back to Station Six at around 2:30 P.M. Intending to have Jesse put his confession in writing, the detectives took him into an empty office, seated him at a table, and presented him with a pencil and a blank sheet of paper.

"What's this for?" Jesse asked.

"We want you to give us a written statement," Wood explained. "Put down everything you said about killing Horace Millen."

"I never said I killed anyone," Jesse replied offhandedly.

Wood looked at his colleagues in astonishment before turning back to Jesse and saying, "You *told* me you killed him."

"No, I didn't," Jesse said. "That's a dirty lie. I'm innocent, and I want to go home."

Restraining his impulse to grab the boy by the shoulders and shake the truth out of him, Wood pulled him roughly from the chair and marched him back to his cell. Something had clearly changed in the short time that the three detectives had been gone for lunch. It didn't take long for Wood to find out what had happened in their absence. Asking around the station house, he was stunned to discover that—in spite of his emphatic request that Jesse not be allowed to see visitors—a man named Stephen G. Deblois, one of the directors of the State Reform School, had been permitted to speak to the boy.

When Wood returned to Jesse's cell and asked about Deblois, the boy readily admitted that the director had come to see him.

"What did he say to you?" Wood demanded.

"He said he is my friend, and that he doesn't believe I am guilty," Jesse answered calmly. "He said that there is nothing against me but circumstantial evidence, and that I should not answer any more questions."

Seething, Wood left the cell and made for the captain's office, where he began remonstrating with Dyer. "Didn't we tell you not to let anyone see him?"

Dyer seemed unfazed. "Yes, but the man is on the board of the state reformatory."

"That doesn't matter a damn," said Wood. "You've done a fine thing. Pomeroy will go on claiming he didn't do it. You'll see. He'll stick to it from now on."

Dyer only answered with a shrug.

Wood felt a dangerous urge rising in his chest—an impulse to shower the captain with curses. Choking it back, he swiveled on his heels and stormed out of Dyer's office.

Detective Wood's prediction that Pomeroy would "stick to" his new claim of innocence was fulfilled on the very next day—Friday, April 24—when the official inquest into the Millen murder got underway. It was held at the Ninth Police Station in the presence of Coroner Allen and his six-man jury. Jesse's mother had retained the services of two South Boston attorneys—Messrs. Joseph H. Cotton and E. G. Walker—who requested the privilege of consulting with their client prior to his testimony in order to discuss his defense. While assuring the lawyers that he "intended to give the lad every opportunity to vindicate himself," the coroner denied the request, explaining that he could "not permit counsel to see the accused until after the jury had listened to his story concerning his whereabouts on the day of his murder."

The proceedings began with the swearing-in of ten witnesses, who were then promptly excluded from the room. A few moments later, Jesse was brought in and seated at a table beside his mother, whose careworn appearance contrasted strikingly with her son's conspicuous nonchalance. Speaking in a cool, absolutely assured voice, Jesse (who'd had two days by this point to work on his alibi) proceeded to relate a story that—though essentially identical to his original version—was far less vague and inconsistent.

During his initial interrogation on Tuesday night, for example, he claimed that he had spent the key hours between 11:30 A.M. and 2:30 P.M. strolling up to and through the Commons. He'd been suspiciously hazy, however, about certain important details, such as the condition of Tremont Street (which was undergoing major construction work). Now, by contrast, he was suddenly able to evoke the scene with a remarkable—indeed photographic—precision.

"On Tremont," he explained, "I noticed that men were digging up the left-hand side going towards the Commons. They were preparing to lay pipes. They were working towards the Scollay Square. When I saw them, I think they were between Winter and Bromfield Streets. Then I crossed to the Commons and sat on a tree stump which was covered with zinc. I noticed that the side of the fence on Tremont Street had been taken away. Some of the walks were covered with tar, and others were covered with boards. After resting a few minutes, I started again and walked along till I came to the Frog Pond. The fountain was not playing when I was there, though the pond was full of water. I did not stop there. I went down by the parade ground. There were some boys playing ball there. Then I went right over to the Public Garden and passed through the fence. I noticed in the doorway of the hothouse a large plant. I don't know the name of it but it was in a large tub, which was painted green."

Altogether, Jesse testified for over an hour. He ended with a firm declaration of his innocence, insisting that he "never saw the murdered boy until I saw him in the coffin at the undertaker's. I am sure I never spoke to him." He also asserted that he was unfamiliar with the spot where the murder took place, having "been out there only once, about two years ago this coming summer."

When Jesse was finished, his chief attorney, Joseph H. Cotton, requested that his testimony be read back by the scribe. Jesse listened attentively, then—after asking for a few minor revisions—signed the transcript with a bold, clean hand. He was remanded to the custody of Captain Hastings of the Ninth Police Station with instructions that no one be allowed to have conversations with him besides his lawyers and mother.

By that point, it was already so late in the afternoon that only two more people had a chance to appear before the jury—Officer Roswell Lyons, the first policeman to arrive at the crime scene, and George Powers, the younger of the two beachcombing brothers who had originally stumbled on Horace Millen's corpse. Following their testimony, the inquest was adjourned until 2:00 P.M. the following Monday.

As soon as the proceedings were over, the newsmen hurried back to their offices to write up their stories. For the most part, these turned out to be straightforward synopses of the day's testimony, though several of the reporters also provided their own impressions of the young suspect's appearance and behavior.

A few of the journalists were especially struck by Jesse's unflappable manner, which—as one of them wrote—was so "candid and explicit" that it was "regarded by some as indicative of his innocence." In 1874, of course, people were far less familiar with the bizarre workings of the psychopathic mind, which makes it possible for these killers to maintain an uncanny composure in the face of the most extraordinary pressures. (For example, when a trio of policemen came to question him about a bleeding, naked fourteen-year-old boy who had just fled in terror from his apartment, Jeffrey Dahmer remained so calm and convincing that the cops turned the boy back over to him—at which point Dahmer promptly tortured, murdered, and dismembered the luckless teenager.)

To other reporters, however, the very cast of Jesse's features was sufficient proclamation of his guilt. In an age that gave serious credence to the pseudoscience of phrenology (according to which a person's mental characteristics could be deduced from the contours of his skull), it was entirely possible to judge someone's innermost nature by his facial appearance. The writer for the *Boston Globe*, for example, needed just a "single glance at the boy's countenance" to "see how it was possible for him to perpetrate the outrages for which he was taken into custody." Pomeroy's innate and incurable degeneracy was, first and foremost, visible in his eyes:

> They are wicked eyes, sullenly, brutishly wicked eyes, and as in moments of wandering thought the boy looks out of them, he seems one who could delight in the writhings of his helpless victims beneath the stab of the knife, the puncture of the awl, or the prick of the pin, as he has so often delighted in. There is nothing interesting in the look. It is altogether unsympathetic, merciless. But worse than all the rest is the sensuality that hangs like lead about those sunken eyes, and that marks every feature of the face. The pallor of his complexion, the lifeless, flabby look that pertains to his cheeks, corresponds with this view; and when the boy walks, it is not the bold, buoyant movement of an innocent lad, but apparently the shuffling of one whose thoughts are of the lowest kind.

With his shuffling gait, sunken eyes, and corpselike complexion, the figure portrayed in this passage sounds less like a severely disturbed adolescent than like the nightmarish creation dreamed up by Mary Shelley fifty years before. And indeed, that is precisely what the press had already begun turning Jesse Pomeroy into—a fourteen-year-old Frankenstein monster, a homegrown horror that would haunt the people of Boston for decades to come.

19

The dime novels came in libraries; for years, until ready for the
sober classes of high school, I devoured such series as the Old Cap
Collier, Old Sleuth, Nick Carter, and Pluck and Luck. Unhappy
was the day when I could not go through at least one of these. What
a phantasmagoria of murder, arson, and sudden death! Yet all it
taught me was a vocabulary of long words and literary clichés.
                                    —Isaac Goldberg, "A Boston Boyhood"

Friday saw another significant development besides the start
of the inquest. Under the headline "A Young Demon," an article
about the Millen murder appeared on the front page of the *New
York Times*. Though preoccupation with the killing continued to be
particularly intense in Boston (where, as one journalist reported,
"the cruel death of the Millen boy remains the general topic of
conversation in the community"), the Pomeroy case was no longer
a matter of merely local interest. It had become national news.

"The story of the Boston child-murderer is one of the most extraordinary of the period," proclaimed the *Times*. Two things
made it so remarkable: the extreme youth of the culprit and the
enormity of his acts, the same factors that have turned the "killer
kid" tragedies of our own day into a source of such widespread
consternation. Indeed, if it proves nothing else, the Pomeroy
case offers striking confirmation of the Scriptural truism that
"there is no new thing under the sun." In every essential respect—from the savage nature of the crimes to the stunned reactions they have provoked—the juvenile atrocities that have
horrified the modern world (and which are often regarded as a
uniquely contemporary phenomenon, a symptom of societal
decay) were prefigured more than a century ago by the deeds of
Jesse Pomeroy.

The modern-day outrage with the closest parallels to the Horace Millen slaying was the 1993 torture-murder of three-year-old James Bulger by a pair of preteen thrill-killers, Jon Venables and Robert Thompson. Indeed, the two crimes bear astonishing similarities. In each case, a little boy, hardly older than a toddler, was lured from a public place in broad daylight (in Bulger's case, from a crowded shopping center just outside Liverpool; in Millen's, from the bustling streets of his South Boston neighborhood). The juvenile abductors then led their little victims by the hand on a meandering trek, pausing occasionally to speak to other people (at one point, Venables and Thompson asked an elderly woman for directions, while Jesse exchanged a few words with a young clam digger on the beach). The victims were eventually brought to isolated locales (Bulger to the verge of a railroad line, Millen to a remote stretch of marshland), where they were tortured and slain. Afterward, the underage killers returned to their homes and families, acting with such perfect nonchalance that they might have been guilty of nothing worse than a day of playing hooky.

In both cases, public reaction was similar, too. Like the people of Great Britain—who were plunged into a state of anguished soul-searching by the Bulger atrocity—the citizens of Boston struggled to make sense of the Millen slaying and of the motives that had (as one reporter put it) "prompted the inhuman wretch, Pomeroy, to deprive the little child of life."

The communal outrage and distress aroused by the crime were summed up by a front-page story that appeared in Saturday's *Boston Herald:*

> It is many a day since anything has happened in Boston which has so wrought upon the feelings and sympathies of the public, as the late terrible tragedy on the beach at the foot of Crescent Avenue. Murder, committed in a heat of passion or when the perpetrator of this greatest of crimes is unmanned by an excessive use of intoxicants, is horrible enough. But when, as in the present instance, a child of less than five years is seduced away by a lad of fourteen and tortured until the little life can no longer dwell within its earthly tenement, and that so inhumanly, what shall be

said? The moral sentiment of the community is
shocked, confounded, and everyone ponders in
vain search for a rational solution of the causes
which could have brought about the death of the
little boy, Millen, at the hand of his supposed
youthful murderer.

Various theories were advanced to account for the crime.
Pomeroy's "mental makeup"—a subject that would generate a
great deal of heated debate in the months to come—was ana-
lyzed by a number of commentators, who concluded that, despite the extreme depravity of his behavior, Jesse was
apparently sane. The writer for the *Herald* offered a typical appraisal: "He does not look like a youth actuated by the spirit
of a fiend, and, with the exception of a peculiarity about the
eyes, he has no marked expression in his face from which one
might read the spirit within. The idea that he is insane is not
supported, except by the extraordinary character of his conduct."

Nor could his family circumstances account for his appalling
behavior. "There was not, so far as is known, any insanity among
his progenitors, so he could not have inherited it," the *Herald* reported. True, there were some questionable factors in Jesse's
background. Probing into his ancestry, the *Boston Globe* discovered a history of family instability that was highly unusual in the
mid-nineteenth century.

At a time when couples rarely split up, the marriages of both
Jesse's parents *and* his paternal grandparents had ended in divorce. (In the era just before and after the Civil War—when the
nation included over fourteen million married couples—there
were only about 10,000 divorces per year in America.) According
to the *Globe*, the "union of Pomeroy's grandparents was not a
happy one, and as the current report has it, the fault was with
the man, not the woman. In some subsequent divorce proceedings, it appeared that the husband ill-treated his wife in various
harsh ways." Following in the old man's footsteps, Jesse's own
father, Thomas, had also been abusive to his wife. "In conse-
quence of their continual quarrels," the *Globe* reported, Jesse's
parents had separated, "leaving the boy to drift pretty much at
his own will. Thus, there seems to have been nothing in the rela-

tions of his home which was calculated to counteract the natural weaknesses of his moral character."

Still, even the "lack of elevating influences" in Jesse's home life could not—in the opinion of most observers—explain the staggering brutality of his crimes. Desperate to construe the horror in rational (or at least comprehensible) terms, the public grasped at increasingly tenuous straws. As soon as it became known, for example, that Thomas Pomeroy worked in the Faneuil Hall meat market, some journalists began proposing that Jesse's bloodthirsty propensities derived from his childhood exposure to butchering.

It wasn't long, however, before a number of commentators came up with another—and, in the minds of many people, far more persuasive—theory. And here, too, the Pomeroy case served as a striking forerunner of contemporary issues. Virtually every notorious case of juvenile murder in recent years has been blamed, at least partly, on media violence. At the height of the Bulger affair, for example, much was made of the fact that one of the young killers, Jon Venables, had reportedly watched the horror video *Child's Play 3* right before the murder. And when a fifteen-year-old New Jersey teenager was arrested in October 1997 for the strangulation-murder of an eleven-year-old neighbor, New York City tabloids ran front-page stories trumpeting the suspect's "violent obsessions with Smashing Pumpkins and Beavis & Butthead."

Within days of the Horace Millen murder, similar accusations were circulating about Jesse Pomeroy. In the pre-electronic era of 1870s America, however, the medium that came under attack was not television, film, gangsta rap, or Nintendo. It was the dime novel.

The dime novel was born in the summer of 1860, when the New York publishing firm of Beadle and Adams put out a cheaply made, paperbound adventure story—Ann Sophia Stephens's *Malaeska, the Indian Wife of the White Hunter*—and priced it at ten cents. ("A dollar book for a dime!" was Beadle's advertising slogan.) Within a few weeks of its appearance, Mrs. Stephens's novel had sold more than sixty-five thousand copies. Beadle immediately followed up with other crudely printed page-turners, published at the rate of two per month. When the eighth title in the series—Edward S. Ellis's *Seth Jones; or, The Captives of the Frontier*—

appeared in October 1860, the American public snapped up half a million copies.

Before long—as other publishers began churning out scores of these throwaway publications—the marketplace became flooded with them. During the Civil War, they were shipped by the freight-car load to Union soldiers, who—starved for escapism—devoured countless works like *Fugitives of the Border, The Phantom Horseman,* and *Bald-Eagle Bob, the Boy Buccanneer.* The product of underpaid and largely talentless hacks, these outlandish fantasies might not have offered much in the way of convincing characters, credible stories, plausible dialogue, or anything resembling literary merit. But—with their extravagant tales of heroic frontiersman, savage "redskins," swashbuckling pirates, and romantic desperadoes— they did offer the kind of easy, fast-paced thrills that, in a subsequent era, would be supplied by superhero comics, television westerns, and action movies. And like those later forms of pop entertainment, they soon came under attack by assorted moral watchdogs—politicians, religious leaders, educators, and the like.

Denunciations of the dime novel's supposedly corrupting effects on young minds began appearing everywhere, from the pulpit to newspaper editorial pages to such venerable publications as *Harper's* and the *Atlantic Monthly.* Writing in the late 1870s, for example, a critic named W. H. Bishop blamed everything from school truancy to petty thievery to parricide on the "sensational romances" peddled in "cheap dime fiction." And in a famous editorial cartoon of the time, a dime novel publisher is shown giving away a free loaded pistol to every young subscriber. The implication was clear: Beadle and his ilk were little more than merchants of death, turning innocent children into cold-blooded killers.

To be sure, there were other commentators who came to the defense of dime novels, most notably a critic named William Everett, who—writing in the distinguished cultural journal *The North American Review*—declared that these crude, wildly popular books "were unobjectionable morally, whatever fault be found with their literary style and composition. They do not even obscurely pander to vice, or excite the passions." Similarly, Edmund Pearson—an early historian of the genre—scoffed at the notion that dime novels were responsible for polluting the morals of the young. To Pearson, the dime novel merely served as a scapegoat, a simple explanation for the troubling complexities of human behavior (and—for young delinquents and their parents alike—a handy way of shirking blame).

"Parents who had shamefully neglected a son and allowed him to stray into mischief," he wryly observed, "found it very convenient to stand in a police court and lay all the blame on dime novels. Inherent deviltry; neglect; selfishness; cruel egotism—oh, dear, no. It was nothing but wicked dime novels. Willy was such a good boy until he began to read them. . . . Judges and teachers and clergymen and Sunday-school superintendents and even police chiefs began to denounce dime novels. It was the most useful explanation of crime, and the easiest excuse for the offender."

Erastus Beadle himself insisted on the purity of his publications, issuing a set of guidelines to his authors that prohibited "all things offensive to good taste," forbade any "subjects or characters that carry an immoral taint," and warned against stories that "cannot be read with satisfaction by every right-minded person, young and old alike." And it was certainly true that readers would have been hard-pressed to find anything even remotely suggestive in a work like *Antelope Abe, the Boy Guide* or *Mohawk Nat: A Tale of the Great Northwest.*

Violence, however—of the ostensibly wholesome, red-blooded, all-American variety—was another matter. As cultural historian Russel Nye has written, the Beadle books were crammed with "blood, bullets, and constant frantic action." According to Nye's estimate, the typical dime novel averaged about twenty killings per book. And the situation became even more extreme as other publishers entered the field and began issuing ever more graphic and sensationalistic stories. To keep up with competitors like George P. Munro, the Beadles were forced to boost the bloodshed in their own publications—"to kill a few more Indians," as Erastus Beadle put it. Before long, the level of violence in books like *Redplume the Renegade, Rangers of the Mohawk,* and *Rattlesnake Ned's Revenge* had reached a dizzying pitch.

In his attack on "cheap dime fiction," W. H. Bishop estimated that among the dozens of books he had purchased while researching his study, "there were not less than ten thousand slain." He then goes on to describe the carnage in one of the most popular dime novels of all time, Edward L. Wheeler's *Deadwood Dick on Deck; or, Calamity Jane, The Heroine of Whoop-Up:*

In the first chapter, seventy road-agents come riding into town. They slay eighteen of the residents and are slain themselves—all but one, who is, by the orders of a leader named Old Bull-whacker, immediately strung up to a tree and pays the earthly penalty for his crimes. And in the next chapter, we find a young man named Charley Davis dashing around a bend, bestriding his horse backwards, and firing at five mounted pursuers. They were twelve originally, but he has gradually picked off the rest. He is joined by Calamity Jane, a beautiful young woman who carries a sixteen-shot Winchester rifle, a brace of pistols in her belt, and another in her holsters, and between the two the pursuing five are easily disposed of. Here are a hundred dead in two chapters only!

In a similar vein, Russell Nye cites a typical passage from one of the later Beadle novels in which the hero—having stumbled upon "the swollen, mutilated corpse of a man, covered with blood and clotted gore"—notes how "the distorted countenance was rendered doubly repulsive by the red streaks where mingled blood and brains had oozed from the shattered skull."

Clearly, the media violence so often deplored by contemporary critics pales by comparison to the slaughter commonly found in dime novels—those immensely popular, escapist entertainments of the pre- and post-Civil era, whose primary audience was young boys.

Given the profuse and extremely graphic violence in dime novels—and the long-standing tendency of moral reformers to blame juvenile aggression on the sensationalistic fantasies of popular culture—it is no surprise that, within days of his arrest, stories began to circulate that Jesse Pomeroy was addicted to these blood-and-thunder publications. "There is plenty of evidence," declared the *Boston Globe*, "to show that the reading of dime novels ... constituted a good share of the boy's mental nourishment, and herein he was not restricted but commended rather for his studious literary disposition."

As a particularly incriminating bit of "evidence," the *Globe* cited the testimony of a boy named George Thompson, supposedly a "chum" of Jesse's, who revealed that the latter "always had a brick-colored 'Beadle' or a white-covered 'Munro' in his pocket or hand. In school, he used to keep a novel in back of his history, grammar, or geography book and devour it while pretending to study his lessons."

To be sure the interviewee himself—along with the rest of his pals—was an equally avid consumer of dime novels, who loved playing games of violent frontier make-believe. "I always insisted on playing Wild Bill, because he had killed thirty-nine men," the young man cheerfully asserted. Other boys in the group preferred such two-fisted, all-American characters as Buffalo Bill, Dashing Charlie Emmett, Texas Jack, Wrestling Joe, and Rattlesnake Ned.

What made Jesse so suspect was his highly unnatural sympathy for the Indians. "Jesse would watch us," said Thompson, "but he thought it unfair that the Indians were always wiped out, while the scouts were victorious. He seemed to think more of the Indians than he did of the scouts. Simon Girty, I remember, was his hero. Jesse used to think it was a fine thing to be a renegade like Girty; to be the one white man in a great Indian tribe like the Shawnees; to have lots of squaws do all the work, while he sat around and discussed roasted venison. Then the fun with the prisoners of war! The running of the gauntlet, and the different modes of putting captives to death!"

Reports like these soon led to authoritative pronouncements—issued by assorted savants—that it was Jesse's fondness for "reading cheap blood-and-thunder stories, particularly those about Indians and the way they torture prisoners" that "first put it in his mind to torture boys."

One of the weirdest news stories on this subject appeared in the April 27 issue of the *Boston Herald,* under the following headline:

THE CHILD MURDER.

**The Dreams of a Spiritual Medium
on the Subject of the Tragedy—
Pomeroy the Agent of Young
Indian Devils Avenging
Themselves on "the Whites"—A
Theory Which Requires Time for
Substantiation.**

According to this article, a reporter for the paper—seeking to shed light on Pomeroy's motivations—had sought out the advice of a "thoroughly reliable trance medium." This unidentified spiritualist had promptly put himself in touch with a mysterious "intelligence" that proceeded to reveal the following information through the medium's lips:

> The intelligence spoke of the recent event and, incidentally, of previous acts of violence committed by the youth Pomeroy. It said that . . . he was to blame and yet not to blame. The law would hold him guilty, but in another sense he was not responsible for the act. He was defective in his mental organization and lacked an appreciation of right and wrong, so that even in the commission of murder he would have no realizing sense of wrongdoing. If his parents had watched him closely in years past, they would probably have observed that he manifested an unnatural fondness for witnessing acts of torture and cruelty, like the excessive beating of horses and the like.
>
> But this was not all that was said in explanation of the affair. Through this weakness, he had attracted about him a spiritual influence of an even worse type, so that in the present act of murder the boy was but the tool of a blood-thirsty and cruel band of spirits. To be more explicit, this band was composed of a number of wild and untutored Indian boys about a dozen years old, led on by another young savage of some seventeen years. Most, if not all, of them had within a few years been massacred by the whites in the far Western plains, and, having been educated to hate the "pale-face," they had gathered about the boy (Pomeroy) and through him sought vengeance upon the oppressors of their people.
>
> In evidence of the truth of this assertion, the intelligence called the writer's attention to the published fact that the boy would dance around his victims, real Indian fashion, and seemingly delight himself as he saw the blood flowing from the wounds of the tortured captives.

Needless to say, the theory that Jesse was demonically possessed by a band of vengeance-crazed Indian spirits was bizarre in the extreme. Nevertheless, some of the medium's comments were surprisingly astute—his observation about Jesse's parents, for example, and their failure to note his early "fondness for witnessing acts of torture and cruelty." The same point is commonly made by modern psychologists, who list childhood sadism as an early warning sign of what is now called "conduct disorder."

Indeed, what strikes a contemporary researcher into the Pomeroy case is that—when it comes to understanding the root causes of sociopathic behavior—things haven't progressed very much in the hundred-plus years since the "boy fiend" was on the prowl. We are still groping for answers, still putting the blame on violent popular entertainment, or neglectful parents, or innate propensities for evil. In fact, there are still people who insist that "the devil made them do it."

In the end, the answer provided in a newspaper editorial that appeared on Friday, April 24, 1874, was as good as anything modern criminology has come up with. There was only one way to explain the atrocious deeds of Jesse Pomeroy, proclaimed the paper. The boy was "a moral monstrosity."

20

Public interest in the tragic death of the child Horace H. Millen does not seem to abate, but, on the contrary, daily grows more intense.
—*Boston Post*, April 27, 1874

The growing notoriety of the Pomeroy case was demonstrated again on Monday, when the *Boston Evening Herald* ran an editorial pertaining to the Millen murder by the Reverend Henry Ward Beecher, the most famous American preacher of the day.

Two days earlier—on Saturday, April 25—the little boy's funeral had taken place. The plight of John and Leonora Millen—so poor that they could not afford a coffin for their four-year-old child—had elicited an outpouring of sympathy from the people of South Boston. The grief-stricken parents had been deluged with notes of condolence, many containing small sums of money. The Millens had also received a purse of $50 from John's fellow-workers at Clark's cabinet factory; while the police officers attached to Station Six had contributed an additional $150.

As a result, the Millens had been able to purchase a handsome casket for their child. Following the funeral service on Saturday morning, at which the Reverend Mr. Rand officiated, Horace's body was transported by train to Wicasset, Maine—John Millen's birthplace—for burial in the family plot.

It was the terrible ordeal of the murdered boy's parents—and especially of Horace's mother, who had been virtually prostrated by the tragedy—that inspired the editorial. The Reverend Mr. Beecher (who was himself at the center of a nationwide scandal at the time of the Pomeroy affair, having been publicly denounced as an adulterer by the flamboyant women's rights crusader, Victoria Woodhull) based his article on a passage from scripture, Hebrews 12: 11: "Now no chastening for the present seemeth to be joyous but grievous; nevertheless, afterward it yieldeth the peaceable fruit of righteousness unto them which are exercised thereby."

The editorial itself—a kind of consolatory sermon, entitled "A Mother's Sorrow"—begins with an evocation of the indescribable raptures of mother-love:

> As the waters roll in on the shore with incessant throbs, night and day, and always, not alone when storms prevail, but in calms as well, so it is with a mother's heart bereaved of her children. There is no grief like unto it—Rachel weeping for her children and refusing to be comforted because they are not! With what long patience, what burden and suffering does the mother wait until the child of her hope is placed in her arms and under the sight of her eyes. She remembereth no more the anguish for joy that a man is born into the world.
>
> Who can read, or, if he saw, could utter the thoughts of a mother during all the days and nights in which she broods the helpless thing. Every true mother takes home the full meaning of the angel's word, that holy thing which shall be born of thee shall be called the Son of God. The mother does not even whisper what she thinks, and the whole air is full of gentle pictures, every one of the background of the blue heavens.
>
> The child grows; grows in favor of God and man—and every admiring look cast upon it, even by a stranger, sends light and gladness to the mother's heart. Wonderful child! The sun is brighter for it! The whole earth is blessed by its presence! Sorrows, pains, weariness, self-denials, for its sake are eagerly sought and delighted in.

Beecher then delineates the crushing sense of grief and self-recrimination that overwhelms the mother when her cherished boy is suddenly snatched away from life:

The mother's heart was like a heaven while it
lived; now it has ascended to God's heaven and
the mother's heart is as the gloom of midnight.
Wild words of self-reproach at length break out,
as when a frozen torrent is set loose by spring
days. She that has lavished her life-force upon the
child turns upon herself with fierce charges of
carelessness, of unskill, of thoughtlessness. She
sees a hundred ways in which the child would
have lived but for her! All love is turned to self-
recrimination. Tears come at last to quench the
fire of purgatory. But grief takes new shapes
every hour, till the nerve has lost its sensibility,
and then she coldly hates her unnatural and inhuman heart that will not feel!

The editorial concludes on a note of solace that suggests the
healing effects which the passage time—and the return to the
mundane routines of everyday life—inevitably bring:

A child dying, dies but once; but the mother
dies a hundred times. When the sharpness is
over, and the dullness of an overspent brain is
passed, and she must take up the shuttle again
and weave the web of daily life, pity her not that
she must work, must join again the discordant
voices, and be forced to duties irksome and hate-
ful. These all are kindly medicines. A new
thought is slowly preparing. It is that immovable
constancy and strength which sorrow gives when
it has wrought the divine intent.

On the same day that this editorial was published, the inquest
into Horace Millen's death resumed at Police Station Nine. The
session, which began shortly after lunch and lasted for about
three hours, was held behind closed doors—a circumstance that
led to a great deal of griping on the part of reporters. "Why the
whole thing needs be shrouded in mystery is unaccountable,"
the reporter for the *Boston Journal* complained; while his colleague at the *Evening Transcript* similarly questioned the purpose

of such "secretive sessions" and denounced them as "stupid proceedings."

Not that the newsmen were the only ones excluded from the inquest on Monday afternoon. Even Jesse's lawyers were obliged to leave the hearing room once the testimony began. Nevertheless, thanks to the persistence of the reporters, who (in the self-congratulatory words of the *Herald*'s man) "lingered about the premises for over three long and weary hours with their customary patience"—the papers were able to provide their readers with a summary of the day's proceedings, gleaned from interviews with participants.

Altogether, the coroner's jury heard testimony from the Powers brothers, Obed Goodspeed, and four other people who had been on the marsh the day of the murder. At least three of the witnesses positively placed Jesse at the crime scene. The casts of Jesse's boot prints were also exhibited, along with the confiscated boots themselves, whose soles were shown to match their plaster counterparts point for point. In addition, the jury learned that Jesse's double-bladed knife had been subjected to a microscopic examination, and that (as the *Herald* reported) "traces of blood were plainly distinguishable on the larger blade."

The inquest concluded on the following day—Tuesday, April 28—with a four-hour session that commenced just after 2:00 P.M. Another half-dozen witnesses were examined, all but one of them police officers involved in the investigation. The most significant testimony of the day was delivered by Detective James Wood, who described the confession Jesse had made to him after viewing Horace Millen's corpse at Waterman's undertaking parlor.

Following the testimony of the final witness—Officer Hood of Police Station Nine—the coroner's six-man jury retired for its deliberation. They returned shortly after 7:00 P.M. with the following verdict: "That the said Horace Holden Millen came to his death between the hours of eleven o'clock in the forenoon and five o'clock in the afternoon of Wednesday, April 22nd, 1874, from loss of blood and injuries received in the neck and chest, which injuries were produced by some sharp-cutting instrument. And the jury further find, from the testimony before them, that they have probable cause to believe said murder was committed by Jesse Harding Pomeroy."

Jesse was returned to his cell to await his arraignment, which took place before Judge Wheelock at the Highlands Municipal Court on Friday morning, May 1. With his lawyer at his side, Jesse pleaded not guilty. He was committed to jail without bail to await the convening of the Grand Jury.

Approximately one month later, at its June term, the Grand Jury found (in the words of the indictment) "That Jesse Harding Pomeroy, April 22, 1874, at Boston, in and upon one Horace H. Millen (age 4 years), feloniously, wilfully, and of his malice afore-thought, an assault did make; and that the said Pomeroy with a certain knife, the said Millen in and upon the throat, breast, hands, and belly of the said Millen, then and there feloniously, wilfully, and of his malice aforethought did strike, cut, stab, and thrust, giving to the said Millen then and there with the knife aforesaid in and upon the throat, breast, hands, and belly of said Millen diverse mortal wounds, of which said mortal wounds, the said Millen of the twenty-second day of April did languish and languishing did live and on the twenty-second day of April, at Boston, the said Millen of the mortal wounds aforesaid, did die."

After entering a plea of not guilty, Jesse was once again de-nied bail and remanded to the Charles Street Jail—this time to await his trial for murder, scheduled to begin in December 1874.

PART 3

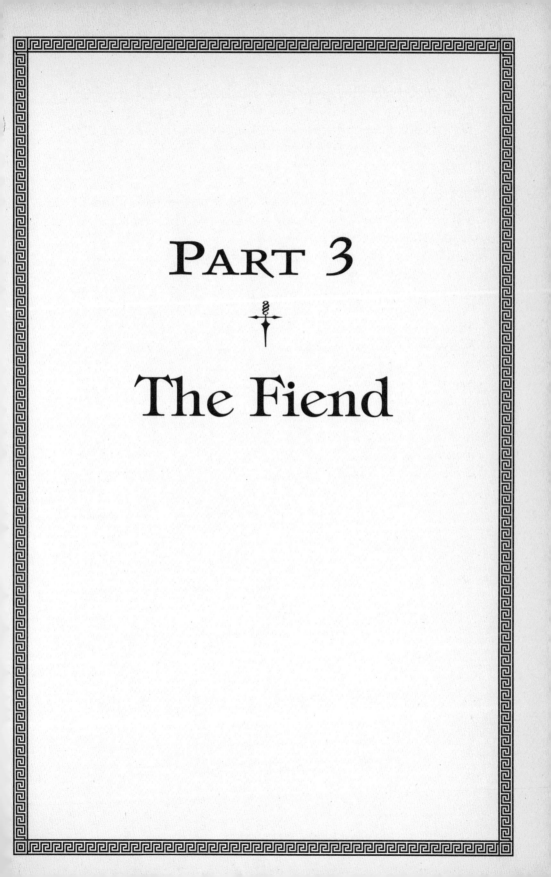

The Fiend

21

Every child is a little criminal. He becomes law-abiding only when we
have grafted inhibitions—"do nots"—upon his impressionable mind.
                                    —Dr. A. A. Brill, "Youthful Killers"

More than a century after the Pomeroy crimes, our country
was rocked by a string of preteen homicides that left countless
Americans groping for both explanations and solutions. Following
the so-called Jonesboro massacre in March 1998, for example—
when two Arkansas schoolboys gunned down four fellow students and a teacher—*Time* magazine ran a piece whose headline
posed a question that had suddenly become an issue of heated, nationwide debate: "What Is Justice for a Sixth-Grade Killer?" At
least one Texas politician, a State Representative named Jim Pitts,
believed he had the answer. A month after the Jonesboro tragedy,
Pitt proposed a bill that would permit the death penalty for murderers as young as eleven—a proposal endorsed by a sizable majority of his constituents.

Others, however, urged a more enlightened approach. Writing
in the *New York Times*, for example, Patrick T. Murphy, the Public
Guardian of Cook County, Illinois, argued that "eleven- and
thirteen-year olds are not short adults. They are children....
Because their characters are not formed, we have a chance to influence them, to divert them from becoming hardened criminals.
Let's not turn the clock back to the harsh justice of the nineteenth
century. Let's treat juveniles who commit crimes like the children
they are. If we as a society are saying that it's too late for an eleven-
and thirteen-year-old, we have a lot of soul-searching to do."

Clearly—along with internet porn, bioterrorism, and conspir-
acy theories—the debate over juvenile crime and punishment
has become a defining feature of our cultural moment. But it is

certainly not unique to modern times. For in this as in other regards, the Pomeroy case precisely foreshadowed the current
controversy over underage killers. No sooner had the Millen inquest ended than a fierce argument erupted over how to deal
with Jesse—and the terms of that dispute were remarkably similar to those heard in the wake of recent juvenile atrocities.

The earliest published call for Jesse's execution appeared on
Tuesday, April 28, on the letters page of the *Boston Daily Advertiser*.
The writer—identified only by the initials "S. M. Q."—pulled out
all the rhetorical stops in arguing that only one remedy, Pomeroy's
death, could guarantee the safety of the children of Boston from
future depredations by the "boy-tiger." The complete text of the
letter—which was headlined "A Mad Dog"—ran as follows:

> As the poor brute in frenzied torment with
> foaming jaws and starting eyes tears victim after
> victim in his headlong course, who can deny that
> he, as well as they, may be the object of legitimate
> pity and compassion? He has done no wrong, has
> been guilty of no offense which punishment will
> prevent him or others from repeating; and if ra-
> bies were a disease from which dogs recovered,
> one might imagine the owner pleading for the
> animal's life with promises of strict confinement
> until a cure is effected and all danger past.
>
> Suppose him to be apparently successful, and
> after the lapse of weeks or months, the beast—to
> all appearances healthy and harmless—is again
> at large. A *second time* the fierce impulse to tear
> living flesh maddens his fevered blood, and a *sec-
> ond time* defenseless and innocent youth fall man-
> gled and mutilated victims of his fury.
>
> "Spare him once more," says the philan-
> thropist, "and this time he shall be more securely
> chained; he is an object of pity and shall be put
> where he can't do such things."
>
> "He shall indeed," reply the parents whose
> darlings have thus far escaped the monster, "he
> shall indeed, and the policeman's revolver shall,
> in accordance with the law, send him there."

That the boy murderer whose fearful mania has found another defenseless victim may well be the object of the same compassion which we extend to the raging brute, none will deny. That the self-defense of society, in accordance with the law, should be the same in both instances, the writer believes to be a terrible but solemn duty. Vengeance is the Lord's, but the protection of innocent and defenseless human life is man's. For such a human tiger—with the beast's craving to tear and rend and the man's intellect to seek methods of gratifying it—there is but one sure prison, and if consigned to any other, more innocent blood will yet cry from the ground against those who might have spared its effusion.

A lunatic, whose insanity is such as to insure his confinement, may without danger be spared, but a person capable of restraining and concealing such horrible propensities for years, until opportunity may be contrived for its indulgence, is accountable for his actions and forfeits his right to an existence incompatible with the safety of his fellows. If two years of good behavior sufficed for the release of the boy-tiger, the lapse of five or ten at most may presumably set the man at liberty— at which period even the advocates of the abolition of the death penalty may do well to keep their children from the streets.

This and other equally emotionalistic cries for Jesse's blood were countered by more measured arguments that focused on the issues of his youth and mental condition. On Friday, May 1, for example, the *Boston Evening Transfer* published an editorial that—beginning with a derisive allusion to the writer of the "Mad Dog" letter—raised the question of Jesse's responsibility for his acts:

A good deal of nonsense is getting into print on account of the horrible developments in the Pomeroy case. In times of hotly excited indignation, the man who says the hardest things is likely to be thought the wisest man. Doubtless extermination is a prompt and sure means of preventing a repetition of offenses by the same offenders. To shoot pickpockets upon first conviction would insure society against trouble a second time from the same sneak. . . . But to sensible minds there are objections to this course.

Law is a general rule of action. It is based on average and aggregate estimates of human nature. It cannot be fitted exactly to every exceptional case. Laws touching homicide and cruelty suppose that those offenses proceed from recognized motives, and propose other motives, such as dread of punishment, to deter offenders from their commission. In the Pomeroy case, there is exceptional *absence* of the ordinary motives for violence. Vindictiveness, cupidity, fear of exposure—these are not present to the mind of the torturer. Nor is any other impulse which would not be promptly overruled by the ordinary sympathies and sensibilities of human nature, did those exist in Pomeroy. It seems plain that these checks do not exist in him, and if it be true that he had done nothing, when his career of violence began, to eradicate these natural instincts of mankind, it would certainly seem that he is not responsible for the absence of them. It may be expedient to exterminate Pomeroy . . . but it should hardly be called exact justice.

As these contrasting opinions make clear, feelings about the right way to punish the "boy killer" ran high from the very start of the case (both the "Mad Dog" letter and the editorial response were published before Jesse was even arraigned). Eventually, these emotions would erupt into a full-scale battle that would engage the passions of people throughout the nation, from ordinary citizens to some of the country's most eminent men.

In the meantime, Jesse languished in jail—reading, brooding, and keeping up a regular correspondence with his mother, brother, and a few staunch (if desperately misguided) supporters who persisted in believing in his innocence. As the spring turned into summer, the Pomeroy case slipped from the papers, supplanted by other more up-to-the-minute crimes, scandals, and atrocities.

In late May—as though to prove that juvenile depravity was not restricted to Boston—a gang of "young ruffians" (as the newspapers put it) attempted to sneak into the opening performance of Montgomery Queen's Circus in San Francisco by crawling under the tent. After being chased from the premises by a watchman named James Ramsey, these "idle and dissolute youths" armed themselves with cobblestones, returned to the circus, and proceeded to stone Ramsey to death.

At almost the same time in New York City, a young nursemaid named Jennie Powell was arrested after dousing an infant boy in coal oil and setting him on fire. Under arrest for the outrage, Powell confessed that, over the years, she had tried to burn a number of babies in her charge, and had also torched several houses. When the police, seeking to fathom her motives, asked "why she had done such horrible things to the babies," the young nursemaid matter-of-factly replied, "I just wanted to burn them."

From Mexico, meanwhile, came tales of ghastly goings-on in a small village in Chihuahua. According to these reports—published in papers throughout the United States, including the *New York Times*—the *alcalde* (or mayor) of the village had begun "to meet his friends late at night at a house on the outskirts of the town for supper." The principal dish at these gatherings was a savory stew, presumably compounded of pork. One day, however—as the *Times* reported—"a neighbor, an Indian woman, missed her little three-year-old child. . . . Then another, and still another, and yet another neighbor, on succeeding days, reported the losses of their tender infants. Great excitement ensued; and at last suspicion fell upon the midnight suppers of the *alcalde* and his companions. The political chief of the section was summoned. Armed with his superior authority, he penetrated the secrecy of the *alcalde*'s mystic rendezvous and there discovered the heads and bones of thirteen children. The *alcalde* confessed that the missing infants had been barbequed, or roasted whole; and the cannibals, just before they were hanged, told the political chief with fiendish joy that 'had he ever tasted the roast, he would have joined the infernal association.' "

And then there was the ongoing spectacle of the Beecher adultery case, which, by the summer of 1874, had turned into the nation's juiciest public melodrama. So intense was America's fascination with the scandal that (as one historian has pointed out) when Beecher spoke at a Brooklyn church in July, 1874, "the Associated Press *alone* sent thirty reporters to take down his words." Ironically, the same grown-ups who never tired of condemning the "lurid rot" found in children's dime novels appeared to have no qualms about wallowing in the sensationalistic details of the reverend's affair that were dished up every day by the press.

Between these and other, far more substantial (if less titilating) events, the story of the infamous "boy killer" had been entirely displaced from the nation's papers by early summer. Even in Boston, the public had, by and large, put the case out of mind.

To be sure, small items about the Katie Curran mystery occasionally showed up in the news. During the first week of May, for example, a report briefly circulated that the missing girl's body had been found in a sandbank near South Boston harbor. But this story turned out to be completely groundless. The prevailing opinion among the Currans' friends and neighbors was that (as the *Boston Globe* reported) "Pomeroy knows something about the case and . . . may someday confess a connection with the disappearance." But most law enforcement officials felt differently. They remained convinced that a nine-year-old girl would have held no interest for Jesse, whose depraved tastes ran entirely (so far as was known) to little boys.

Among the police and much of the public the consensus continued to be that "a difference of religious opinions" was at the bottom of Katie's disappearance—that the child had been caught in the middle of a nasty dispute between her Protestant mother and Catholic father and had been spirited off to a convent. In short, for most Bostonians, the Curran case wasn't a crime story at all, but rather a kind of cautionary tale about the evils of intermarriage—about the misery that is bound to result when a Protestant commits the grievous mistake of wedding a Catholic.

22

Truth will come to light; murder cannot be hid long.
—Shakespeare, *The Merchant of Venice*

While the public at large had turned its attention to other matters by early summer, things were different in the South Boston neighborhood where the Millen, Curran, and Pomeroy families resided within a short distance of each other. There, community indignation against the "boy killer" and his relations continued to run high. The situation wasn't helped by the attitude of Mrs. Pomeroy, who persisted in proclaiming her son's innocence to anyone who would listen. Far from displaying any sympathy for the Millens and Currans, she openly blamed them for her poor Jesse's travails.

Needless to say, such callousness did not endear her to her neighbors. Business at the Pomeroys' dressmaking/periodical store at 327 Broadway dropped off precipitously. People still came by the store—but only to gawk at the place where the notorious killer had once worked as a newsboy. Before long, Mrs. Pomeroy couldn't afford to keep paying the rent. On Sunday, May 31, she and Charles moved her dummies and sewing machine across the street to their little frame house at 312 Broadway and closed up the shop for good. For the next few weeks, she struggled—with meager success—to operate the business from her home.

The two-story frame building that housed the vacated shop had been on the market for months. The ground floor was divided in half by a metal partition. One side had been occupied by the Pomeroys' store; the other by a defunct little jewelry business run by a man named E. C. Mitchell. The owners of the premises, a couple named Margerson, lived on the second floor.

The building—originally L-shaped—had been renovated a few years earlier. The long, narrow rear had been broadened to the same width as the front, so that the entire structure was now rectangular. The cellar, however, had not been expanded accordingly. A dank, airless vault that stretched beneath the original floor-space of the building, it contained two gas meters; a rank little privy; a faucet that discharged a continual drip; a pair of storage bins containing the Margersons' monthly supplies of wood and coal; and—in one pitch-dark corner—a sizable heap of ashes and refuse. It was the kind of cellar that unnerved even grown-ups; for children, descending into that fetid gloom, where the vermin scurried at the first sound of human intrusion, was creepy enough to cause nightmares.

Situated a few doors down from the Margersons' building—at 342 Broadway—was a little grocery, owned by an enterprising gentleman named James Nash. Nash, whose business was booming, had been looking for a larger space in the neighborhood, and when Mrs. Pomeroy's store became available, he saw his opportunity. In mid-June, several weeks after she abandoned the shop, Nash purchased the entire building from the Margersons and began to renovate the premises. Foreseeing the need for increased storage facilities, he decided to begin by enlarging the cellar. And so, during the last week of June, a pair of workmen named Charles McGinnis and Patrick O'Connell made their way down into the cellar to begin the excavation.

The smell hit them even before they reached the bottom of the stairs—a carrion stench that caused the two men to screw up their nostrils.

"What's that stink?" asked O'Connell.

McGinnis shook his head, then hurried off to fetch Nash, who returned a short while later with the workmen. Armed with oil lamps, the three men made a search of the cellar but found nothing to account for the fetor. Heading upstairs, Nash spoke to Mr. Margerson, who acknowledged that he, too, had noticed a rotten smell in the cellar the last time he'd been down there. But, assuming that some small creature—a rat or possibly a cat—had crawled into a corner and died, he had paid little attention to the matter.

Nash and his workers did what they could to dispel the odor.

They propped open the five tiny windows spaced around the basement walls, and gave the foul little water closet a thorough cleaning. The excavation work helped, too. Within days of beginning the job, McGinnis and O'Connell had torn down most of one outer wall, letting in plenty of fresh air. They also dug up part of the hard-packed dirt floor, releasing the aroma of newly turned earth into their work area. By the second week of July, the two laborers had largely forgotten about the stink.

And then, on Saturday, July 18, they uncovered its source.

It was McGinnis who actually made the discovery. He was still hard at work at around 5:00 P.M., demolishing a wall in the far corner of the cellar where the ash-and-refuse pile lay. At one point—weary from his long day of labor—he took an errant swing, striking the heap with his pick blade. Something small and spherical went flying into the air. McGinnis, who caught only a glimpse of the object as it sailed to one side, assumed it was an old tin bowl or water dipper, discolored with rust.

The next blow of his pick dislodged a large chunk of the wall, which dropped into the ashes. As McGinnis raised his implement again, he glanced down and noticed something odd that had been exposed by the falling debris. Frowning, he bent to take a closer look—then let out a startled cry.

The thing sticking out of the ashes was a skeletal human forearm, black with putrefied flesh and partially clothed in decaying fabric.

McGinnis staggered back a few steps. As he did, he caught sight of the small, rounded object he had taken for a rusty bowl. It took him a few seconds to understand what he was looking at. When the realization hit him, he dropped his pick, stumbled upstairs, and ran off to find James Nash.

The round, dirt-covered object was a small human skull. Tufts of wavy brown hair still clung to the cranium in patches.

McGinnis and his employer were back within minutes, along with Officer John H. Foote of the Sixth Police Station. Using a shovel, Foote carefully uncovered the entire remains, which (as the *Boston Post* would later report) "emitted a disgusting odor—for there was still something left of the intestines."

A short while later, three other men arrived at the scene—Captain Dyer, Patrolman Thomas Adams, and Coroner Ingalls. Adams, who had been deeply involved in the search for Katie

Curran, required only a glance at the corpse's green-and-black-plaid dress to identify the victim. The ten-year-old girl who had been missing for months—ever since she had left home one spring morning in search of a new schoolbook—had just been found under a fetid ash heap in the cellar of the shop that had once been the workplace of Jesse Harding Pomeroy.

23

†

If the Pomeroy boy had fallen at this time into the hands of an average assembly of citizens of ever quiet Massachusetts, the chances are
that he would have been torn limb from limb, like some furious
beast which had fallen among those upon whom he had preyed.
—Anonymous, *The Life of Jesse H. Pomeroy, The Boy Fiend* (1875)

For John and Katherine Curran, the months since their little
girl vanished had been a time of unremitting torment—made even
worse by the rumors that they themselves were at the bottom of
the terrible mystery. It was hard enough to live with the horror of
Katie's disappearance. Having to endure the public's wholly
groundless suspicion that she had fallen victim to her own father's
religious zeal made the situation that much more agonizing.

Knowing full well that the story was a bigoted lie, the
Currans could only imagine what had really happened—and by
the beginning of summer, they had given up hope that their
daughter would ever be found alive. They knew how much she
loved to wander by the wharves. For the parents of South
Boston, the nearby waters of Dorchester Bay were an ever-
present danger that had claimed the lives of many local children.

It was dreadful to think of their pretty ten-year-old girl dying
that way. But after so much time without a hint of her whereabouts, they had begun to resign themselves to the likelihood
that Katie had fallen into the water and drowned. Though her
loss would scar their hearts forever, the lapse of four months had
(as one newspaper put it) "begun somewhat to assuage the
poignancy of their grief."

And then, at around 6:00 P.M. on Saturday, July 18, Officer
Thomas Adams knocked on their door.

He did not break the awful news right away, saying only that some evidence relating to Katie had just been discovered, and that their presence was needed at once. Still, the stricken parents must have guessed the truth. By the time they descended into the dismal basement of the house across the street, Mrs. Curran was already trembling violently.

Captain Dyer led them to a remote corner of the cellar, as far away as possible from the spot where a group of policemen stood in grim silence around the ash heap. First, Dyer showed Mrs. Curran a soiled scarf that she instantly recognized as the one her daughter had been wearing on the morning of her disappearance. Next, she identified the old-fashioned jacket, or sacque, Katie had thrown on just before leaving the house. As Mrs. Curran examined this garment, sounds of barely stifled anguish began to arise from deep within her throat. When Dyer finally held out a rotting scrap of Katie's black-and-green-plaid dress, the heartsick woman let out a groan and fainted.

She revived a minute later. Leaping to her feet, she sprang toward the ash pile and attempted to break through the cluster of policemen blocking her way. "Let me see her!" she screamed. But the officers held her back. Her husband came up behind her and, taking her by the shoulders, led her back across the cellar. Sobbing convulsively, Mrs. Curran begged Captain Dyer to let her take her daughter's body home. As gently as possible, he explained why he could not honor her request. The child's remains had to be examined by a specialist. Arrangements had already been made to transport it to J. B. Cole's undertaking parlor. But the captain promised that every care would be taken with the body.

Dyer, of course, had another reason for refusing Mrs. Curran's plea. After four months in the cellar, her daughter's corpse was in such unspeakable shape that the mere sight of it would have been more than either parent could bear. But, of course, Dyer said nothing about this to the Currans.

At last, the sorrowing woman allowed her husband to lead her back home. As she mounted the cellar steps, she threw back her head and cried out: "If only she had drowned! Anything but a death like this!"

The bustle of activity at 327 Broadway—the comings-and-goings of the police, the entrance of the Currans in the company of Patrolman Adams, the arrival of reporters who had gotten wind of the story—alerted the neighborhood residents that something dramatic had happened. Within the hour, a large and increasingly restive crowd had gathered outside the building. When the Currans finally reemerged—the grim-faced husband with his arm around his wailing, barely ambulatory wife—the sight of the devastated couple confirmed the rumor that had already spread through the crowd: that the body of the missing Curran girl had been unearthed in the cellar of Mrs. Pomeroy's former shop.

All at once, the crowd let out an angry roar and surged across the street. Men and boys snatched stones, trash, and mud from the gutter and began pelting the Pomeroy house, while others cried out angrily for vigilante justice. It seemed, as one newsman reported, "as if the excited mass of humanity would wreak its vengeance on all the Pomeroy family. Had not restraint prevailed, Judge Lynch would, undoubtedly, have held high carnival at this time."

By that time, around 6:00 P.M., Chief Savage had been notified of the developments in South Boston and was on his way to Station Six. The moment he arrived, he dispatched a contingent of officers to the Pomeroy home. While several of the men stood guard outside, keeping the clamorous mob at bay, two others—Officers Bragdon and Foote—entered the house and asked Jesse's mother to accompany them to the police station.

With her usual sullenness, Ruth Pomeroy refused to cooperate, folding her arms across her chest and declaring that "she could not imagine what she was wanted for." The officers—indicating the commotion outside—explained that they were taking her into custody as much for her own safety as for any other reason. Mrs. Pomeroy simply glanced out the window and muttered curses at the mob.

His impatience rising, Foote finally announced to the ill-tempered woman that they were there to arrest her "on suspicion of being connected to a felony." Mrs. Pomeroy sputtered indignantly, uttered a few more curses, and glowered at the officers. But in the end, she was taken away.

A short while later, a pair of officers named Mountain and Deveny were sent back to the house to await the arrival of Jesse's brother, Charles, who was out delivering his evening papers. As soon as Charles returned from his route, he, too, was arrested and taken to Station Six.

In the meantime (as the *Boston Globe* reported) "a strong detail of men remained posted at Mrs. Pomeroy's house, as rumors were current throughout the evening that her home and all it contained would be destroyed by the outraged populace."

At approximately 8:00 P.M., Chief Savage—accompanied by Chief of Detectives Jason W. Twombly—arrived at the Charles Street jail to interview Jesse. Dressed in his shabby street clothes and wearing his usual surly expression, Jesse was led into Sheriff Clark's office and seated across a table from the two officials.

"Do you know who I am, Jesse?" Savage began by asking.

"Sure," Jesse said. "Mr. Savage."

"What do you think I came to see you about?"

Jesse shrugged. "The dead boy, I guess."

"No, Jesse," said the chief. "I have come to tell you that the body of Katie Curran has been found in your mother's cellar. She was murdered and buried down there. I came to ask if you knew anything about it."

"No," said Jesse. "I don't."

"I see," Savage said, regarding the boy closely. "Jesse," he continued after a moment, "can you guess where her body was found?"

Jesse only shook his head.

Concealing his exasperation at the boy's stubborn reticence, Savage asked: "Jesse, where do you put your ashes that come from burning coal?"

"Down in the cellar," Jesse answered matter-of-factly.

Folding his hands on the table, Savage leaned forward and—speaking in an even voice—said, "Jesse, your mother and brother have been arrested for the murder. *Now* can you tell me anything that will throw light upon the subject?"

If Savage was hoping that this intelligence would give the boy a jolt and loosen his tongue, he was disappointed. Keeping his unnerving gaze fixed directly on Savage, Jesse coolly replied: "No. I can't."

For a long moment, the chief simply stared back at the coarse-featured boy—at the oversized head, the bulldog jaw, the pallid eye. Then, slapping his hands on his thighs, he rose from his chair and motioned to Twombly, who quickly got to his feet. With his subordinate following close behind, Savage turned on his heels and strode from the room, leaving the sullen young felon to brood on the bad news.

By nine o'clock the following morning—Sunday, July 19—an immense crowd had already gathered outside the Pomeroy house, which remained guarded by a large detail of policemen. Unable to vent their wrath against the property of the detested family, several dozen people swarmed along Broadway, as though bent on storming the police station, seizing Ruth Pomeroy, and stringing her up. They were met by a line of officers, who quickly dispersed the infuriated mob.

Throughout the day, people came to gawk at the house where the little girl's body had been found. By late afternoon, according to the *Boston Post*, the murder scene had been "visited by thousands of men and women, many of whom expressed themselves very forcibly regarding the disposition they would like to make of the whole Pomeroy clan." Scandalous stories about Ruth Pomeroy circulated among the crowd—that she was a woman of shockingly loose morals; that she revelled in the sight of blood and liked to frequent the Brighton slaughterhouses; that she had spewed vicious curses at the mothers of her son's little victims.

Other rumors were bandied about and immediately picked up by the papers. South Boston suddenly seemed to be populated by young children who had barely escaped from the murderous designs of Jesse Pomeroy. Several months earlier (according to one widely reported story), Jesse—who was alone in his brother's shop—had looked out the window and spotted two little girls playing hopscotch on the sidewalk. Going to the door, he had beckoned to the girls and—handing them a few coins—persuaded them to run across the street to the grocers and buy him some oranges. When the children returned with the fruit, Jesse was in the rear of the store, lowering the window-curtains. The little girls immediately became suspicious and, "instead of entering the shop, tossed the oranges into the place and ran away, greatly frightened."

Another neighborhood child, a nine-year-old girl named Minnie Tappan, claimed that, shortly after Katie Curran's disappeared, Jesse had asked her to come into his store, "as he had some papers for her brother which he wished her to carry to him." Minnie, however, had been so alarmed by the strange look on Jesse's face that she had immediatiely turned and dashed for home—"whereupon he became enraged and chased her down the street, threatening to drag her back into the store whether she would or not."

How much truth there was to any of these claims is, of course, an open question, since sensational crimes have a way of generating overheated—and often hysterical—mass fantasies. Still, the newspapers could not resist plastering their front pages with these and similar stories, titillating readers with lurid speculations about the dreadful fate that would surely have befallen "the little innocents, had they been induced to enter the store on those occasions."

In the meantime, the remains of the "little innocent" who really *had* fallen into Jesse Pomeroy's clutches had been transferred to J. B. Cole's undertaking establishment, where—starting at approximately two o'clock on Sunday afternoon—the autopsy took place. The examination was conducted by a pair of physicians, Drs. E. A. Gilman and Hugh Doherty, and viewed by Coroner Richard M. Ingalls and his jury.

The flesh of the upper body was so badly decomposed that it was impossible to determine the precise nature and extent of the wounds that had been inflicted on the child. Her skull, which Charles McGinnis had inadvertently struck while excavating the cellar, was completely separated from the body—but the doctors couldn't say whether it had been severed by her killer or by the blow from McGinnis's pickaxe. Still, there were unmistakable signs that the child had been brutally slashed about the neck.

The lower body was in a substantially better state of preservation than the upper. As a result, the doctors were able to discover a critical—and thoroughly appalling—fact. Whoever murdered Katie Curran had sliced open her dress and undergarments with a sharp implement—presumably the same weapon used to cut her throat. Then—in an apparent frenzy of bloodlust—he had savagely mutilated the ten-year-old girl's lower abdomen, thighs, and genitals.

24

I felt bad that they were arrested, and I resolved to do all I could to get them out, so I kept in mind that proverb, "One may as well be hanged for stealing a sheep as for stealing a lamb," altering it to suit my case: "One may as well be hanged for killing one as two."
—*Autobiography of Jesse H. Pomeroy*

Early Monday morning, Chief Savage—having given Jesse two days to mull things over—returned to the Charles Street jail. Chief of Detectives Twombly had asked to come along, but Savage—believing that the boy might speak more freely if no one else was present—thought it best to handle the interview by himself.

As before, the meeting took place in Sheriff Clark's office. This time, however, instead of confronting Jesse across the table, Savage seated himself directly beside the boy.

"Jesse," Savage solemnly began, "I have come to give you one more chance to clear your mother. It seems to me that you must know something about the little girl, and I would like you to tell me the facts of the case."

For a moment, Jesse—head bowed, hands clasped on his lap—did not answer. Then, he slowly looked up at the older man and said: "Well, Mr. Savage, I killed her, but I don't want to say how."

"Jesse," the chief said firmly, "that just won't do. You must tell me how you killed her." He paused for a moment, then, in a voice full of calm but compelling authority, asked: "Now, at what time did you open the store?"

After a brief silence, Jesse softly replied: "At half past seven."

Savage nodded in encouragement. "And exactly what happened after that?" he asked.

"Well," Jesse began, "the little girl came into the store, and I was standing over near the far end of—" All of a sudden, he broke off his recitation and said, "I have made a little drawing of the store. It is in my cell, if you will let me go get it."

"All right," said Savage. Stepping to the door, he beckoned to the jail-keeper, who escorted Jesse from the office. Several minutes later, Jesse returned with a small piece of notepaper that he laid out on the table in front of Savage. Sketched on the sheet was a simple floor plan of the cellar and store. Pointing out the various locations as he spoke—and displaying no more emotion than if he had been describing a typical workday—Jesse proceeded to relate the events of that ghastly morning back in March, when he had slaughtered the ten-year-old girl who had wandered into his store in search of a notebook.

When Jesse was done, Savage regarded him in silence for a long moment. Then—speaking in a tone that suggested he only had the boy's best interests at heart—he said: "Jesse, this is an important case. I would like to write down exactly what you said, so as to get the facts of the case just right when I speak to the jury of inquest this afternoon."

"I don't want to want to have it in the papers," Jesse said warily.

"That is something I cannot control," Savage answered. "But I want to tell your story to the jury just as you told it to me."

After considering the chief's words for a moment, Jesse agreed. Savage pulled out a notepad and pencil. Then—with the same bizarre, matter-of-fact demeanor as before—Jesse repeated his appalling tale, while the older man transcribed the statement word for word.

At four o'clock that afternoon, the coroner's jury met in the guardroom of Police Station Six. Unlike the proceedings in the Millen case, which had been conducted behind closed doors, the Curran inquest was open to the public—a circumstance that elicited warm praise for Coroner Ingalls from members of the press. Still, not everyone was happy. The crowd of people gathered outside the station house was so enormous that only a fraction gained admission to the show.

Mrs. Curran spoke first. Attired in funereal garb—a steel-gray dress with a border of black, a black sacque, a dark straw hat with a heavy black veil that obscured much of her haggard face—the heartbroken mother, whose voice quavered audibly throughout her testimony, began by describing her murdered child, who had turned ten the previous December 21.

"She was always at home," Mrs. Curran told the jury, "never out of my sight from the day she was born until the day I missed her, except she was at school or unless I knew where she was. . . . I am positive that my girl was not in any way acquainted with the Pomeroy boy. My child didn't know there was such a person. She might have gone into the store for a paper for her father, but she never knew there was such a person as Jesse Pomeroy. She was smart and bright, but innocent. She was one of the gentlest persons I ever knew. I suppose she can be no gentler now she is in heaven than when she was on earth."

After pausing for a moment to regain control of her voice—which had begun to tremble so violently that her last few words could barely be understood—Mrs. Curran continued by recounting her experiences following the disappearance of her daughter: her frantic visit to the police when Katie failed to return; her subsequent trip to the home of the delivery boy, Rudolph Kohr, who insisted that he had seen Katie in Jesse Pomeroy's store on the morning of her disappearance; the reaction of Officer Adams, who assured her that Kohr was a known liar, that Jesse Pomeroy had "nothing more to do with your Katie than I had," and that she should put all her trust in the police. "We will bring your little girl back to you without any doubt," Adams had promised her.

"Everyone advised me to go see Chief Savage for a warrant to have the place thoroughly searched," Mrs. Curran testified bitterly. "But I depended on Mr. Adams because he had kept me hoping, and I thought he was my true friend."

Exhaling a tremulous sigh, she added: "It is a sad ending to all my sorrow."

With that, her testimony ended. She was followed by her husband, who quietly explained that, on the day his little girl vanished, he had been away at work and knew nothing beyond the facts related by his wife. As Coroner Ingalls offered a final word of condolence—assuring them that "everything possible would be done to account for the manner of their little girl's death"—John Curran signed his wife's statement. Then he helped her to her feet and led her from the room.

* * *

From a purely emotional standpoint, Mrs. Curran's heart-wrenching testimony was the most dramatic moment of the day. But it was the next witness, Police Chief Savage, who created the biggest sensation when he revealed that Jesse Pomeroy had finally confessed to Katie Curran's murder.

After announcing that he was "in possession of facts that would greatly aid the jury," Savage gave a brief summary of his involvement in the case. Following Pomeroy's arrest for the Millen murder, Savage told the jury, he had begun to suspect that Jesse might "have some possible relation to the disappearance of the Curran girl." Accordingly, he "gave Captain Dyer and also the other officers of the adjoining territory instructions to make a thorough investigation of every cellar, well, or ditch that could be searched."

Savage had also talked directly to Officer Thomas Adams, asking him "if he supposed it was possible to go into the Pomeroys' cellar and search it without making any particular sensation about it." Adams said he could. Shortly thereafter, Adams told the chief that he had visited the Pomeroys' shop, looked into the cellar, and concluded that "it was so open it seemed almost impossible that anything could be hidden down there." Neverthless, Savage ordered him to pay another visit to the store and "search the cellar thoroughly."

A few days later, Adams reported that he had "searched every part of the cellar and was satisfied that there was nothing there."

"I will say," added Savage, "that when Mr. Adams was in our office, we always found him a very thorough man. I had considerable, I may say a great deal of, confidence in his thoroughness." Clearly, the chief felt it necessary to defend his faith in Adams's competence—a faith that had turned out to be egregiously misplaced.

Savage went on to describe his initial interview with Pomeroy; the boy's stubborn insistence that he knew nothing about the Curran girl; and his stony response to the news of his mother's arrest.

"This morning, I went to see him again," Savage continued. Then—after pausing briefly, as if for dramatic effect—he proceeded to describe his ensuing conversation with Jesse, and the pivotal moment when the boy finally dropped his pretense of innocence and admitted that he had killed Katie Curran.

The chief's disclosure sent a ripple of excitement through the crowd. Raising his voice slightly to be heard above the buzz, Savage announced, "We prepared the following statement, which I will now read."

Then—as the newsmen strained forward in their seats, poised to transcribe every word—the chief reached into his coat pocket, extracted Jesse's confession, and began to read it aloud:

> I opened my mother's store that morning at half past seven o'clock. The girl came in for papers. I told her there was a store downstairs.

Here, the chief interrupted himself to say that he had originally written *cellar* instead of *stairs*. Jesse, however, had quickly corrected him. "If I had told her 'in the cellar,' she wouldn't have gone down," Jesse had calmly explained, with no apparent awareness that he was revealing himself as a creature of monstrous cunning.

After giving his listeners a moment to absorb the chilling implications of Jesse's remark, Savage returned to his reading, with occasional pauses to point out the relevant spots on the hand-drawn diagram the boy had provided:

> She went down to about the middle of the cellar and stood facing Broadway. I followed her, put my arm about her neck, my hand over her mouth, and with my knife cut her throat, holding my knife in my right hand.

At this point, several sharp gasps arose from the crowd, but Savage, ignoring the disturbance, continued to read:

> I then dragged her to behind the water closet, laying her head furtherest up the place, and I put some stones and some ashes on the body. I took the ashes from a box in the cellar. I [had] bought the knife about a week before for twenty-five cents. The knife was taken from me when I was arrested in April last.
>
> When I was in the cellar I heard my brother at the outside door which I had locked after the girl came in. I ran upstairs and found him going towards the cellar in Mitchell's part, and he came back. Two girls worked in the store for mother.

They usually got there about nine o'clock. Mother came later. Brother Charles and I took turns opening the store till about April. My mother and brother never knew of this affair.

Looking up from the page, Savage explained that, after dictating his confession, Jesse had checked it over and approved it, adding only a single additional detail: before emerging from the cellar, he had washed his bloody knife and hands at the pipe in the water closet.

"This statement was given to me frankly, without holding out any inducement whatever," Savage declared. "I have always felt that confessions should be free or they would be good for nothing, and this one is perfectly free, so far as I can tell."

Raising a finger to attract the chief's attention, one of the jury members, Isaac Campbell, asked if Jesse had provided any explanation for his actions. It was a question that people had been asking about Pomeroy ever since his days as the notorious "boy torturer" of Chelsea.

Savage had, in fact, asked the boy about his motives. At first, Jesse gave the same answer as always: "I couldn't help it." A few minutes later, however, when the chief asked again, Jesse offered another explanation—one that a *New York Times* editorial would describe as "a marvel of cold diabolism." "I wanted to see how she would act," the boy had said calmly.

Jesse himself, along with his mother, was scheduled to appear before the jury that afternoon. But Chief Savage's testimony had proved so significant that, after a brief consultation, Coroner Ingalls decide to postpone the proceedings, in order to give the jurors "sufficient time to digest what had been told them." Accordingly, the inquest was adjourned until four o'clock on Wednesday afternoon.

Though Savage's revelation only confirmed what everyone already believed, the news of the confession created an immediate uproar. As the *Boston Globe* reported, "The crowd outside the station continued to increase during the holding of the inquest, and when it was known that Pomeroy had confessed, the people seemed almost crazy with excitement and rushed about, spreading the news rapidly, commenting on the terrible story and discussing the probable fate of the author of the horrible deed."

Before the day was over, one enterprising local newspaper, the *South Boston Inquirer*, had rushed out an "extra" containing the substance of Jesse's confession. Printed on a two-column, five-by-seven-inch sheet and costing two cents a copy, the entire edition sold out immediately.

It was from the newsies peddling this broadside that Jesse's mother first learned about the confession. After having been briefly locked in a cell following her arrest, she—along with her older boy, Charles—had been transferred to more comfortable quarters on the second floor of the station. At around 6:00 P.M. on Monday, she was seated by an open window that overlooked Broadway, when she heard the newsboys crying below: "Extra! Extra! Pomeroy confesses!"

Gazing at Charles, who had turned very pale, she curled her lips into an ugly snarl and said: "It's a lie."

The sentiments of the people of the Twelfth Ward—already inflamed against the police—were aroused to an ever greater pitch of fury by Savage's testimony. Though the most inexplicable blunder had been committed by Officer Adams—whose "thorough search" of the cellar had somehow failed to turn up the decaying, hastily concealed corpse—it was his superior, Captain Dyer, who bore the brunt of the public's anger.

Even before the Pomeroy affair erupted, the fifty-seven-year-old Dyer had been a target of community ire. A mason by trade, he had joined the police force in 1849. Five years later, he was promoted to lieutenant and assigned to Station Six in South Boston, where he would spend the remainder of his career.

It was a career marked by controversy. In June 1856—for reasons that were never made public—he was demoted to the rank of patrol officer. Two years later, when a new administration took power, his lieutenancy was reinstated, and in 1866—when old Captain Taylor of Station Six died—Dyer was appointed his successor. He quickly came to be seen, however, as a singularly ineffectual commander. Indeed his reputation was such that, when Mayor Pierce decided to transfer him to Dorchester, the people of that district objected so vehemently that Dyer was forced to remain in South Boston.

In the wake of the Millen murder, Dyer had been widely denounced for his reputed support of Jesse Pomeroy's early parole from reform school. Now, there were new, inflammatory charges against him. It was rumored that on Saturday evening—when as many as ten thousand enraged people had poured onto the streets following the discovery of Katie Curran's body—Dyer had gone home and retired for the night, in spite of the very real danger (as one newspaper put it) of "imminent riotous proceedings."

Indeed, by the day of the inquest, a serious movement was afoot to get rid of Dyer. Petitions calling for his removal were circulated throughout the district, while a delegation of prominent citizens, led by Councilman Flynn, visited the office of Mayor Cobb and demanded Dyer's immediate resignation.

Eager to get Dyer's side of the story, a reporter for the *Post* visited his home on Dorchester Street early Monday evening and managed to secure an exclusive interview with the beleaguered captain.

Though Dyer received his visitor very courteously, he was deeply agitated throughout the interview. He stammered, sputtered, and had trouble controlling the quaking of his voice. Though he insisted that he had "made every possible effort to unravel the mystery" of Katie Curran's disappearance—and indignantly denied the rumors that he and Ruth Pomeroy were on "intimate terms"—the case had clearly taken a serious toll on the man's equilibrium.

When the reporter questioned his "conduct in leaving the station house at six o'clock Saturday evening during the extreme excitement," for example, Dyer defended himself by claiming that his nerves were too fragile to tolerate the strain. He had been "completely prostrated at the discovery," he explained in a tremulous voice. "To think that all our investigations to find Katie Curran had been such a horrible failure. I am of a very nervous temperament, and upon this denouement I was very nearly unmanned. I was unfit for further duty and turned over the care of the situation to Lieutenant Emerson and then went home." That this pitiable self-portrait—this image of a police captain reduced to a state of complete emotional debility—might fail to win public sympathy appears not to have occurred to the overwrought captain.

Shortly thereafter, the reporter took his leave. Dyer bid him farewell with a final, plaintive remark. "I know that we have made a miserable failure of the case," he said, his voice cracking slightly. "But I did my best to solve the mystery concerning her." Gazing into his face, the reporter saw an expression of hopeless resignation—the look of a man who knows that his professional days are numbered.

25

The great characteristic of American society is an increase of immorality and infidelity. Are our young men growing up in such a way that they will be able to bear the burdens borne by their fathers? Are our young women growing up with the charms of modesty and feminine grace and domestic virtue? Away with all the absurd fashions, follies, and frivolities of society, behind which all kinds of vice and crime lurk and conceal themselves!
—Reverend W. E. Copeland, June 21, 1865

Whatever faint hope Dyer might have had about holding on to his job was dashed on Tuesday morning, July 21, when the *New York Times* ran an editorial on the Pomeroy case that leveled a stinging rebuke at the Boston police. "In passing," read the piece, "it may be said that Boston is not to be congratulated on the skill of its detective Police. A four months' search for a missing child failed to discover anything, though her remains were thinly buried in an ash heap in the cellar of the home in which a boy charged with the murder lived when the child disappeared."

The editorial was the final nail in Dyer's professional coffin. He had not only antagonized the people of his district; he had made the whole department a national laughingstock. As the *Boston Herald* put it in its own editorial demanding his dismissal, Dyer had "put a stain on the department which should cause every official connected with it to wince."

The inevitable climax came before noon. Summoned to City Hall by Mayor Cobb, Dyer acknowledged that he had gone home to bed during the near-riot on Saturday evening because of "a nervousness that he could not overcome." Regarding this behavior as "sufficent evidence that he was unfit to hold the responsible position of captain," the mayor offered Dyer a classic

Hobson's choice: he could resign within the hour or be summarily discharged. Dyer opted for the former, whereupon Lieutent E. Y. Graves was immediately put in charge of Station Six.

The response to Dyer's ouster was positively jubilant. A typical headline in Tuesday's *Boston Herald* crowed: "Off Goes His Head!"

Though every bit as culpable as his boss, Officer Thomas Adams—the man who had actually conducted the bungled search of the Pomeroys' cellar—somehow managed to elude the axe. Like Dyer, he was approached by reporters and given the chance to present his side of the story to the public.

Adams explained that—although he was a "regular patrol officer"—he was frequently employed in detective work and was "given the duty of finding Katie Curran." He insisted that he had "worked on the case zealously and did his best to discover her whereabouts, but was misled by the stories of different persons who stated positively that they had seen the girl taken into a carriage." Adams had done "all he could to keep up Mrs. Curran's hopes, because he did not think her child had been foully dealt with. He was at her house two, three, and even four times a week, and—along with an officer named Griggs—had searched the cellar under Mrs. Pomeroy's store a few days after Mrs. Curran told him her suspicions."

As for the most critical issue—how he could have possibly missed the little girl's remains—Adams offered the following, highly questionable excuse:

> Officer Griggs and I searched the cellar, as we thought, thoroughly. There were no indications that the ground of the cellar had been upturned, nor was there any offensive smell to be perceived. The ground where the body was finally found was, at the time of the search, as hard and as solid as any other part of the cellar. We did our best, and it is unfortunate that we did not succeed. The body may have been deeper in the ground when we searched than when it was discovered, as the heavy rain which came down a day or two previous poured into the cellar and washed away some of the dirt which covered the body.

In spite of its flaws (Adams's suggestion that "the body may have been deeper in the ground" at the time of his search was disingenuous at best, since the corpse had not been buried in the ground at all, but rather dumped in an ash heap), the mayor and Chief Savage evidently chose to accept this explanation. Or perhaps the public's demand for accountability had been sufficiently appeased by Captain Dyer's removal. Whatever the case, Adams avoided his superior's fate and was allowed to remain on the force.

In our own time, the sites of sensational murders—John Wayne Gacy's suburban "house of horrors," for example, or the squalid little apartment where Jeffrey Dahmer committed his unspeakable crimes—have become such morbid attractions that they have had to be demolished just to keep the crowds away. The situation was no different back in 1874. For days after the discovery of Katie Curran's body, hordes of curiosity-seekers would congregate outside Mrs. Pomeroy's former shop and (as the *Boston Herald* reported) "gaze with apparent awe through the cellar windows, as though expecting to see the original tragedy enacted before their eyes."

As it happened, the cellar was already in the process of being torn up by workmen—a circumstance that allowed the ghoulish sightseers to collect macabre souvenirs: small bits of masonry from the depths of the cellar, or pieces of excavated rubbish that were often rumored to possess a particular, grisly significance.

At one point on Tuesday, for example, the workmen turned up a few tattered old copies of the *Boston Herald*, discolored with reddish stains. In a flash, the story spread throughout the neighborhood that the papers had been used by young Pomeroy to wipe the gore from his bloody hands and knife blade. After examining this supposedly damning evidence of Jesse's guilt, however, Coroner Ingalls concluded that the reddish marks were probably cherry stains and chucked the mildewed papers in the trash.

Later that same day, a reporter for the *Herald* managed to sneak down into the cellar for a quick, furtive look around the murder site. No sooner did he emerge than he announced to the world that he had discovered convincing "proof of the truth of Jesse's story that he cut his victim's throat."

Remarkably, the reporter's "proof" hinged on the fact that he had *not* been able to find any evidence of bloodstains in the cellar. Instead—conducting his search "by the fleeting light of burning matches" (as he described it)—he had perceived a bunch of nicks on one of the grimy brick walls. Considering that two workmen had been wielding pickaxes in the basement for nearly three weeks, the fact that there were gouges on the walls should not have been terribly surprising. To the reporter, however, the marks indicated only one thing—that, in an effort to obliterate all traces of his crime, Jesse had taken his pocketknife and methodically "chipped off every spot of blood that had accidentally become spattered upon the wall when he cut his victim's throat." Needless to say, this theory was exceptionally dubious, if not completely far-fetched. But it was precisely the sort of lurid speculation that helped to sell papers to a public that couldn't seem to get enough of the Pomeroy story.

Indeed, the fascination with the Boston "boy fiend" (as the papers had taken to calling Jesse) was so intense that it struck most news commentators as unprecedented. Searching for parallels, a few editorialists compared it to the uproar over the Abijah Ellis murder in 1872. Others looked even farther back, to another grisly child-slaying that had transfixed the city a decade earlier. This was the appalling murder of the Joyce siblings in the summer of 1865.

On Monday, June 12, of that year, twelve-year-old John S. Joyce and his fifteen-year-old sister, Isabella, were visiting their grandmother in Boston. At around 11:30 in the morning, they expressed a desire to explore a forested area known as May's Woods in nearby Roxbury. After some initial reluctance, the grandmother finally relented. She packed them a lunch, gave them ten cents each for trolley fare, and told them to return no later than 2:00 P.M. She never saw them again.

When the children failed to return, their grandmother became frantic. For the next five days, search parties scoured the woods around Roxbury. It wasn't until Sunday, June 18, however, that two men, John Sawtelle and J. F. Jameson—while hiking across the wooded estate of the Bussey family in West Roxbury—stumbled upon the remains of the missing children.

From the evidence, it seemed clear that Isabella and her brother had been playing happily in the woods—creating a little hillock of moss and fashioning hatbands out of oak leaves and twigs—when they were unexpectedly set upon. Their assailant—a "fiend in human shape," as the newspapers called him—attacked the girl first, savaging her body with a dagger, then tearing off her undergarments and raping her. There were twenty-seven stab wounds on her torso, and another sixteen on her neck. The ground all around her corpse was clotted with blood. She had apparently put up a desperate fight, grabbing the long blade of the dagger and attempting to wrest it from her killer. The index finger of her right hand was completely severed, and the rest nearly cut off. Her clothes were soaked in blood, and clumps of grass had been shoved into her mouth to stifle her cries.

Apparently, her brother had stood paralyzed for a few moments with terror. When he finally turned to run, it was too late. He was found lying facedown, having evidently tripped over a tree root while attempting to escape. His killer had pounced on the prostrate boy and stabbed him through the back a half-dozen times. The wounds were so deep that, in several instances, the blade had gone all the way through the little victim's body, coming out the skin in front.

There were two houses within a few hundred yards of the scene. But the inhabitants were so accustomed to shouts, laughter, and yells from picnic and excursion groups that, as the newspapers noted, "they would not have paid any attention even if they had heard screams on this occasion."

The appalling savagery of the Joyce murders provoked a city-wide furor. From their pulpits, ministers decried the murders as a sign of the growing degeneracy of the age—of the country's deplorable descent into vice, immorality, and crime. An enormous manhunt was undertaken to track down the "inhuman wretch" who had committed the "fiendish deed." But—though the police issued many confident pronouncements, assuring the public that the culprit could not possibly get away with his crime—no one was ever arrested. The ghastly deaths of the Joyce children would remain forever unsolved.

The Millen-Curran slayings were undoubtedly the most sensational Boston child-murders since the Joyce atrocities. But there was one significant difference between the two cases: in the former, the public knew exactly whom to blame. Indeed, they had not one but *two* targets for their outrage: the "boy fiend" himself and his grim, unrepentent mother.

The public's antipathy toward Mrs. Pomeroy was vividly demonstrated early Tuesday morning, when a large, noisy crowd gathered outside Station Six to denounce the police for their mishandling of the Curran affair. All at once, several of the protestors spotted Ruth Pomeroy staring down at them from an open second-story window. One glimpse of her face was all it took to send the crowd into a frenzy. They began screaming, hooting, demanding that the police remove the hated woman from their sight.

Far from being intimidated by the mob, Jesse's mother seemed intent on inciting them to even greater heights of fury. She leaned her head out the window and answered their jeers and insults with imprecations of her own. The scene turned so ugly that some observers were convinced that a riot was about to break out. It wasn't until several police officers forced Jesse's mother away from the window that the crowd finally quieted down.

Given the public's feelings about Ruth Pomeroy, it's no surprise that a story quickly sprang up linking her child's blood-crazed behavior directly to her own presumed penchant for butchery. The story—which had already gained citywide circulation by late Monday afternoon—was summed up in Tuesday's early edition of the *Boston Globe:*

> Directly after Pomeroy was first arrested after torturing a number of children in Chelsea and South Boston, three well-known physicians, who were anxious to learn all that they could about the boy, called upon his mother and had a candid interview with her. They told her their errand, and she gave them all the information in her power.
>
> Among other things, she said that her husband was a butcher, and that during the period of her pregnancy she went daily to the the slaughterhouse to witness the killing of the animals, and that somehow she took a particular delight in seeing her husband butcher the sheep, the calves, and the cattle, and not infrequently she assisted him in this bloody work. She also said that after Jesse was born and became old enough to hold a knife in his hands, he was all the time, when opportunity offered, jabbing a knife into pieces of

meat, and when still older and about his father's market, he did the same thing.

These facts certainly explain in some measure why Jesse "could not help" committing his crimes, as he told the court. He was simply *marked* by his mother, as other children had been, only in a different way.

The theory that Jesse was "marked" by his mother—i.e., born with an innate penchant for violence because of his prenatal exposure to animal-butchering—was quickly discounted by Coronor Ingalls and other medical experts. Ingalls was especially disdainful of the idea, comparing it to the primitive folk-belief that, should a woman have a tooth extracted during her pregnancy, her infant will be born with a harelip. In his fifteen years of practice, Dr. Ingalls declared, he had "never met with such a case, and scientific research has never revealed a single instance in which some secret influence has affected offspring."

Ruth Pomeroy herself was given an opportunity to address the issue on Tuesday morning, when—at the request of several reporters—Jesse's lawyer, Joseph H. Cotton, paid her a visit to ask about the rumor. Mrs. Pomeroy immediately composed a reply, which—while convincingly refuting the slaughterhouse story—proposed an equally reductive theory of her own. (In its reference to the "absurd requests" she had been receiving from all over the country, her reply also makes clear that—like the psycho-killers of our own day, who invariably attract the perverse devotion of various "groupies"—Jesse Pomeroy had already achieved a macabre celebrity.)

Mrs. Pomeroy's answer, which appeared in every major daily in Boston, as well as in the *New York Times* and other papers throughout the nation, went as follows:

> Before going into the butcher business, my husband worked in the Navy Yard at Charlestown, where he was employed for a period of ten years. He was at work there four years before Jesse was born, and remained there until [Jesse] was nearly six years of age. It was after this he went into the butcher business. He did not kill

cattle, but carried the carcasses about the market. *I never saw an animal of any kind slaughtered.* I do not believe in the theory of being marked.

The statement regarding the visit of the three physicians is false. The only gentleman of science that questioned me on the subject of Jesse was a phrenologist, and he did not seem to be able to understand Jesse's mania at all.

I have frequently received letters from persons in all parts of the country, principally in the West, asking for some of Jesse's hair and other absurd requests that I have not paid any attention to.

The story of Jesse sticking knives into raw flesh is also false. I think his vaccination had more effect on him than anything else. He was vaccinated when he was four weeks old, and shortly after, his face broke out and had the appearance of raw flesh, and some fluid issued from the wounds that burned my arm when it dropped on it, from which fact I judge the fluid was poison. This lasted until he was six months old, when his whole body was covered with large abscesses, one of which was over the eye.and occasioned that cast or fallen appearance that it wears at present. At the time, it was thought he would die, but he recovered slowly, and Dr. Lane, who attended him, stated that the sickness was occasioned by vaccination.

Both the slaughterhouse story and Ruth Pomeroy's own theory that her son had been poisoned by a smallpox vaccination represented only two of countless efforts to comprehend the mystery of Jesse Pomeroy's actions. In the end, these efforts—which would continue for many months—weren't especially productive. For the most part, they consisted of describing Jesse's bizarre personality in the colorful, prepsychiatric lingo of the day: "moral malformation," "horrible monomania," "innate depravity," etc.

Perhaps the most intriguing early comments on the Pomeroy case appeared on the editorial page of Tuesday's *Boston Globe.*

The piece, headlined "A Curious Case," compared Jesse to a number of notorious figures, including Gilles de Rais—the fifteenth-century nobleman who reputedly butchered more than one hundred young boys and who is generally regarded as the model for the fairy-tale monster Bluebeard—and Martin Dumollard, a French lust-murderer responsible for the deaths of at least ten servant girls in the mid-1800s.

True, the editorial did not shed any new light on Jesse's motivations. But it astutely placed him in the correct behavioral context—within that criminological category we now call serial sex-murder. (The editorial—published in July 1874—also makes it very clear that, far from being a uniquely contemporary phenomenon, serial homicide has always been a feature of human society.)

In the end, it was Jesse himself who offered what might have been the only possible explanation for his acts. Shortly after noon on Tuesday, he was visited by his lawyer, Joseph H. Cotton, who gave the boy a rundown of the previous day's proceedings. Just before he departed, Cotton asked Jesse the question that was on everyone's mind: Why had he killed Katie Curran? What made him do it?

At first, Jesse gave the same answer as always: "I do not know. I couldn't help it." Then, raising his right hand, he pointed to the side of his head and added: "It is in here."

26

I had heard of the loss of the Curran girl, but never suspected that Jesse had anything to do with her. I never saw anything in connection with Jesse that led me to think that he had done wrong, and never thought he had a propensity for doing wrong.

—Ruth Pomeroy

On Wednesday, July 22—four days after the discovery of her body and more than four months since she vanished from sight—Katie Curran was finally laid to rest. At approximately half past three in the afternoon, Undertaker Cole delivered the little girl's encoffined remains to the home of her grief-numbed parents. Wishing to bury their child with as much dignity as possible, John and Katherine Curran had taken pains to keep the funeral a secret, particularly from the press. As a result, few people observing the mournful little cortege as it passed along the streets on its way to Holyhood Cemetery had any idea that it bore the pathetic remains of the "boy fiend's" penultimate victim.

Only a few people were present at the burial site—Katie's parents, a priest, and a handful of relatives and friends. The scene was so somber and hushed that Mrs. Curran's heartbroken whimpers resounded through the graveyard as she watched her daughter's white-painted coffin being lowered into the ground.

The solemnity of the funeral was in marked contrast to the tumultuous scene taking place simultaneously at Police Station Six, where the coroner's inquest into Katie Curran's murder was about to resume. Hoping for a glimpse of the infamous "boy fiend"—who was supposedly slated to appear before the jury—an enormous crowd had gathered on the sidewalk, clamoring for admission. They jostled and shoved their way into the building, quickly filling up every available seat in the guardroom and occupying every inch of standing space in the outer offices and hallways.

Among those who managed to make it inside the room was the same "well-known spiritualist" who had announced that Jesse was controlled by a band of bloodthirsty Indian spirits. But the presence of this publicity-hungry charlatan was deemed to be so distracting to the jury that Coroner Ingalls demanded his removal before the proceedings began.

As it turned out—and much to the disappointment of the spectators—Jesse didn't put in an appearance. Still, the afternoon's proceedings—which lasted one and a half hours, beginning at 4:00 P.M.—weren't entirely without interest. Though the star attraction never showed up, the audience *did* get to witness the next best thing: the testimony of his mother, Mrs. Ruth Ann Pomeroy, who—by this time—had achieved nearly as much notoriety as her son.

She wore a plain, dark dress and a deeply careworn expression. Surprisingly, she showed none of her normal pugnacity, delivering her remarks in a low, even voice. Essentially, her testimony consisted of a string of denials. She did "not recollect seeing anything unusual" when she arrived at her shop on the morning of March 18, the day of Katie Curran's disappearance. She did not "remember whether anyone was in the store" when she came in. She did not "recollect anything about Jesse on the 18th of March." She "did not go into the cellar" until the following week. She "never saw anything that led me to think there was anything wrong in the cellar." She "never to my knowledge saw this Curran girl." She "never perceived any bad smells in the store that led me to think there was something wrong." She "never knew of Jesse's being in the cellar more than he ought to be, or saw any efforts made to conceal anything that might have been done." She "never saw on Jesse's clothing or on the floor of the cellar anything in the shape of blood."

Jesse, she insisted, was a "good and clever boy, and never quarreled with his brother more than boys generally will." She knew that he "carried a small knife" but always "trusted him, and never thought there was anything wrong."

With her subdued, ladylike demeanor, Mrs. Pomeroy made a surprisingly favorable expression on the spectators, who were expecting a harridan. The case was precisely the opposite with the next witness, her older son, Charles. Consistently portrayed in the papers as a model of youthful diligence, the sixteen-year-old boy turned out to be a sullen adolescent, who slouched in his seat, chewed on a toothpick throughout his testimony, and spoke with such careless indifference that Coroner Ingalls felt obliged to admonish him repeatedly that he was under oath.

Charles's testimony, like his mother's, was a litany of negation. He "didn't recollect who opened the store" on the morning of March 18, nor did he remember "anything else about this day." He "did not know where Jesse was, what he was doing, or whether he was in the store." He couldn't remember whether he "found the door locked that morning." He "never smelled anything bad in the cellar, never looked behind the water closet, never thought Jesse had anything to do with the Curran girl, never saw any blood on his clothes, sleeves, or elsewhere."

Two more witnesses spoke briefly after Charles. Sergeant Hood of Police Station Nine testified that—shortly after being arrested for the Millen murder—Jesse had hinted that he knew something about the missing Curran girl and was willing to reveal this information "if he could be sure that his mother would get the reward." Next, one of Katie's schoolmates, a little girl named Emma Lee, made a brief statement. Early on the morning of March 18, she had spotted Katie looking into a store window on Broadway, near D Street. Though the six-year-old was not officially sworn, her testimony was regarded as important for one reason: apart from the killer himself, little Emma Lee was the last person known to have seen the murdered child alive.

At that point—at around 5:30 P.M.—the inquest was adjourned until Friday afternoon. Immediately following the conclusion of the day's proceedings, Mrs. Pomeroy and Charles were escorted—not back to their second-story quarters—but to the Charles Street jail. Given the uproar that Jesse's mother was capable of provoking in the local populace, the authorities felt it best—for her own protection, as well for the good of the community—to remove her from the neighborhood and keep her locked in a cell.

Immediately after the proceedings ended, a reporter for the *Boston Herald* sought an interview with Edward Mitchell, the man who had operated a little jewelry business directly adjacent to the Pomeroys' shop at the time of the murders. Mitchell's comments, which focused mainly on Jesse's relationship with Charles, revealed a pattern of sibling hostility that was considerably uglier than the benign teenage bickering their mother had described at the inquest.

According to Mitchell, the two brothers were constantly at each others' throats. Mitchell had a particularly detailed memory of a vicious (though by no means atypical) fight that took place on April 22—the day of Horace Millen's murder. Mitchell was still in his store at about half past nine that evening, removing his display goods from the window and storing them away in his safe, when he heard a squabble break out between Jesse and Charlie. There was nothing unusual about that—"quarrels between the two were frequent," Mitchell explained to the reporter. On this occasion, however, their struggle turned especially violent. The two boys began "scuffling and tumbling against the thin board partition that separated the two stores." Mitchell—"afraid that they might break through the partition"— left his shop and headed next door, intent on breaking up the fight. He had just reached the sidewalk when Charlie stormed out of the shop, dragging his younger brother by one ear.

"What the devil is going on?" Mitchell demanded.

Yanking himself free of Charlie's grasp, Jesse turned to lash out at his big brother, who shoved Jesse so hard that the boy went crashing into Mitchell.

"What the hell are you doing?" Mitchell cried, pushing Jesse away.

"You son of a bitch!" Jesse shouted, turning his rage on the jeweller. "You are always putting your big nose in other people's business."

Infuriated at the boy's insolence, Mitchell slapped him sharply across the face. Jesse, eyes tearing, dropped the older man's lapel and whimpered: "My mother will have you arrested, you son of a bitch." Then he turned on his heels and headed up Broadway.

Mitchell—so worked up that his voice quivered slightly— turned to the older boy and barked: "What in blazes are you two fighting for all the time?"

"I don't know," Charlie snarled. "There's something the matter with him."

Not long afterward, Mitchell—still shaken from the episode—

FIEND

closed up his shop and bent his steps toward home. As he approached E Street, he spotted Jesse leaning against a building. As Mitchell walked passed, Jesse glared at him balefully, then immediately turned and started back down Broadway, in the direction of the shop.

There was so much malice in Jesse's look that Mitchell—convinced the boy had mischief in mind—decided to follow him from a slight distance. Mitchell hadn't proceeded very far when he spotted a neighborhood patrolman named Leighton on the opposite corner. Crossing the street, he told Officer Leighton about his troubles with Jesse.

"I am afraid the young ruffian means to return to my shop and break the windows," the jeweller explained.

"I will go have a talk with him," said Leighton, then headed after the receding figure of the boy.

Reassured, Mitchell continued home and went to bed. It wasn't until the next day, when he read his morning paper, that he learned about Jesse's arrest for the Millen slaying. Like everyone else in the neighborhood, Mitchell knew all about Pomeroy's criminal history. Given his own, firsthand experience of the boy's vile temperament, the notion that Jesse might be guilty of murder was all too easy for the jeweller to believe.

With Ruth Pomeroy sequestered in the Charles Street jail and removed from public sight, the violent, neighborhood protests incited by her presence came to an end. But nothing could stop the rumors that continued to spring up around her. A particularly sensational one made the rounds late Tuesday afternoon. According to this story (which did, indeed, have some basis in fact), Mrs. Pomeroy had been informed by Jesse's lawyers that her son had finally made a full, highly graphic confession to the murder of Horace Millen.

The "essential particulars" of this statement were published in the following day's edition of the *Boston Daily Advertiser*:

> On the morning of the 22 of April, Jesse rose early and went to the store, and afterwards went to the city, returning home about 9 o'clock. He remained at the store until 11½ o'clock, when he told his mother he was going to the city. She gave

145

her permission, and he went over to his mother's house, where he remained a few moments, and then started for the city proper. He, however, went up Dorchester Avenue to Eighth Street, where he saw the little Millen boy, and immediately his evil genius got possession of him and he determined to torture him, if not kill him.

He asked the boy if he would like to see the steamer, and the boy said he would, and both started off in the direction of the marshes. When they arrived at the spot where the body was found, Jesse told the Millen boy to lie down, and the little fellow, not dreaming of his danger, did so. The young fiend then immediately sprang upon him, clapped his left hand over the little innocent's mouth to stop his outcries, and then, with the same jack-knife that had but a month before been used to murder the unfortunate Katie Curran, the monster deliberately cut the throat of the little boy that had so implicitly trusted him.

The boy struggled fearfully, and the murderer, desperate at his failure in not at the first blow killing his victim, stabbed him repeatedly in the bowels and chest. He mutilated the body in a frightful manner, but does not know, as he says, to what extent, and finally left his victim in a dying condition. He cleaned his knife and person as well as he could, and then took a car for Boston proper, going to the Common, where he remained some time, and then returned home.

Stripped of its florid journalistic touches ("the young fiend, "the little innocent," etc.), this statement proved to be essentially a faithful account of the atrocity commited upon the Millen child. Publicly, Jesse would always maintain his innocence. But there were certain individuals to whom he sometimes confided otherwise. One of these was an elderly fellow familiarly known as "Uncle Cook," the chaplain of the Charles Street jail. According to news accounts, it was Uncle Cook who had elicited this confession. It happened Tuesday, when the chaplain made his customary evening rounds and found Jesse in an unusually somber mood.

"Is something the matter, Jesse?" the older man asked, seating himself beside the boy on the edge of the bunk.

After hesitating briefly, Jesse acknowledged that he was "feeling uneasy" about the death of the Millen boy. The chaplain assured him that he would "feel better if he told exactly what had happened"—whereupon Jesse drew a deep breath and proceeded to unburden himself.

Uncle Cook listened to the story in silence, then quietly asked the boy what he "felt should be done with him." Jesse—who had obviously given the matter some thought—promptly replied that he "should be sent to prison for five or six years." When he got out, he would "then go to sea for two or three years"—by which time he would be a "fully grown man and strong enough to resist the temptation to do such bloody deeds."

It was a revealing answer. Like all sociopathic lust-killers, Pomeroy was clearly incapable of grasping either the true enormity of his acts (for which he felt that a few years behind bars would be sufficient punishment) or the dark, implacable forces that fueled his mania—forces which, however dormant they might sometimes lay, could never be entirely expunged or outgrown.

27

It is unfortunately true, as most of us know by observation, that the cruelest of living animals is a boy.

—*The New York Times*, July 26, 1874

Seeking to avoid a repetition of Wednesday's mob scene—when a horde of people had shown up at the station house in the hope of glimpsing the "boy fiend"—Coroner Ingalls had tried to arrange a trip to the Charles Street jail, where his jury could hear Jesse's testimony in private. When the proceedings resumed on Friday afternoon, however, Ingalls had a disappointing announcement to make. He had sent a note to Sheriff Clark, asking for permission to visit Jesse in jail. Much to Ingall's chagrin, Clark had declined the request. "While it would be pleasant for me to do anything to favor you," the sheriff had written in reply, "I feel obliged to decline, because the boy does not wish to appear before a coroner's jury to be seen or to be asked any questions. And as he could not be compelled by any court to testify in a case against himself, it is not right for me to exercise my power and take him before you or for you to take the jury before him."

Ingalls explained to the jurors that—although he had the "power to require the attendance of Jesse at the inquest, as of any other person"—he thought it best not to do so. Since Jesse clearly had no intention of volunteering any useful information, there was no point in dragging him down to the station house, particularly since his presence in South Boston was bound to cause an uproar.

Having taken care of these preliminaries, Ingalls called the first witness of the day, Dr. E. A. Gilman, the physician who had conducted the autopsy on Katie Curran's remains. Though the essentials of the Curran murder had been public knowledge for days, Gilman's official report—which he read aloud to the jurors—revealed grim, new details:

> The appearance of the remains was that of a body in a stage of decomposition, with clothing also in a decayed condition; the skull detached from the trunk; the flesh, with some exceptions, rotted away from the bones; and the whole mixed with a quantity of moist coal, ashes, cinders, etc. The above was the remains of a young girl.

Gilman then proceeded to describe the victim's garments—her sacque (or outer jacket) of cheap, "gray shaggy goods"; her dress "trimmed with wide strips of plaid"; her blue flannel petticoat; her white cotton chemise, drawers, and stockings. Though the decayed condition of the remains made it difficult "to ascertain the precise cause of death," Gilman's investigation made it clear that the young victim had suffered an appalling degree of violence at her killer's hands:

> The clothing of this girl was found to have been either forcibly pulled open or cut apart, up and down in front. The sacque and waist of the dress were unfastened and appeared as if pulled apart without time being given to unbutton the sacque or unhook the waist. The front of the waist of the petticoat and a part of the skirt had been cut down the middle, as was also the waist of the drawers, the two cuts corresponding. The chemise was in such a dilapidated condition that it was difficult to say whether it was cut or torn, but one or the other had been done. The right side of the drawers was buttoned to the waist, while the left side was not, but appeared as if torn down the outside of the leg to the bottom.
>
> The skin and flesh of the lower part of the abdomen was in a remarkable state of preservation in comparison with the other parts of the body. Here were found evidence of wounds inflicted with a cutting instrument. On the left thigh, a little below the groin, was a stab. In a line directly upwards and continuous with the opening of the external genitalia was the plainest cut, which extended through the skin and cellular tissues and into the abdominal cavity; but how far upwards this

cut was carried it was impossible to determine, as the skin a few inches above was decayed away.

Another cut of four or five inches in extent, over the right iliac fossa, or the right lower part of the abdomen, and in an oblique direction, was quite plain to be seen. As regards the middle and upper part of the abdomen and the chest and neck, the skin and tissues being entirely destroyed by decomposition, it is impossible to say what wounds might have been inflicted in those parts. There was found no fracture of the skull or of any other bone.

I examined very carefully for evidence of stabs made through the clothing, but saw nothing which I could call a stab, except a hole through the left leg of the drawers, which might have been over the stab in the thigh. The clothing was evidently opened before any wound was inflicted below the neck. . . .

This is a direct description of all the facts which the autopsy revealed.

After giving the jurors a few moments to absorb the ghastly specifics of this report—with its horrific depiction of butchery and sexual mutilation perpetrated on a ten-year-old girl—Ingalls called the next witness, the onetime jeweller Edward Mitchell, whose recollection of Jesse's vicious altercation with Charlie on the night of the Millen murder had appeared in the *Boston Herald* that very morning. Mitchell now related the same story to the jurors, along with some additional accounts of Jesse's loutish behavior.

According to his testimony, Michell began to notice a "bad smell, like the smell of offal" wafting up through his floorboards a few days after Jesse got out of reform school and went to work in his brother's shop. Descending into the cellar with a candle, he found the toilet completely stopped up with paper. After clearing it out with a stick, he went back upstairs to have a talk with Charles, who acknowledged that his younger brother seemed to spend an inordinate amount of time in the bathroom. Just then, Jesse came into the store.

"Young man," Mitchell said to him sternly, "if you don't use that water closet in a different way, I shall nail it up."

Jesse's response was to mutter something nasty under his breath, turn his back on the jeweller, and slouch away.

Several weeks later, on a Saturday morning in mid-March, Jesse got embroiled in a fight with his brother, who flung him

JESSE POMEROY.

An engraved portrait of Jesse Harding Pomeroy, based on a photograph taken at the time of his arrest for the Millen murder, 1874.

"WITH MY KNIFE I CUT HER THROAT."

Illustration from the 1875 crime pamphlet *The Life of Jesse H. Pomeroy, The Boy Fiend.* (*Rare Books Division/New York Public Library/Astor, Lenox and Tilden Foundations*)

Jesse's mother, Ruth Ann Pomeroy. *(Corbis Images)*

One of the penciled notes written by Jesse to his young jail-mate, Willie Baxter, in 1875.

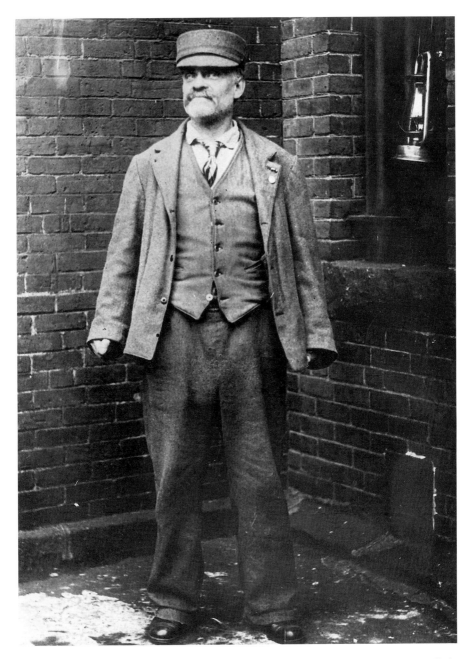

After forty-one years, Pomeroy is finally released from his solitary cell in January 1917. *(Corbis Images)*

Pomeroy poses with one of the many modern wonders he has never seen—a motion picture camera. *(The Boston Herald)*

Frontispiece portrait from Pomeroy's 1920 book of poetry, *Selections from the Writings of Jesse Harding Pomeroy, Life Prisoner Since 1874.*

After more than fifty years in Charlestown prison, Jesse Pomeroy (center) is transferred to the state farm at Bridgewater in July 1929. *(Corbis Images)*

out onto the street. A late-winter storm had hit Boston a few days earlier. Scooping up handfuls of filthy snow, Jesse began to mold them into balls and hurl them at the open door of his brother's shop. When one of these missiles shattered against the partition separating the two stores and sent chunks of grimy snow spattering onto Mitchell's showcase, the older man strode to the doorway and warned Jesse to stop.

"Shut your damned door if you don't want it thrown in," was Jesse insolent reply.

"Young man," Mitchell said, his voice tight with anger, "you have been in the House of Correction once, and if you don't take care, you will get there again."

"It's none of your damned business," sneered Jesse.

"It is mine or *any* good citizen's business," answered Mitchell. Then—resisting the impulse to go outside and give the impertinent teenager a well-deserved whack in the face—the jeweller stepped back into his store and slammed the door behind him.

Mitchell (who had given up the jewelry business and was now employed as a special police officer in Chester Square) concluded his testimony by stating that—for all his trouble with the vile-tempered boy—it had never occurred to him that Jesse might have done away with the Curran girl. "If I *had* suspected him," Mitchell told the jury, "I would have searched the cellar myself."

The remaining witnesses at Friday's session had few new revelations to offer. Officer Thomas Adams repeated the story he had already told to the papers. Under sharp questioning by the jurors, he continued to maintain that his examination of the cellar—conducted with a kerosene lamp and a long, pointed stick—had been thoroughly professional, in spite of his failure to detect the fetid, clumsily concealed corpse. His colleague, Asel B. Griggs, who had assisted with the search, corroborated Adams's story.

Next, Charles McGinnis, the laborer who had uncovered the Curran girl's remains, gave a graphic account of his discovery, describing the horrifying moment when he had come upon the child's moldering skull and arm. Finally, two more policemen— Officer John Foote and Sergeant George Hersey of Station Six— described a visit they had paid to Ruth Pomeroy's residence at 312 Broadway, where they had fruitlessly searched the cellar for evidence.

At that point the inquest was adjourned until 4:00 P.M. the following Monday.

Perusing their weekend papers, Bostonians would have been briefly distracted from the grim business of the Pomeroy case by a blaring, front-page announcement. Though designed to resemble a major news story, this item was actually a paid advertisement, trumpeting the upcoming, three-week run of what was being ballyhooed as "The Event of 1874!"

"BARNUM IN BOSTON," screamed the headline. "GREAT ROMAN HIPPODROME! INVOLVING A CAPITAL OF ONE MILLION DOLLARS!!! OCCUPYING FOUR BLOCKS ON BACK BAY, ADJOINING COLOSSEUM GROUNDS!"

A few months earlier, in late April, P. T. Barnum's Hippodrome had opened in New York City. Staged inside a colossal structure that could seat as many as 12,000 spectators at each sold-out performance, the show drew raves from audiences and critics alike. "It is unquestionably the most magnificent entertainment ever introduced to an American audience," cheered the *Sunday Democrat.* "Altogether making up an exhibition never before equalled in this country," exclaimed the *Brooklyn Union.* "The magnificence of this last venture of Barnum cannot be understood unless seen," declared the *Commercial Advertiser.* Even the straitlaced *New York Evangelist* had warm words for the show, pronouncing it "free from those evil associations which cluster around ordinary amusements and make them so often ministers to vice."

Regarding the Hippodrome as the "crowning effort" of his long and celebrated career, Barnum had pulled out all the stops for the occasion. He imported $50,000 worth of chariots, armor, flags, and historical costumes from England, shipped scores of exotic animals to New York from all over the world, and in general spared no effort or expense to mount the most dazzling spectacle ever presented—"a startling novelty, far beyond anything ever seen in this country," as advertisements proclaimed.

Each performance began with an hour-long "Congress of Nations," a pageant whose "splendor and variety" (as one reviewer wrote with inadvertent irony) "seemed almost interminable." Thousands of lavishly costumed performers representing the "Kings, Queens, Emperors, and other potentates of the civilized world" paraded around the arena in a grand procession that invariably brought gasps of awe from the wonder-struck crowds. Following this magnificent spectacle, the audience was treated to a dizzying assortment of races (involving camels, elephants, monkeys, ostriches, ponies, and Roman chariots driven by "Amazonian women"); an English hunt featuring real stags and more than 150 authentically costumed riders; a balloon ascension; a Western show with scores of real Indians and buffaloes; and much more.

In addition to these "splendid and exciting scenes," the Hippodrome also featured a menagerie, a museum, an aquarium, and of course, Barnum's beloved sideshow, where visitors could gawk at such celebrated "human oddities" as "English Jack," the frog-swallower; the armless wonder, Charles Tripp; and Ana Swann, the Nova Scotia giantess.

While the Great Hippodrome Building on Vanderbilt Square in Manhattan was being renovated for the winter, Barnum sent the show on the road. A pioneering manipulator of the media, the "great showman" knew precisely how to whip up audience anticipation. Ads for the Hippodrome began running in Boston papers more than a week before it was scheduled to open. In the meantime—while waiting for the "Grand Spectacle" to commence its three-week run—Bostonians could continue to divert themselves with their own "human oddity": the "boy-tiger," the "moral monstrosity," the "white-eyed demon," who exerted a primal fascination every bit as intense as anything in Barnum's sideshow.

That his contemporaries regarded Jesse as a kind of carnival freak—the criminal equivalent of one of Barnum's sideshow "curiosities"—was confirmed on Sunday, July 26, when the *New York Times* ran another lengthy editorial on the Boston murders. Pomeroy's case, declared the writer, was "one not only of extraordinary atrocity in crime but of singular interest in psychology." What could possibly explain the motivations of a fourteen-year-old boy "who kills other boys and girls for no other reason than the love of inflicting torture and death, and a curiosity to see how they will act while he cuts their throats and stabs them?" The phenomenon was so monstrous—such a shocking "exhibition of the fiendish capacity of human nature"—that anyone looking for an answer might almost be tempted to revert to "the old beliefs in werewolves and possession by devils."

Of course, the writer continued, there were other possibilities. In contrast to the medieval, superstitious belief in demonic possession, there was the modern scientific theory of "Darwinian development." According to this theory, Jesse's crimes could be seen "as an outbreak of the savage nature inherited from that hairy wild beast with a tail from which the [followers of Darwin] insist we are all descended." To be sure, the writer added, "there are few, if any, wild beasts that kill for the mere sake of killing." But no one could deny "that there are men, women, and children who seem to delight in giving pain for the mere sake of giving it; which would seem, according to Mr. Darwin's theory, to involve the conclusion that the wild beast of which man is the final result was the vilest and bloodiest of all the brute creation."

In the end, however, the writer rejected both the "gloomy beliefs of the old theology" and the "new and dreary science" of "Darwinian development" in favor of a more novel explanation. Jesse's behavior, he argued, could "reasonably be accounted for" by the unfortunate fact that, of all "living animals," the absolutely cruelest is a young boy "in that dreadful period between six and twelve years of age. Few of us" the writer continued, "if we have been reflective observers of our kind, can fail to remember cases of boys who have been wantonly and atrociously cruel to inferior animals, and even to younger children. . . . Why boys are thus cruel is a question involving discussion beyond the province of journalism. But that they are so is a fact to be accepted. And this boy, Pomeroy, is probably a mere example, or 'case,' of the existence of this cruelty of disposition in an exaggerated and hideously monstrous development."

The editorial concluded by recommending a punishment in keeping with its view of Jesse as an example of freakish human development, a specimen to be isolated and put under observation. "For the world's sake as well as his own," the writer urged, "he should be imprisoned and watched and studied as a monstrous moral phenomenon."

The inquest lasted two more days before reaching its preordained conclusion. A half-dozen witnesses testified on Monday afternoon, July 27, most significantly John and Millie Margerson, the original owners of the house at 327 Broadway, who had been living above Mrs. Pomeroy's shop at the time of the murder. Both husband and wife stated that, in the latter part of May, they became aware of a rank odor emanating from below stairs. Assuming that it was coming from the water closet, Mr. Margerson had gone down into the cellar and unclogged the toilet. Over the next few weeks, however, the smell just got worse. Thinking that some sort of dead animal might be rotting in the cellar, he checked again in mid-June—but by then, the stench was so overwhelming that he couldn't bear to stay down there for more than a few minutes. According to Margerson, it had crossed his mind that the missing Curran girl might be buried below the Pomeroys' shop (by that time, of course, Jesse was already infamous as the prime suspect in the Millen slaying). But since the police had already made a supposedly thorough search of the cellar, he had shrugged off his suspicions.

At the final session of the inquest on Wednesday afternoon, July 30, the jurors heard from James Nash, who had purchased the building from the Margersons, and who offered a corroborating account of the discovery of Katie's remains; Willie Kohr, the newspaper delivery boy, who testified to having seen Katie in the shop with Jesse right before her disappearance; and Thomas Tobin, owner of the neighborhood stationery store, who stated that a little girl matching Katie Curran's description had come into his shop early on the morning of March 18, looking for a notebook. Tobin had shown her three different kinds, but none proved to her liking. When he last saw her—through the window of his store—she was heading up Broadway in the direction of the Pomeroys' shop.

At approximately 5:30 P.M., following a brief deliberation, the jurors returned their verdict: "That the said Katie Mary Curran came to her death on or about the 18th of March, 1874, at No. 327 Broadway, South Boston, by the hand of Jesse H. Pomeroy; that he has acknowledged the crime, and the evidence obtained corroborates his statement. And the jury further find that either before or after the commission of the murder, the girl's person was mutilated with a knife or some sharp instrument."

The public's obsession with Jesse Pomeroy wasn't over. Far from it. In another few months, with the start of his trial, his case would explode back onto the front pages and excite communal passions all over again.

But with the end of the Curran inquest, the story temporarily faded from the news. On Thursday, July 31, the papers offered the final glimpse of the "boy fiend" that readers would get for a while—a glimpse that reinforced the popular view of Jesse as a prodigy of both fiendish crime and diabolical cunning.

According to an unnamed but apparently reliable source, Jesse was devoting the bulk of his time to the preparation of a lengthy manuscript intended to establish his innocence. Entitled "Jesse H. Pomeroy's Defense," this nearly book-length work offered a "minutely detailed" account of his actions at the time of the Millen murder and exhibited "a remarkable shrewdness" in rebutting nearly every accusation leveled against him.

When not engaged in composing this work (supposedly intended for the use of his lawyers), Jesse passed his time sleeping, eating, and reading the only books permitted to him—religious tracts supplied by Uncle Cook, the chaplain. (As the newspapers noted, these uplifting works "were not much relished by Jesse," whose tastes ran to the lurid pleasures of Beadle's blood-and-thunder stories.) Occasionally, he also wrote a letter to his mother, who always answered promptly. Every day, Sheriff Clark was besieged by visitors seeking access to Jesse—reporters, photographers, and ordinary citizens hoping for a glimpse of the caged "boy-tiger." All such petitioners, without exception, were politely but firmly turned away.

Jesse himself was generally on his best behavior—"courteous and respectful in his address." Even so, there was something vaguely unsettling about him. Interviewed by a reporter from the *Boston Post*, the jail turnkey, an old-timer named Bradley, described Jesse's peculiar effect on the people around him.

The boy "never causes trouble," Bradley observed. But "beneath his placid appearance," there was "something in his manner which caused aversion" in those who came in daily contact with him—"something which old officers cannot describe, but which causes an innate feeling of distrust and dread."

PART 4

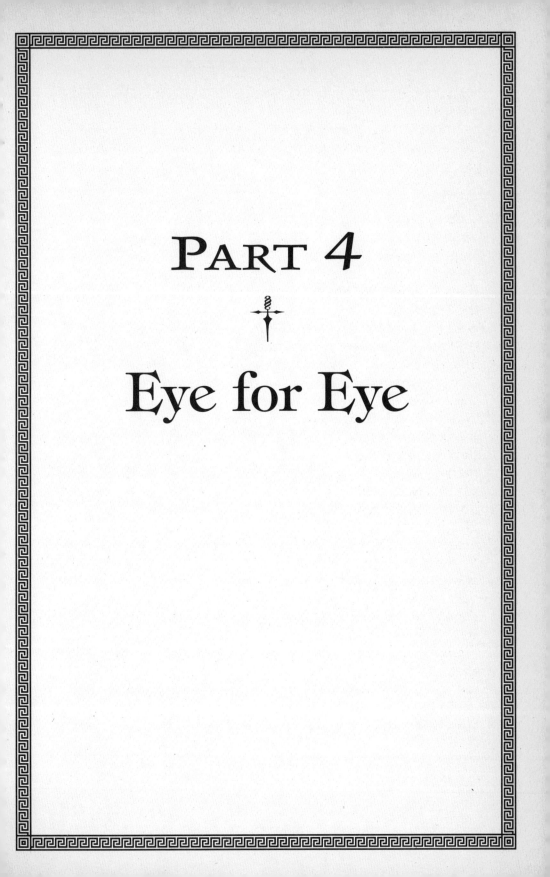

Eye for Eye

28

Now, are we not each and all a little insane; that is to say, of unsound and imperfect mind, impelled by defects of will to constant variations from the straightforward course? Well then, suppose some of the worst of these defects greatly aggravated in our constitution. Imagine a strong inclination to cruelty, a passion for destroying, united with dull perceptions of moral rectitude and a weak will. Who shall say that the perpetrator has not the same right to claim that he could not help it that we have in our everyday peccadilloes?

—*The Boston Daily Globe*, May 7, 1874

It was clear that—if Jesse's lawyers hoped to save him from the gallows—they would have to mount an insanity defense. And indeed, from the moment of his arrest, the debate over the boy's mental condition—and the extent to which he could be held responsible for his acts—had raged in the press. On one side stood those who believed that—though clearly afflicted with "a morbid condition of the mind"—Jesse did not suffer from the radical "disorganization of the faculties" that constitutes true insanity. To these commentators, there was only one sure way to "protect society against the recurrence of future atrocities by Pomeroy," and that was "to put him out of the world." Executing Jesse would also serve as a powerful deterrent to others "who might be led to imitate his example." As an editorialist for the *Boston Post* argued:

> This plea of criminals, whether juveniles or adult,
> that they cannot help it is a dangerous one. It may
> be that they are driven on by an impulse to evil
> that seems to them uncontrollable, but we are in-
> clined to think that means might be found to
> check this indulgence in evil propensities. If there

was the certainty of severe punishment before
them, they could probably, by a strong effort,
keep their hands off their fellow creatures. We
think they might even be induced to abstain from
enticing little children away and sticking knives
into them, if they were sure that indulgence in
such pastimes would bring a severe penalty.

On the other side of the debate were those who argued that—
as the victim of a "horrible monomania which he had neither the
moral force nor the training to control"—Jesse was no more responsible for his acts "than a young tiger." His treatment by civilized beings, therefore, should be analogous to that which a
jungle cat would receive in a zoo—*i.e.*, lifelong incarceration behind bars (either in a prison or mental hospital). These observers
expressed grave doubts that Jesse's destruction would "deter
others of a like evil nature from committing similar crimes," for
the simple reason that such killers—while perfectly aware of the
wickedness and potential legal consequences of their acts—"are
impelled by dreadful promptings they are powerless to resist.
They know what they are doing, and yet they cannot help it."

And then there were those editorialists who declined to take
sides until the issue was resolved at Jesse's trial. This more mod-
erate position was epitomized by a piece in the *Boston Globe*,
whose writer acknowledged the extreme difficulty of diagnosing
a killer like Pomeroy—a person whose "mental structure" was
apparently intact but who was nevertheless subject to "an uncontrollable passion for inflicting pain." True, Jesse appeared
sane enough to know what he was doing and to understand "the
heinous character of his acts." Even so—since the boy was
clearly in the grip of "evil passions and propensities"—it was
"not easy to say whether he could help it or not." In the end, this
writer insisted, the question of Jesse's sanity (and moral responsibility) could only be answered by trained "alienists"—medical
experts specializing in the study of mental disease.

In the months preceding his trial, three such experts visited
Jesse in his cell—Drs. Clement Walker and John E. Tyler (who
had been retained by the defense) and a physician named
George T. Choate, who was working for the prosecution. Among
them, the three alienists would conduct fourteen separate inter-

views with the young prisoner—enough (as Jesse would later report) "to make me nearly insane, if I was not already so." By the time the doctors were done with him, he felt as if he had been operated on with the mental equivalent of a stomach pump.

Though Walker paid the greatest number of visits to Jesse—seven in all, between mid-September and early December—it was Tyler, a portly little man with a ready wit and an easygoing style, that Jesse felt most comfortable with. During their first meeting, on September 16, Jesse gave Tyler a detailed account of his attacks on the young boys in Chelsea and South Boston, insisting that he had initially approached them "just out of mere companionship," with "no more idea of whipping and torturing them than I had of jumping up to the moon." It wasn't until he had led the little victims to a remote locale that a "sudden impulse or feeling came over me."

When Tyler pressed the boy for more information about this "feeling," Jesse pointed to his head and explained that, immediately before each of his crimes, he had experienced a sudden pain that began just over his left ear and passed from one side of his head to the other. This pain, Jesse said, was always the harbinger of violence. "The feeling which accompanied [the headache] was that I must . . . whip or kill the boy or girl, as the case was, and it seemed to me that I could not help doing it."

Though Jesse claimed he retained only an "indistinct" recollection of his victims—and of the precise torments he had inflicted on them—he freely confessed to the crimes, not only to Tyler but to Walker and Choate as well. In mid-November, however, his story suddenly changed. According to his later account, he began to doubt his own memory after receiving a note from his mother which counseled him "not to say I did it unless I did, and to say I didn't if I didn't." Mulling over this advice, the boy was forced to acknowledge that—though he "really *did* think" he had committed the crimes he was accused of—there was a small voice inside his head that sometimes said, "Jesse, you know you did not do these things, so why do you not stand up and try to clear yourself?" For a while, however, he resisted this inner prompting, fearing that, if he recanted, his mother and brother might fall under suspicion.

When Dr. Tyler visited him in mid-October, however, and began questioning him about the Curran murder, Jesse—almost without intending to—abruptly denied that he had committed it.

Tyler stared at him for a long moment. "Are you saying now

that you did *not* kill the little girl?" the doctor asked, his eyebrows raised.

"That's right," Jesse said.

"But you have said that you *did*, Jesse," Tyler protested. "Which story am I to believe?"

"You must believe me now," said the boy.

"Well, then," Tyler said after a momentary pause, "if you didn't kill her, who did? Your mother?"

Jesse grew instantly incensed. "No gentleman would say such a thing."

A few days later, Tyler examined him again, but Jesse continued to stick to his new version of events. Indeed, he now claimed that he hadn't killed either Katie Curran *or* Horace Millen, and that "this was the truth."

Tyler didn't try to hide his disbelief. On October 16, during his fifth visit, he took a few more futile stabs at getting Jesse to retract his new claim. When Jesse stubbornly insisted on his innocence, Tyler left and never returned.

Several weeks later, on November 6—just a few weeks shy of Jesse's fifteenth birthday—Tyler submitted his written report to the defense lawyer, Joseph Cotton. It is a revealing document, offering insight into both Jesse's pathology and the state of psychiatric knowledge in 1874. It begins with a few brief observations about the subject's physical condition and mental capacities, both of which were, in Tyler's estimation, unexceptional. Jesse's "general health" was "fair though not robust"; his memory "accurate but not quick"; and his learning limited to "some knowledge of the elementary branches of education." In short—apart from his blighted right eye (which Jesse claimed "was a result of vaccination")—he was physically and intellectually average.

By contrast, his "moral sensibility" was strikingly aberrant. Though able to discriminate between right and wrong when presented with various hypothetical cases, Jesse was absolutely "obtuse" when it came to his own crimes. "He evinces no pity for the boys tortured or for the victims of his homicide," Tyler writes, "and no remorse or sorrow for his acts." Moreover, his wildly "contradictory statements"—his detailed "account of killing the children and subsequent denial of any agency therein"—were the sign of a deeply duplicitous nature.

After describing the "peculiar sensation" that "always preceded" Jesse's outbursts of violence, Tyler goes on to offer his diagnosis. An especially significant aspect of the case, he notes, was that Pomeroy's victims "were persons whom he did not even know and towards whom he had no malice or ill-will. . . . None of the usual incentives to crime appear: no offense had been taken, no grudge, no envy felt, no hope of gain or advantage appears." When queried about his motives, Jesse could only say "I *had* to." Tyler correctly concludes that since "no reasonable and satisfactory *external* motive for these extraordinary acts exists or can be found," there must be some *internal* cause, in the form of a mental disease. He then attempts to place Pomeroy within a category of pathological behavior by citing what he takes to be analogous instances:

> Cases similar to this are recorded, and a number have been known to the writer, which, however, differed in this—that the impulse was to commit acts comparatively inoffensive, and of which the results were comparatively unimportant. For instance, the child or youth is impelled to wash and re-wash his hands, his clothes, the chair he sits upon, the food he eats. He is disturbed if interfered with, and will seek to do it privately. The only reason he can give for his doing so is, "I *had* to." So it is with the propensity to cut up clothing, to fire buildings, to steal articles of which no use is ever made and the interest in which ceases with the act.

The problem with this passage, of course, is its indiscriminate lumping together of several distinct mental disorders, from obsessive-compulsive behavior to kleptomania and pyromania—none of which is especially pertinent to Jesse's pathology. With his complete lack of conscience and deeply sadistic appetites, Jesse was a classic (if unusually precocious) sexual sociopath—a juvenile lust-murderer who delighted in torture and bloodshed, and who certainly would have preyed on other victims had he not been stopped so early in his appalling career. Though Tyler can be commended for recognizing that Jesse's crimes were the product of a profound psychological disorder, his attempt at diagnosis ultimately misses the mark, equating the atrocities of a serial sex-killer with the acts of a neurotic who is compelled to scrub his hands a hundred times a day or to avoid stepping on sidewalk cracks when he walks along a street.

Tyler's ultimate opinion is also open to question. There is no evidence to suggest that Jesse suffered from a psychosis—that he had paranoid delusions, experienced bizarre hallucinations, or heard voices commanding him to kill. And according to the results of Tyler's own testing, Jesse had no trouble discriminating between right and wrong. Given these findings, the doctor's conclusion comes as something of a surprise:

"It is evident that such a boy as this should be carefully restrained of his liberty that others may not be endangered. . . . In my belief, he is *insane.*"

29

Six miners went into the mountains
To hunt for precious gold;
It was the middle of the winter,
The weather was dreadful cold.
Six miners went into the mountains
They had nor food nor shack—
Six miners went into the mountains,
But only one came back.
                    —"Ballad of Alfred Packer"

In the weeks preceding the start of Jesse's trial, there was no
shortage of lurid news to keep the public diverted—grisly acci-
dents, ghastly crimes, a sensational case of frontier cannibalism,
and the long-running sex scandal featuring America's most popular man of the cloth, the Reverend Henry Ward Beecher.

From Omaha came reports of a bizarre and bewildering
tragedy—a devastating act of God inexplicably visited upon several of His most devout servants. According to the account in
the *New York Times*—headlined "A CLERGYMAN AND HIS
WIFE KILLED BY A THUNDERBOLT WHILE AT WORSHIP"—
a Methodist minister named Richard S. Shreve had just seated
himself at the dinner table, along with his wife and older brother,
John, who was also a preacher. Outside the cozy refuge of the little house, a thunderstorm was brewing. The sky was "overcast
with dark, angry clouds, and a few large, scattering drops of
water had begun to fall." Before partaking of their evening meal,
the Reverend Shreve proposed that the little party join together
in a family prayer. No sooner had he opened his Bible, however,
than a "death-dealing" bolt of electricity exploded through the
dining window and smote the seated trio. John Shreve eventu-

ally recovered, but his brother and sister-in-law were killed instantly—"furnishing one of the most startling exemplifications on record," as the *Times* put it, "of the truth of the line in the *Book of Common Prayer,* to wit, 'In the midst of life we are in death.' "

News of another tragic accident—this one exemplifying the daily perils of nineteenth-century industrial labor—was reported from Vermont. A middle-aged factory worker named Elbridge Williams and his nineteen-year-old son, Edwin—"sober and industrious men," according to the papers—were working together at the Cook Slate Works in Rutland when the younger of the pair, attempting to adjust the gear in the feeder of a slate planer, got his right hand caught in the moving cogs. When he shouted for help, his father dashed to his side. Instead of reversing the machinery, however, the elder Williams stuck his own right hand into the apparatus and attempted to pull his son free. "In doing this," the papers reported, "his own hand became entangled, and both were slowly drawn in and crushed in the gear." Hearing their screams, the factory foreman managed to stop the machine and freed the two men. Though both survived the accident, their mangled right hands had to be amputated—a catastrophic misfortune, since, as the papers reported, "father and son were the only means of support to a poor and worthy family."

Infanticide was much in the news, particularly in New York City, where the sinister practice of "baby-farming" suddenly began to receive widespread attention after the suspicious death of a seventeen-day-old infant named Charles Corey. At the request of Dr. Harris of the New York City Board of Health, Coroner Wolfman and his associate, Dr. William Shine, visited the child's supposed caretaker, a middle-aged woman named Kate Kilbride, who occupied a dismal apartment in the basement of a West Side tenement. Under intense questioning by the investigators, Mrs. Kilbride revealed that she had received the infant from a woman named Mary H. Doran, who ran a private "lying-in asylum" on West Twenty-Sixth Street. Further investigation revealed what the *New York Times* called "the shocking details of a most aggravated case of 'baby-farming.' "

Mary Doran's establishment, it turned out, was nothing but a kind of squalid little dormitory, patronized by poor, unwed women in advanced stages of pregnancy. For the price of five dollars per week, each of these unfortunates got an iron-framed cot outfitted with a fetid straw mattress and dilapidated bed-clothes. Once they gave birth, their babies were turned over to Mrs. Doran to dispose of as she saw fit. The newborns were generally advertised for adoption at the price of twenty-five dollars apiece. When there were no interested takers, the infants were "farmed out" to people like Mrs. Kilbride, who received a small monthly stipend for "taking care" of the babies—meaning that the women were expected to do everything possible, short of outright murder, to make sure the infants didn't survive.

Mrs. Kilbride's method was to nurse her little charges on a diet of "poisonous soothing syrup." In another, equally shocking case, a "baby-farmer" named Elizabeth Graham starved her infants by feeding them nothing but a spoonful of condensed milk and a half-pint of water twice a day. The precise extent of this "nefarious practice" was unknown, but—in a city with more than 5,000 illegitimate births per year (out of an annual total of 34,000 newborns), there were "grave apprehensions among experts of its being very widespread."

Accounts of other shocking crimes filled the New York and Boston dailies. Within the course of a few weeks in fall of 1874, the front pages were packed with blaring headlines: "ATROCIOUS MURDER IN HACKENSACK, N.J.," "DOUBLE MURDER AT NEW ROCHELLE," "MURDER AND LYNCH LAW IN TENNESSEE," "A WOMAN BRUTALLY MURDERED BY HER HUSBAND," "A CONDEMNED MURDERER KILLS HIS KEEPER," "AN ENTIRE FAMILY MURDERED AND BURNED," "MORE WHOLESALE MURDER AND CREMATION," and others. One of the more shocking stories came from Topeka, Kansas, where a teenaged grocery clerk named Fred Olds—after arguing with his employer over a checkers game—shot the older man with a carbine, finished him off with a cheese knife, then buried his corpse in the cellar. The next morning, Olds calmly reopened the store, telling customers that his boss had suddenly been called East on personal business.

Most appalling of all, however, was the case of the Colorado man-eater, Alfred (aka "Alferd") Packer. Though his crimes had first come to light in the spring of 1874, it wasn't until mid-October—when *Harper's Weekly* ran a gruesomely illustrated, front-page account—that the case gained nationwide notoriety.

Born in 1842, Packer had started his career as a shoemaker, a trade he abandoned for good after enlisting in the Union army during the Civil War. (It was during his military stint that he began to be known as "Alferd," supposedly after a semiliterate tattoo artist etched the misspelling onto Packer's forearm.) Following his disability discharge (for epilepsy), Packer headed out West to try his hand at gold mining. By 1873, he was working as a wilderness guide in Utah and Colorado.

On November 17 of that year, he set out from Provo, Utah, as the leader of a twenty-one-man prospecting party headed for the gold fields near Breckenridge, Colorado. Two months later—after an arduous trek during which they were reduced to subsisting on their horses' feed—the exhausted band straggled into a camp of Ute Indians near the confluence of the Gunnison and Uncompaghre Rivers. They were welcomed by Chief Ouray—widely known throughout the West for his friendly relations with whites—who advised them to wait until spring before attempting to negotiate the snow-covered mountains. After a few restless weeks, however, Packer and five of his companions—Shannon Bell, James Humphreys, Frank Miller, George Noon, and Israel Swan—decided to risk the journey. On a mild day in early February, 1874, the six men bid farewell to their Indian hosts and headed off into the mountains.

Only one of them was ever seen alive again. Sixty-six days after leaving the Ute camp—on April 17, 1874—Packer alone appeared at the Los Pinos Indian Agency. When questioned about the fate of his five comrades, he initially claimed that—after becoming too footsore and snow-blind to travel—he had been abandoned by the others, who had gone off in search of food and shelter. When it became clear that they had no intention of returning for him, he had somehow managed to fight his way out of the mountains.

This story was greeted with a good deal of skepticism. Among other things, Packer looked suspiciously fit for a man who had supposedly suffered near-starvation; he was also equipped with Frank Miller's hunting knife and Israel Swan's rifle, and had a pocketful of money that he began spending freely at a frontier saloon. Subjected to a second, far more grueling interrogation, he related a grisly tale of bloodshed and cannibalism.

According to Packer's confession, he and his five companions had become snowbound in the mountains not long after leaving the camp of Chief Ouray. Within two weeks, their food supplies had run out. When Israel Swan, the oldest of the group, perished of hunger and exposure, the others—Packer included—had feasted on his flesh. Humphreys died next, then Miller. Their bodies, too, served to keep the survivors alive. George Noon was the fourth to go—killed, according to Packer, by Bell. When the two survivors had picked Noon's body clean of meat, Bell tried to murder Packer, who slew his attacker in self-defense, then cannibalized his corpse.

Several months later, in early August, a magazine illustrator named J. A. Randolph—working on a story about the ill-fated expedition for *Harper's Weekly*—stumbled on the remains of Packer's five companions. The article—complete with Randolph's graphic engravings of the decomposed corpses—appeared in the October 17, 1874, issue, sending shockwaves of horror throughout the country.

Packer was ultimately sentenced to hang by Judge Melville Gerry, who—according to legend—indignantly declared: "Packer, there were only seven Democrats in all of Hinsdale County, and you ate five of them, you son of a bitch!" Three years later, defense lawyers managed to obtain a retrial. This time, the "man-eater" was sentenced to forty years in the state penitentiary. Paroled in 1901, he settled in Littleton, Colorado, just south of Denver, where he lived out his days regaling the local youngsters with colorful tales of life in the old West.

Sensational violence, of course, was only one of the topics that kept the country riveted in the fall of 1874. Intense as it was, the morbid fascination exerted by the Packer case was overshadowed by the public's unbridled obsession with the scandalous allegations surrounding the Reverend Henry Ward Beecher. Then, as now, few things sold more newspapers than lurid accounts of sexual misconduct among the nation's most eminent men.

Beecher wasn't merely eminent; he was a major celebrity, whose "Gospel of Love"—spread through his sermons, speeches, newspaper columns, and magazine articles—struck a powerfully responsive chord in his Gilded Age contemporaries. His weekly services at the Plymouth Church in the fashionable neighborhood of Brooklyn Heights drew admirers by the thousands. Though unremarkable in appearance—in 1874, he was a portly, moon-faced sixty-one-year-old—he possessed a charismatic appeal, particularly to women. His flowery orations, delivered with a showman's flair, inspired the kind of female adulation that, in future generations, would be lavished on crooners, movie idols, and rock stars.

One of his most ardent followers was thirty-five-year-old Elizabeth Tilton, whose husband, Theodore, was Beecher's closest friend. In 1868—after turning to Beecher for solace following the death of her newborn son—Elizabeth embarked on an eighteen-month affair with the older man (whose own marriage, to an aloof and censorious woman named Eunice, had been emotionally bankrupt for years). Their illicit relationship remained a secret until 1870, when a guilt-ridden Elizabeth finally confessed to her husband, who in turn confided in a number of prominent friends. Before long, Beecher's adultery had been exposed in the press, precipitating the greatest sex scandal of the era.

For months, accusations and denials flew back and forth, with Beecher indignantly denying the charges, and his supporters (including his famous sister, Harriet Beecher Stowe) rallying to his defense. In the fall of 1874, matters came to a head when Tilton brought suit against Beecher, charging him with adultery and demanding $100,000 in damages. Eventually (and in spite of the overwhelming evidence of his guilt), Beecher would be acquitted. His wildy sensational trial (covered by the press with a prurient zeal that made it the late-nineteenth-century equivalent of the O.J. Simpson media circus) kept the nation transfixed from January through July, 1875, a six-month span that coincided with a period of renewed furor over another sensational story—the crimes, accountability, and punishment of the Boston "boy fiend," Jesse Harding Pomeroy.

30

Christine: Tell me, do children ever commit murders? Or is crime something that's learned gradually, so that only adults do really dreadful things?

Tasker: Well, I have thought about that, and so have several authorities I've consulted lately. Yes, children have often committed murders, and quite clever ones, too.

—Maxwell Anderson, *The Bad Seed*

For the three days of its duration, the trial of Jesse Harding Pomeroy for the murder of Horace H. Millen was not only front-page news in every Boston paper but also the hottest show in town. So many people clamored for admission each morning that the courthouse guards—unable to handle the crowds—had to be assisted by a special detail of police. Still, the *real* commotion wouldn't begin until after the verdict was rendered—and it wouldn't subside for more than a year.

With the Supreme Judicial Courtroom packed to capacity, the proceedings got underway on Tuesday, December 8, 1874, at precisely 9:30 A.M. As Jesse was led to the dock, several hundred spectators half-rose from their seats, straining to get a better look at the notorious "boy fiend," who hadn't been seen in public since the previous spring. Except for his jailhouse pallor, he looked essentially the same. His preternatural composure hadn't changed, either. Throughout the trial, he seemed coolly indifferent to—even bored by—the proceedings.

At least one observer, however—a reporter for the *Globe*—claimed to perceive an occasional crack in Jesse's stolid demeanor, one that exposed the prisoner's deep, underlying malevolence. According to this writer, "While the counsel were relating his atrocities and the manner in which they were committed, Pomeroy found it difficult to restrain his laughter, and his face gave evidence of a secret pleasure."

The empanelling process went briskly, and by 11:00 A.M., twelve jurors had been selected and sworn in: Moses H. Libby, Ira E. Sanborn, Reuben Rice, Warren J. Poor, Charles H. Joy, George D. Wise, Henry H. Chandler, Eugene T. Hosford, Samuel Mills, Otis Dudley, W. Eames Stillman, and Henry S. Linnell, who was appointed foreman by the Court. The clerk then read the indictment. Immediately afterward, District Attorney John W. May rose to deliver the opening argument for the Commonwealth.

May's statement (which typified the entire trial) was a brisk, no-nonsense affair that wasted little energy on courtroom histrionics or sentimental appeals. He began by explaining that, in earlier ages, no distinctions were drawn between different types of homicide (which he defined as "the intentional killing of a fellow being"). Murder—"even its least aggravated form"—had invariably been punished by death.

As civilization developed, however, and the "spirit of Christianity" modified the harsh practices of former times, a "more humane view" gradually arose. "It was found," May observed, "that there were degrees of depravity even in murder itself." Eventually, the law had come to discriminate between killings committed in the heat of passion and those perpetrated "with deliberately premeditated malice aforethought, or with extreme atrocity or cruelty." Only the latter crimes were defined as murder in the first degree. The evidence to be presented to the jurors, May suggested, would leave no doubt in their minds that the present case fell into that category.

May then proceeded to recount the "main facts" of the crime, beginning with the discovery of the little boy's savaged corpse—the body still warm, the throat cut, the chest punctured with "fifteen or twenty" stab-wounds, the genitals horribly mutilated. After being removed to Police Station Nine in Roxbury and "thence to the undertaker's," the body was identified as that of little Horace Millen—"an infant, I might call him, four years and three months old"—whose parents had only recently moved to South Boston.

Next, May summarized the evidence against the defendant: the testimony of various witnesses who had seen the older boy leading the younger one onto the marsh; the precise correspondence between Pomeroy's boots and the footprints found at the murder scene; the findings of the inquest. As if all this weren't compelling enough, the "Commonwealth will also introduce to you another and distinct species of evidence," proclaimed the D. A. "This is a confession!" Though this confession alone was sufficient to convict Pomeroy, May continued, "it was thought the prudent and the better course to present to you, substantially, everything that was known about the matter. And it is with that view that I have detailed to you the evidence which the Commonwealth believes will satisfy you that Horace H. Millen was murdered by Jesse Harding Pomeroy!"

After appealing to the jurors to discharge "faithfully and fearlessly" the duty they had undertaken—a duty they owed to themselves, to society, and to public justice—the D.A. concluded his statement and rejoined his colleague, Attorney General Charles Train, at the prosecutor's table.

The Commonwealth's case began with the testimony of Horace H. Moses, a civil engineer and surveyor who had mapped out the localities involved in the case, from Mrs. Pomeroy's shop on Broadway to the place where the victim's body had been found. Moses's diagram hung on the wall facing the jury box and would serve as a crucial reference chart throughout the trial.

The remainder of the morning session was taken up by a string of government witnesses who—under questioning by District Attorney May—methodically traced the events of that raw April morning, eight months earlier, when little Horace Millen had been led to his death. Referring to Moses's map, twelve-year-old George Powers indicated the exact spot on the marshland—"about half a mile from the railroad" and "within twelve feet of the waterline"—where he and his deaf-mute brother, James, had stumbled on the body. He then told how he had alerted two older men who were out shooting on the marsh. The latter—Patrick Wise and Obed Goodspeed—corroborated Powers's testimony, adding detailed descriptions of the conditon of the corpse: the blood issuing from the eyes, the throat slashed, the hands badly cut.

Two policemen were the next to testify: Officer Roswell Lyons, who had been summoned to the murder site by James Powers; and Sergeant Henry O. Goodwin, who had taken the victim's body to Waterman's undertaking parlor and been present when the plaster casts were made of Jesse's bootprints on the marsh. Coroner Ira Allen followed the policemen to the stand. His graphic description of the terrible wounds inflicted on the victim—and particularly of the child's partially castrated genitals—brought gasps of dismay from the crowd, who also reacted with audible shock when Horace Millen's blood-stiffened shirt was held up for display.

Mrs. Eleanor Fosdick, the next witness, testified that—around 11:00 A.M. on the day of the murder—she had been seated at the window of her residence on the corner of Dorchester and Eighth Streets when she saw the Millen boy enter the bakeshop across the street. Another, much larger boy huddled in a nearby doorway. According to Mrs. Fosdick, there was something so strange about the bigger boy's expression that she put on her glasses to study him more closely. As she did, he suddenly glanced up at her window, and she "noticed that he had a white eye." A few moments later, the Millen boy reappeared with a drop cake. After breaking off half for himself, the older boy led the younger one away.

Asked by District Attorney May if she saw the older boy in the courtroom, Mrs. Fosdick raised a finger toward the prisoner's dock and, in a voice quivering with emotion, exclaimed: "There, in that box, is the big boy—the boy Jesse Pomeroy, who took the cake and went off with the little child!"

The most heartwrenching moment of the day occurred when Mrs. Leonora Millen took the stand. Clad entirely in black—as though still deep in mourning for her murdered son—she described, in a faltering voice, the final morning of his life. She had given him a few pennies to buy a treat at the bakeshop, expecting him to return within minutes. Instead, she had never seen her little boy again.

When the district attorney held up Horace's mangled, bloodstained garments and asked her to identify them, Mrs. Millen broke into piteous sobs. The sight was so affecting that it elicited tears from many of the spectactors. The district attorney himself seemed deeply moved, and—acting with what one reporter described as "commendable delicacy"—excused the anguished woman from further testimony.

Three more witnesses testified before the afternoon break: Elias Ashcroft, who had spotted Pomeroy leading Horace Millen by the hand along the Old Colony Railroad track; Robert Benson, the fifteen-year-old who had encountered the pair by a little creek on the marsh and was able to identify Jesse by the "white spot on his eye"; and Edward H. Harrington, the clam digger who had seen Pomeroy fleeing from the spot where Horace Millen's body was subsequently found.

At 3:00 P.M., following a one-hour recess, the Commonwealth resumed its case with the testimony of several police officers—Thomas Adams, John Foote, and James Wood—who traced the chain of events from the time of Jesse's arrest to his viewing of the corpse at Waterman's undertaking partlor. They were followed to the stand by the undertaker's son, George, who offered corroborating testimony, and a South Boston physician named Horace Everett, who had made a microscopic examination of Jesse's pocketknife and told the jury that the reddish-brown substance staining the smaller of its blades was, in his opinion, human blood.

After Everett left the witness box, May stood before the jury and read them the testimony Jesse had given at the coroner's inquest, in which he had denied any involvement in the murder. Then, the D.A. played his trump card.

As his next witness, he summoned the chaplain of the county jail, "Uncle" Rufus P. Cook, who testified that the previous July—without any prompting or "inducement"—Jesse had offered him a radically different account of the Millen slaying, in which he freely confessed to the murder. After showing a sheet of paper to Cook—who identified it as Jesse's handwritten version of this confession—May proceeded to read it aloud to the court.

Essentially it was the same statement that had been widely reported in the press five months earlier, in which Jesse graphically described how—after luring Horace Millen onto the marsh by promising to show him a steamboat—he had overpowered the struggling child, slashed his throat with a pocketknife, stabbed him again and again in the chest, and savagely mutilated his lower body.

At the end of May's recital, there was a protracted silence in the courtroom, as spectators, reporters, and even some of the jurors fixed their gaze on the prisoner, curious to see his reaction. But if they were expecting that this last and single most damning piece of evidence would somehow shake his composure, they were gravely mistaken. Head back, hands laced behind his neck, Jesse stared up at the ceiling with a look of perfect noncha-lance—the very picture of a young lad with not a trace of care in the world.

"Uncle" Cook turned out to be the prosecution's final witness. At approximately 4:45 P.M.—less than six hours after the district attorney made his opening argument—the Commonwealth rested its case.

No sooner had May reseated himself at the prosecution table than Jesse's senior counsel, Charles W. Robinson, Jr. (who had joined the defense team in the fall), rose to make his opening re-marks. It immediately became clear that—as the press had long speculated—an insanity argument was the only recourse open to Jesse's defenders.

Addressing the jury in a solemn voice, Robinson began by de-scribing Pomeroy's case as "the most remarkable in the history of crime or criminal law." Two factors made it so unusual: the ex-treme youth of the offender (who, at fourteen years and five months old, had only just reached the age "when the law says he can be held responsible") and the motiveless malignity of his acts. Indeed, Robinson—whose tone made it clear that he de-plored his client's behavior as much as any man—made no effort to mitigate the awfulness of Jesse's crimes. On the contrary, his speech (which several commentators characterized as "inge-nious") consisted largely of a detailed itemization of every atroc-ity Pomeroy had been accused of committing, beginning with the series of assaults that had landed him in reform school.

After describing each of these incidents in turn, Robinson pro-ceeded to summarize Pomeroy's time at Westborough, recount-ing—among other disconcerting episodes—the time that Jesse had taken such savage delight in pounding a snake to death that he had to be dragged away from the creature's mangled carcass.

It was soon after his release that Jesse committed the first of his two homicidal "transactions" (as Robinson, in jarring legalese, persisted in calling the murders). "This transaction oc-curred . . . on the 8th day of March. On that day, he did kill the Curran girl." Jesse, of course, was not on trial for the slaying of Katie Curran. Neverthless, Robinson proceeded to provide the jurors with a dramatic précis of her death.

At half past eight on that morning, he explained, Jesse had gone across the street as usual to open his mother's store. "While he was there, engaged in sweeping it out, the Curran girl came in. She was an entire stranger to him, and he to her, and before her coming in there, he did not know there was a Curran girl in the world.

"Instantly, the thought came to him, and he told her to go into the cellar. And then, within three minutes from the time the girl went into that cellar, she was dead!

"She went and asked for some article. He told her it was downstairs. She went down and he immediately locked the front door. As I understand, she stepped down and stood right in the center of the place below, facing Broadway. He stepped up behind her and in an instant cut her throat.

"It was done in an instant! She died quite suddenly, without any great struggle. He then took her and drew her on one side and covered her over with some few things and left her.

"The next transaction was this transaction of which you have heard today. These are the particular transactions connected with this boy."

Having given the jury the gruesome details of Pomeroy's "transactions," Robinson then got down to the crux of his case—that Jesse, as a being who could not control his most violent impulses, fell under the legal definition of insanity.

It was not, Robinson stressed, that the boy lacked intelligence. "He understands what is wrong and what is right. He understands that if he does an act, he is liable to be punished for it. He was in school and learned rapidly." Nor was the lawyer suggesting that Jesse ever be set free. "This boy cannot go out safely. It would not be safe to the community to have him at large."

Indeed, if Jesse moved into Robinson's own neighborhood, "where I have my children, I would move, because there is no more safety with that boy around than there is with powder and fire in close proximity." At one point, Robinson told the jurors, he had put a question to Jesse—"If it was *my* little boy, and I should leave him here with you, would he be safe?" Jesse had looked him in the eye and answered "No." He might not *mean* to do anything bad, he told the lawyer. But if the "feeling came over him, which he could not control, he would do these things again." In a period of approximately two months from the time of his discharge from the State Reform School, he had killed two children. "As I understand it," Robinson said, "if he had had an opportunity within the last six months, he might have killed six more."

What made Pomeroy so dangerous was precisely his bizarre mental makeup—his manifest intelligence combined with an absolute "want of capacity" to resist his savage impulses. Where this deficiency came from Robinson could not say. Perhaps it was an innate defect and there "was always something wanting in him." Or perhaps he'd been "born with evil powers." Or his incapacity might have resulted from a childhood disease. Whatever the case, there was no doubt that Jesse Pomeroy was "not a responsible being."

Having sketched out his argument—that Jesse, by virtue of his "unsound mind," should be found not guilty by reason of insanity—Robinson concluded by stressing that such a verdict would not result in Pomeroy's freedom. "The legislature has passed a law to meet just such a case," he assured the jurors. "That law reads: 'When a person indicted for murder or manslaughter is acquitted by the jury by reason of insanity, the court shall order such person to be committed to one of the State Lunatic Hospitals *during his natural life.*"

Immediately following his remarks, Robinson called his first witness, Ruth Ann Pomeroy. There was a great deal of public curiosity about Jesse's mother—whose foul-tempered manner and ferocious loyalty to her son had earned her a notoriety nearly equal to his own—and every eye in the courtroom was riveted on the small, hard-featured woman as she rose to take the stand. Every eye, that is, except the disquieting pair belonging to Jesse, who—seemingly lost in some strange reverie of his own—sat in the prisoner's dock, staring off into space.

Under questioning by Robinson—who was clearly trying to establish that Jesse had been aberrant since birth—Mrs. Pomeroy described several near-fatal childhood illnesses that had left her son both physically scarred and emotionally damaged. At three months of age, he had come down with a terrible infection that ulcerated his face, permanently damaged his eyesight, and "almost reduced him to a skeleton." Just before his first birthday, he had been afflicted with another, equally dire disease that plunged him into a three-day delirium and caused "his head to shake constantly" for weeks. Since that time, he had suffered from a range of afflictions—bouts of dizziness and insomnia, "pains in his eyes," and frequent, violent headaches. He was "addicted to dreaming extravagant dreams, which would usually haunt him the following day."

In school, he was known as a somewhat eccentric child (though not, Mrs. Pomeroy insisted, a *bad* one). During the past three or four years, his "peculiarities" had grown more extreme. Mrs. Pomeroy continued to believe that her son was innocent of the charges that had sent him to reform school—that every one of the half-dozen little boys who had identified him as their assailant was mistaken. But if Jesse *had* committed those crimes, he must have done so while suffering from one of his increasingly frequent "spells."

After a sharp cross-examination by Attorney General Charles Train (who got her to admit that, since starting school at five, Jesse had always been a quick learner and capable student), Mrs. Pomeroy was excused. She was followed by three more witnesses who were asked about Jesse's eccentricities. An officer of the Charles Street jail, John F. Bailey, testified to Jesse's "unnatural indifference" to his crimes. Mrs. Helen Brown, a former neighbor of the Pomeroys, told of the time that she had seen a cat dash from the alleyway, pursued by Jesse, whose face wore a "wild" expression. Another former neighbor, Mr. Francis J. Almeder, described Jesse's "peculiar actions while at play. He would break off suddenly from his games, run away by himself, and sit down and hold onto his head, which would shake violently." When one of these attacks came on, Jesse's bad eye would blaze "like a ball of fire."

Almeder brought down the house when, at one point in his testimony, he remarked that "Jesse had a dog, a little pup, and he had a fit that lasted nearly all night."

Jesse's lawyer, Charles Robinson, gave the witness a puzzled look for a moment before asking, "Well, who had the fit, the dog or Jesse?"

"The dog," answered Almeder.

"Well, what has that got to do with Jesse?" Robinson exclaimed.

Almeder shrugged. "I don't know."

This exchange triggered such an uproarious burst of laughter in the courtroom that Chief Justice Gray had to pound his gavel for a full half minute before order was restored.

It was on that raucous note that the first day of Jesse's trial ended. By then, the time was nearly 7:00 P.M. Almeder was dismissed without cross-examination, and the proceedings were adjourned until the following morning at nine o'clock.

31

Cruelty ever proceeds from a vile mind.
—Ludovico Ariosto, *Orlando Furioso*

The second day of the trial, like the first, drew a large, eager crowd to the courthouse. The spectator gallery filled up as soon as the doors were opened, leaving dozens of disgruntled people milling outside the building until they were dispersed by the police.

The proceedings, which began promptly at 9:00 A.M., picked up where they had left off on the previous day. Mrs. Hannah F. Almeder—wife of the last witness to testify on Tuesday—seconded her husband's recollections. She had always considered Jesse "a very strange child," she declared, "and at times thought him insane."

Another woman who had known Jesse as a child—Mrs. Lucy Ann Kelly, wife of a Charlestown policeman—took the stand next and offered a vivid instance of the boy's precocious cruelty, his "peculiar thirst for blood." Years before, when Jesse was only four or five, she had caught him one day in the yard with a small, piteously mewling kitten in his hands. The cat, whose coat was dabbled with blood, had clearly been tortured: stabbed in the throat, chest, and other parts of its body. When Mrs. Kelly asked the little boy what in the world he was doing, Jesse looked at her with a weird, unnerving smile and said: "This is my little kitty."

One of Jesse's former teachers at the Winthrop School, Mrs. Abbie M. Clark, confirmed that—while Jesse had always been an "apt student"—he was also an extremely difficult one to manage. On various occasions, she had been compelled to whip him with a rattan for whispering in class, annoying his schoolmates, and other infractions. He also had a bizarre, disruptive habit of "making strange faces" at her during lessons. He never displayed the slightest remorse for any of his misdemeanors. On the contrary, he regarded any sort of punishment as an utter injustice, insisting—whenever he misbehaved—that he "could not help it."

At this point in the proceedings—and over the objections of Attorney General Train—Jesse's counsel, Mr. Robinson, was permitted to read from the official record of Pomeroy's earlier crimes, the ones for which he'd been sent to reform school. This recitation was followed by what the *Boston Globe* (in an unabashedly Barnum-esque phrase) trumpeted as the "feature attraction" of the morning session—the testimony of the little boys "who had been tortured by the young fiend."

In having these juvenile victims give detailed accounts of their sufferings, Jesse's lawyer was clearly trying to establish that his client was insane—that only a person suffering from a severe mental disturbance could commit such atrocities. But (as Robinson must surely have known) it was the kind of tactic that could easily backfire, working the jury into such a pitch of indignation against Jesse that they would never acquit him, no matter *how* crazy he seemed. In any case, the little boys' testimony turned out to be the dramatic highlight of the day, and (as the *Globe* reported) "the most perfect silence prevailed during its progress."

Tracy Hayden, Pomeroy's second known victim—who had been seven at the time he was assaulted—spoke first. Pointing to the prisoner's dock, he identified Jesse as the "bad boy" who had taken him to an outhouse on Powder Horn Hill, then stripped him naked, lashed his wrists together with a rope, hung him from an overhead beam, whipped him with a "hard stick," and threatened to cut off his penis.

Hayden was followed by five more schoolboys from Chelsea and South Boston, each with a tale of abduction and torture more appalling than the last. Johnny Balch—who had been lured to the same outhouse and subjected to even greater cruelties—began speaking in what the papers characterized as a "clear, ringing voice." As he described a particularly horrific moment, however—when Jesse, after cutting him down from the beam, laid him on the ground and began stomping on his naked body until he nearly fainted—his voice became so choked with emotion that he had trouble continuing.

Robert Maier conjured up a picture of Jesse as a being of almost preternatural cruelty, "jumping around" with demonic glee as he flogged his little victim and made him say "naughty words, like 'kiss my ass' and 'shit.' " Several jurors seemed openly appalled as the next witness, George Pratt, described the way Jesse had tortured him—whipping him with a strap, "meddling" with private parts, puncturing his cheeks and eyelids with a needle, and biting him "right in the rump."

Joseph Kennedy—who had been stabbed in the hands with a horseshoe nail, slashed on the face with a pocketknife, and forced to recite an obscene version of the Lord's Prayer—also had a visibly dismaying effect on the jury. "He cut me here," Kennedy said in a faltering voice, pointing down at his crotch. "Then he made me say my prayers and naughty words, and said he was going to kill me, and that I would never see my father and mother any more."

Robert Gould, the last of the little victims to take the stand, elicited shocked reactions in the courtroom before he even spoke. Gould still bore the scars of the knife-wounds inflicted by Jesse, and the mere sight of the child's mutilated face brought scattered gasps of horror from the audience.

After the Gould boy finished speaking, Robinson summoned one more witness with firsthand experience of the defendant's explosively violent temperament—Laura Clarke, a teacher at Westborough, who recalled the time that Jesse had gone into a frenzy of bloodlust while killing a snake in the school garden. Mrs. Clarke also described another occasion, when—just days after Jesse's arrival at the reform school—she was walking past the chair shop and noticed a sobbing young boy, who claimed that Jesse had been hurting him. When she approached Jesse to ask "why he had done so," Pomeroy—a "wild look in his eyes"—brandished a knife that he'd evidently stolen from the shoe shop. Certain that he meant to attack her, Mrs. Clarke froze in her tracks. But after a brief, terrifying moment, the crazed expression evaporated from his eyes, and—lowering his weapon—he returned to his work as though nothing had happened.

Aside from those two incidents, Mrs. Clarke testified, Jesse's "conduct was good."

Following the brief and wholly inconsequential testimony of William Lee Miller—the principal of Westborough at the time of Pomeroy's incarceration—Robinson proposed to submit Jesse's confession to the Katie Curran murder. His intent, the lawyer explained, was to offer "further evidence of my client's insanity." Attorney General Train vehemently objected on the ground that the document "had no reference whatever to the trial in progress." Chief Justice Gray, however, ruled in favor of the defense—whereupon Robinson proceeded to read aloud the same chillingly matter-of-fact statement that Chief Savage had first made public at the Curran inquest.

The time had now arrived for the defense to summon its psychiatric specialists. And here, too, the situation in 1874 was remarkably similar to the way things are now. Like their counterparts today, the opposing lawyers in Pomeroy's trial managed to find experts who completely contradicted each other—"men of a quarter-of-a-century's experience" (as the *Boston Globe* dryly noted) who were brought in "to swear positively on both sides and to put in evidence of an almost diametrically opposite character."

Dr. John E. Tyler was the first of the "insane experts" to take the stand, and his testimony was essentially a verbal recapitulation of the written report he had submitted to Jesse's lawyer a few months earlier. After describing the handful of visits he had paid to the defendant in the county jail, Tyler stated his belief that the boy was insane and "not responsible for his actions." His opinion was based on a number of factors: the bizarre nature and extraordinary barbarity of the crimes; the absence of any discernible motive; and Jesse's complete lack of any "feeling in regard to the murder." Tyler acknowledged that, by themselves, none of these things necessarily "denoted insanity." But "taken together," they offered a clear indication of an "unsound mind."

Another sign of the boy's "mental derangement" was his insistence that he "could not help" committing his atrocities—that he *"had* to." Tyler cited the cases of several patients he had known who suffered similar—if "less disastrous"—compulsions, such as the need to wash their hands dozens of times a day. Like these unfortunate people, Jesse, too, was the victim of an "uncontrollable impulse"—albeit one with infinitely more dire consquences.

In response to Robinson's questions, Tyler insisted that the ability to distinguish between right and wrong was not necessarily a sign of sanity. "Insane persons," he declared, "may have their own idea of what is right and what is wrong." They are also able to "carry out a preconceived plan of murder," and often display a "great deal of cunning in concealing their crimes." Moreover, the fact that Jesse appeared to be perfectly rational most of the time proved nothing about his mental condition, since "a man may be insane on one subject and not another. " Indeed, Tyler insisted, "there are insane persons who would not be recognized as such by any but experts."

Following a one-hour recess that lasted until 3:00 P.M., Tyler was subjected to a rigorous—indeed, often grueling—thirty-minute cross-examination by Attorney General Train. Train began by asking if Tyler knew of any facts in the boy's life—apart from his crimes—that indicated an unsound mind.

"I know of none," Tyler conceded.

Tyler was also compelled to admit that Jesse knew his acts were wrong, and that the "circumstances attendant to his crimes"—the cunning he'd shown in luring his victims to secluded spots, the care he'd taken to clean his weapon, his efforts to avoid detection following the murders—were consistent not only with a "sane mind" but with "mental capacities of a high order."

After getting Tyler to acknowledge that "merely killing some-one was not in itself evidence of insanity," the attorney general asked what distinguished Jesse from other murderers. Tyler, who seemed a bit rattled by this point, reiterated that it was the "ac-cumulation of unnatural barbarities"—as well as the sheer "mo-tivelessness" of the crimes—that "gave doubts as to his sanity."

"But it does not necessarily follow," said Train, "that because you could not detect a motive, there was none. Isn't that so, Dr. Tyler?"

Tyler admitted that it was.

"Could not the love of cruelty for its own sake be a motive?" Train inquired.

"Yes, I suppose so," said the psychiatrist, shifting uncomfort-ably in his seat.

After wresting one final concession from the witness—that "an examination in a jail cell might not be the best means of judging a prisoner's mental condition"—Train excused him from the stand. It was the general consensus among observers that the cross-examination represented a solid victory for the prosecutor, who had (as the *Boston Globe* reported) compelled Dr. Tyler to make a number of key "admissions which consider-ably shook his direct testimony in many of its vital points."

Tyler was followed to the stand by his colleague, Dr. Clement A. Walker. Superintendent of the Boston Lunatic Hospital since 1851, Dr. Walker stated that he had "given the subject of insanity his attention almost exclusively for twenty-five years, and during that time had treated some two thousand patients both in the hospital and outside."

It was his belief—based on his examination of Jesse, as well as on "the evidence thus far presented at the trial"—that "at the time the deed was committed, its perpetrator was laboring under a mental disease." Like Dr. Tyler, he based this opinion on the "apparent want of motive, the peculiar age of the boy, and the extraordinary number and character of his crimes."

Jesse, moreover, had never displayed "any sorrow or pity for his wrong acts." He showed "no visible sign of any such thing as moral responsibility and seemed dead to all the finer emotions which are met with in sane persons." During one of their interviews, for example, Walker had asked him how he felt about the "wretchedness he had caused the Millen family."

"I hardly ever think of it," Jesse replied with a shrug. Then, expelling a little snort of bemusement, he added: "It's funny, isn't it?"

It was Dr. Walker's belief that Jesse might be suffering from an obscure form of epilepsy, a condition that would account for the various symptoms the boy complained of—the frequent headaches, the bizarre dreams, and the peculiar, "misty" sensation that seemed to come over him right before he engaged in one of his crimes. If this were the case, "it followed as a matter of course that he had commited his acts through a lack of control." A person suffering from such a condition, Walker explained, "might be able to determine as between right and wrong, and *still* be compelled, by the violence of his mental disease, to adopt the wrong." Dr. Walker concluded by reiterating his "firm belief" that Pomeroy "was not responsible when he committed the acts charged against him."

Under a relentless cross-examination by Attorney General Train, Walker held firm to his conviction that Jesse's motiveless atrocities were "indicative of a mental disease." Indeed, Walker opined, Jesse's disorder might well eventuate in his "total loss of mind."

Even so, Train forced the witness to admit that "the mere evidence presented at the trial was not, in itself, sufficient to establish insanity." Walker also conceded that "the fact that the boy ran away after committing the acts, so as to escape punishment, was clear evidence of his power to distinguish between right and wrong, and established that he was fully conscious of his responsibility."

With the conclusion of Dr. Walker's testimony, the defense rested its case. The time was a little before 5:00 P.M. The jurors were allowed a five-minute recess, after which the government's rebuttal witness, Dr. George T. Choate, was sworn in.

A self-described "expert in insanity," Dr. Choate had served as superintendent of the State Lunatic Asylum in Taunton for seventeen years before establishing a private sanitarium about thirty miles north of New York City, on the Hudson River. In the course of his career, he had treated hundreds of patients, among them the renowned journalist and statesman, Horace Greeley.

He began by explaining that he had interviewed Jesse twice in October. During his first visit, Jesse had freely confessed to the Millen murder and demonstrated at least a modicum of remorse, "acknowledging that what he'd done was wrong." Choate had been struck by the boy's "intelligence and shrewdness." Evidently, Jesse had been spending his time in jail "investigating the legal aspects of his case." With cool, even cocky, self-assurance, Jesse had stated "that the authorities will never hang me, as I am too young. They have never hung a boy as young as fourteen in Massachusetts, and I do not believe they will begin with me." Instead, he expected to be sentenced to either the state prison or a lunatic asylum—though he firmly believed that "if he could be sent away to sea, he would get over his desire to commit cruelties." When Choate had remarked that "it would be difficult for you to get a chance, since a captain might have fears that you would kill him in the night," Jesse had replied: "I have no desire to injure men. Only boys."

Choate was taken aback when—at the start of their second interview a few days later—Jesse completely retracted his confession, claiming that he had only admitted to the murder to clear his mother and brother from suspicion. In Choate's view, this was further evidence of Jesse's cunning, deeply manipulative mind. Unsurprisingly, Dr. Choate's ultimate diagnosis completely contradicted the opinion of the two defense experts. In his view, Jesse was not suffering from a mental disease. "There is no insane temperament or taint of hereditary insanity in the boy," he testified. To be sure, Pomeroy's mind was "different"— but it was different in its *"moral* qualities, in its proneness to certain forms of sin and its weakness in resisting those impulses." Jesse had "a weak character—not a weak intellect." In short, it was Dr. Choate's conviction that on April 22, 1874, the day of Horace Millen's murder, Jesse Pomeroy was not insane.

Robinson cross-examined Choate at some length, but the alienist didn't waver from his opinion that Pomeroy—though possessed of a "weak moral nature"—was "not *mentally* unsound." It was nearly six when his testimony ended. There were no further witnesses to be heard on either side. Having begun only the day before, the trial of the Boston "boy fiend" was already drawing to an end.

A few minutes after Choate left the stand, court was adjourned for the day. Beginning at nine o'clock on Thursday morning, the jury would listen to the final arguments before retiring to deliberate on Jesse Pomeroy's fate.

32

Any person [who] shall commit the Crime of Willful Murder . . . who, in the Supreme Judicial Court, shall be duly convicted . . . shall suffer the punishment of death.
                —Declaration of the Massachusetts State Legislature, 1804

To more than one observer, the scene inside the courtroom on Thursday morning resembled a packed downtown theater during the sold-out performance of a hit show. "Not only every seat," reported the *Boston Herald*, "but every inch of standing room was occupied as well." The crowd had clearly flocked to the final session of the trial in the hope of seeing something dramatic—and they were not disappointed. For in the closing arguments of the opposing attorneys, the audience was treated to a pair of speeches that were (according to one journalist) "masterpieces of legal acumen," containing "many brilliant passages," as well as "wonderfully ingenious pleas and interpretations of evidence."

Jesse's lawyer, Charles Robinson, spoke first. Addressing the jury in sonorous tones, he began by recapping the salient points of Pomeroy's life—his childhood illnesses, his mental idiosyncrasies, his perverse nature, his "love of blood and cruelty." "All the evidence introduced during the trial," he declared, "clearly establishes the fact that at the time the homicidal act was committed, the accused was not responsible, for the reason that his mind was diseased."

In a voice tinged with incredulity, he asked: "Could a boy of fourteen be in his senses and drag away a bright little child, the delight of his home and the hope of his fond parents, and—without any motive or provocation and with premeditated malice aforethought—cut, mangle, and murder him in cold blood?"

Shaking his head "no," as though in answer to his own question, he urged the jury to find a verdict of not guilty by reason of insanity. "I am asking it not for the prisoner," Robinson said, "but in the name of humanity and justice." He stressed that, in reaching such a decision, the jurors would not be setting Pomeroy free. "I would not for a moment ask that such a being be let loose upon society." The law had sound provisions for dealing with "deranged" individuals like the prisoner. Pomeroy would be sent to an insane asylum, where he would be "taken care of with as great a security to himself and the public as if he was sent to another world." He would never again "be able to do harm to innocent children."

Robinson also cautioned the jury against convicting Jesse as a form of deterrent—as a way of sending a warning to other potential killers. "No crime," he proclaimed, "will be deterred by the punishment of an irresponsible person."

Gesturing toward the prosecution table where his opposite number sat, Robinson observed that the attorney general would undoubtedly attempt to portray Jesse as a monster. But the boy was "not a monster born under barbarous influences," Robinson declared. He was "a product of Massachusetts—an outgrowth of her civilization for the last fourteen years, a pupil of her schools, a son of one of her citizens." It was plain that he was "not naturally wicked. Neither was he so from example, but rather from an unfortunate disease of the mind which rendered him irresponsible.

"It was not the boy alone who was on trial," said Robinson. "The intelligence, the humanity, the Christian principles of the Commonwealth were also on the stand." With the jury lay the power of decision, and their "verdict would be the verdict of Massachusetts."

After pausing for a moment, as though to let the full import and gravity of his words sink in, Robinson continued by repeating that the "lack of any motive to impel the boy to commit his acts of atrocity" was the "pivot upon which the whole argument of insanity hinged." Briefly reviewing the psychiatric testimony, he argued that the jurors were duty-bound to give particular weight to the opinions of the defense experts, Drs. Tyler and Walker. "When these learned physicians, who have had a quarter-of-a-century's experience with all classes of insanity, come before a court of the Commonwealth and—after a careful study and frequent examinations—swear that it is their opinion that the boy was insane at the time of the murder, the presumption is that they are right." That opinion, moreover, was bolstered "by the long chain of evidence presented at the trial."

By contrast, said Robinson, the testimony of the government's expert could not be accepted at face value. Though Dr. Choate "was doubtless an honest and a learned man," he could not, under the circumstances, be regarded as a strictly objective one. After all, Robinson insisted, Dr. Choate "had been brought from New York by the attorney general precisely because it was expected that he would look upon the case in the same way as the prosecutors."

Robinson's tone became increasingly fervent as he reached the end of his speech. "The whole history of criminal trials in Massachusetts," he declared, "did not show a case like this." It was "a mountain rising higher than any other crime." Faced with such a momentous decision, the jurors had a sacred obligation "to weigh very carefully the question of the boy's sanity."

Robinson closed with a powerful appeal "for a kindly feeling towards the unfortunate boy, whose mind was impelled to evil by an unseen and inexplicable power." In a voice full of emotion, he urged the jurors to arrive at a verdict "consistent with religion, law, justice, and the highest humanity." So affecting were his final words that, as he returned to his seat, a chorus of sniffles broke out in the courtroom, and a number of women—including Jesse's mother—raised handkerchiefs to their faces to dab away the tears that Robinson's peroration had brought to their eyes.

Moments later, at approximately 12: 45 P.M., Attorney General Train began his address to the jury. Alluding to Robinson's concluding remarks, Train asserted that the Commonwealth, every bit as much as the defense, "wished for a verdict consistent with humanity and justice." But what precisely did justice *mean?*

"It means," he asserted, "that the Commonwealth shall make laws for the government of society, and that the individual shall be beholden to those laws. This is the method by which society seeks to protect itself." All members of society, young and old, boy and girl, are "amenable to its rules." The defendant was no different in this regard from anyone else.

Of course, said Train, it was only natural that the lawyers for the defendant "should appeal to the juror's sympathies." But he emphatically denied the suggestion that the state was somehow *un*sympathetic—that it was actuated by motives of "malice or re-venge." On the contrary, the prosecution had gone to considerable lengths to make certain that the defendant received the fairest trial possible. Though the attorney general "could have tried the case within sixty days of the issuing of the indictment," he had held off the trial for *six months* in order to give Jesse's lawyers every opportunity to mount the strongest possible defense.

Turning to the crux of the case, Train, like Robinson, declared that "the question to be resolved was the responsibility of the person who committed the homicide." The law was very clear in stating "that murder committed with premeditated malice afore-thought shall be considered the highest degree of murder." This law, Train repeated, "applies to all members of society." No one was exempt from it—not even a fourteen-year-old boy.

Put in the simplest terms, "the boy was either sane, or he was a lunatic." And the testimony set forth at the trial led to only one possible conclusion. The state had shown beyond any doubt that—though possessed "of a heart devoid of social duty and wickedly defiant of any restraints"—Jesse Pomeroy was *not* in-sane. The murder of the little Millen boy was not only "premed-itated but committed with atrocity and cruelty."

Train did not claim the boy's acts "weren't extraordinary—for they *were*. But they are accounted for on the ground of *depravity*, not insanity—and society has a right to protect itself from such acts." It was for this reason, Train said gravely, that he must "de-mand a verdict of murder in the first degree."

Proceeding to review the facts of Jesse's life, Train argued that there was nothing about the defendant's behavior that was differ-ent from that of many other young boys. It was not unusual for children to suffer from headaches, or to make funny faces at their classmates. Nor was there anything remarkable about his "doing wrong and then saying he did not know why he'd done it."

Even the story of his maltreatment of the kitten proved noth-ing, given the casual cruelties that so many little boys inflict on small creatures—pulling the wings off flies and so forth. If the story proved anything, Train quipped, it showed that Jesse did not suffer from epilepsy but rather from *cat*alepsy. The attorney general's little pun drew appreciative chuckles from several of the jurors. Even Jesse broke into a big grin and, turning to his lawyer, said: "That's a good one."

Resuming his most solemn mien, Train went on to remind the jurors that Jesse's own mother had testified to her son's intellectual capacities. In reform school, he had been regarded "not only as a good but a remarkably good boy." Did the jury really believe, asked Train, "that the officers of the reform school would turn out an insane maniac of fourteen into the community of South Boston? No! It is a well-known fact that the trustees believed that they were releasing a sane man upon society."

But the most compelling proof of Jesse's sanity was the very fiendishness of his crimes. "Every circumstance connected with the torture of the little boys showed sanity and reasoning." The fact, for example, "that he had taken a little boy, a boy smaller than he was, to Powder Horn Hill, brought a rope with him, took the boy to a retired place, put a handkerchief in his mouth, and so on"—all these things indicated that the defendant "had reason and reasoned very clearly." Indeed, far from being signs of insanity, they served to prove that Jesse Pomeroy possessed "mental capacities of more than ordinary force."

Since it was already 2:00 P.M. by this point, the the judge called a one-hour recess. When the trial resumed at 3:00, Train proceeded with his summation.

He commenced by rebutting one of Robinson's key points— that the "motivelessness" of the Millen killing was proof of Jesse's insanity. "On the contrary," said Train, "an insane man nearly always gives a reason for his crimes." Citing several well-known homicides committed by certified madmen, Train pointed out that, in each case, the perpetrator had taken great pains to justify his deeds—usually by insisting that he was acting under orders from God. If Jesse were truly insane, then he, too, "would have assigned an insane reason for his acts." Thus, argued Train, the boy's "inability to provide a motive could not be construed into an element of insanity."

It was now Train's turn to wring tears from his listeners. Presumably by way of stressing the cold-blooded nature of the Millen slaying, Train proceeded to "draw a graphic picture of the struggles of the little innocent while the fiend was mangling his body and slashing him with a knife in the most demoniac fashion" (as the Boston Globe reported). This "all too vivid picture affected every person in court and brought tears and sobs from the ladies."

In reality, there were at least two people in attendance who were conspicuously *un*affected by this part of Train's performance—Ruth Pomeroy (who had wept during Charles Robinson's climactic plea but now sat in stony-faced silence) and Jesse himself, who, as he had throughout most of the proceedings, appeared vaguely bored.

Train continued by arguing that the entire insanity plea was a last, desperate recourse on the part of Jesse's counsel. It was not until Mr. Robinson had failed to come up with any other feasible line of defense—four full months after starting work on the case—that he called in Drs. Walker and Tyler. Those two "learned gentlemen," Train asserted, "knew perfectly well" that the defense was relying on them to arrive at a diagnosis of insanity.

"The difference between the testimony of the experts," said Train, "was that Dr. Tyler and Dr. Walker took a series of sane acts and constructed therefrom a proof of insanity; whereas Dr. Choate concluded from the same materials that, at the time of the commission of the homicide, its perpetrator was in the enjoyment of all the faculties of his mind, and in a healthy and sound condition." Indeed, Train pointed out, even Drs. Tyler and Walker had been forced to admit under cross-examination that Jesse's behavior during his crimes was, by and large, "consistent with a sane mind."

Train concluded his summation by calling on the jury to render a verdict based strictly on the evidence presented at the trial. Clearly, the attorney general did not wish the jury to be swayed by any qualms about sending a fourteen-year-old boy to the gallows. The age of the defendant, he argued, "was of no account in the case; and his punishment should not form any consideration in making up a verdict." It was solely "to the interest of the community" and "to the vindication of law and order" that the jurors "should turn their minds." They must return a verdict of guilty "in order to restrain thousands of men from acts similar to those for which the defendant is being tried. It was for the fathers and mothers who had sons who might be abused as the prisoner's victims had been that the jury should do its manful duty."

It was nearly 5:30 P.M. when the attorney general reseated himself at the prosecutor's table. Turning to the prisoner, Chief Justice Gray informed Jesse that he now had the right to address the jury on his own behalf, if he so desired.

"I have nothing to say," Jesse answered with a little shrug.

Judge Gray then proceeded to deliver his charge to the jury. Though the trial had, in fact, been conducted with remarkable dispatch—proceeding from opening statements to closing arguments in just two days—the judge began by complimenting the jurors on their patience and promising not to detain them with "any lengthy review of the testimony."

It was not the jury's business to question the wisdom of the law, he explained, but rather to ascertain whether the accused person had violated it. In the present case, "the first question to be asked was, did the defendant kill the boy? And the answer, he averred, was self-evident, since "the testimony of the various witnesses, as well as the confession of the accused, left no doubt on that point."

The next question to be decided was, "what degree of murder it was." The law, he explained, stipulated that anyone fourteen years or older was responsible for his acts, so long as he was "of ordinary capacities and sound mind." Thus, if the defendant was sane at the time of the slaying, the verdict must be murder in the first degree. But if there was a doubt as to his sanity—if he was acting under an irresistible impulse—the prisoner should be found not guilty by reason of insanity.

In a brief review of the psychiatric arguments, Judge Gray reminded the jurors that "counsel for the defense had claimed that their client knew that his acts were wrong, but that he was nevertheless drawn on by an irresistible impulse and was actually forced into their commission. Dr. Tyler and Dr. Walker testified that the boy was insane; while Dr. Choate was of the opinion that he was possessed of all his mental faculties and in a sound condition." Ultimately it was for the jury to decide "how far the expert testimony should go in deciding on the question of the defendant's sanity."

Altogether, the judge's remarks lasted less than a half hour. At a few minutes before 6:00 P.M.—after committing the case to the jury—Chief Justice Gray and his associate, Judge Morton, rose from the bench and retired to their chambers without adjourning the court.

Though a number of spectators took their leave at that point, most remained in their seats, keeping up—as the *Herald*'s reporter noted—"a steady buzz of conversation." For the most part, the crowd remained "very decorous and orderly, as they had been all through the trial." Even so, there was a good deal of heated—and occasionally contentious—debate about "which verdict the jury would bring in." Taking an informal poll as he moved around the room, the reporter discovered a notable lack of consensus among the spectators—"opinions being almost equally divided between verdicts of guilty in the first degree and not guilty by reason of insanity."

The split opinion of the spectators at the 1874 trial of Jesse Harding Pomeroy reflected the extreme difficulty of fathoming the bizarre mentality of sociopathic murderers—the kind of "human monsters" we now call serial killers. What makes the psychology of these beings so hard to understand is precisely their bewildering combination of rationality and madness—their terrifyingly cool and cunning ability to plan, execute, and cover up the most hideous crimes imaginable.

Indeed, one of the most astute discussions of this phenomenon was composed not many years after the Pomeroy trial by the great American novelist, Herman Melville. In his last, posthumously published masterpiece, *Billy Budd*, Melville creates a portrait of sheer, personified evil in the figure of John Claggart, the malevolent master-at-arms who sets about, with fiendish calculation, to utterly destroy the naive title character. Seeking to comprehend the viciously depraved nature of creatures like Claggart, Melville offers an analysis that stands, even today, as one of the best definitions of the sociopathic mind ever written:

But the thing which in eminent instances signalizes so exceptional a nature is this: Though the man's even temper and discreet bearing would seem to indicate a mind peculiarly subject to the law of reason, not less in heart would he seem to riot in complete exemption from that law, having apparently little to do with reason further than to employ it as an ambidexter implement for effecting the irrational. That is to say: Toward the accomplishment of an aim which in wantonness of atrocity would seem to partake of the insane, he will direct a cool judgment sagacious and sound. These men are madmen, and the most dangerous sort, for their lunacy is not continuous, but occasional, evoked by some special object; it is protectively secret, which is as much to say it is self-contained, so that when,

moreover, most active it is to the average mind not distinguishable from sanity, and for the reason above suggested:
that whatever its aims may be . . . the method and the outward
proceeding are always perfectly rational.

Though the term "serial murder" is of relatively recent origin
(dating back only to the early 1970s, when it was coined by FBI
Special Agent Robert Ressler), Melville's description, written more
than a hundred years ago, makes it clear that psychopathic criminals have always existed. And it also explains why the ordinary
person finds it so hard to judge the mental state of such beings.
Though a killer like Jeffrey Dahmer might engage in acts whose
"wantonness of atrocity," as Melville puts it, "partakes of the
insane"—mutilation-murder, cannibalism, necrophilia, sexual torture, etc.—he will generally operate with a high degree of rationality and shrewdness: "a cool judgment, sagacious and sound."
Moreover, as Melville perceives, such killers, for the most part,
present a perfectly normal facade to the world, their "lunacy" remaining dormant until triggered "by some special object."

Clearly, judging the mental soundness of a person whose intelligence and reason are employed in the service of insanely violent drives is no easy task. So it is not at all surprising that,
when the reporter for the *Boston Herald* polled the crowd at the
Pomeroy trial, he found a good deal of disagreement over the
question of Jesse's responsibility. And though the jury itself
would quickly arrive at a unanimous decision, a certain measure
of ambivalence would be apparent in their verdict as well.

Shortly before 8:30 P.M., Chief Justice Gray and Associate
Justice Morton reentered the courtroom, having been informed
that the jurors required clarification on two key points. A minute
later, the jury emerged from the deliberation room and put two
questions to the judges. First: "If the prisoner took the Millen
boy down to the marsh with the intention of inflicting torture on
him, such as he'd inflicted on the other boys, and after getting
him there, he concluded at the last moment to kill him, would
such an act be premeditated aforethought?" Their second question was: "Does a homicide committed under circumstances of
extreme atrocity, unaccompanied by premeditation, constitute
murder in the first degree?"

After a brief, whispered consultation with his associate, Judge Gray explained to the jurors that "it did not require any specified time to constitute premeditation. If the resoluton to kill was clearly and definitively formed at *any* moment before the act was committed, it would be malice aforethought."

As for the second issue, the judge replied that, according to statute, "a homicide committed under circumstances of extreme atrocity *or* with premeditated malice aforethought constituted murder in the first degree. *Either* of these elements, therefore, was sufficient."

Having obtained these answers, the jury then retired again to resume its deliberations.

Shortly before 10:00 P.M., there was sudden stir in the courtroom. The clerk, the sheriffs, and other officials began to move about, as though making ready for the entrance of the judges and jury. Excited whispers ran through the crowd: A verdict had been reached—guilty of murder in the first degree!

A few minutes later, Jesse was led back into the courtroom and seated himself in the dock. Every eye studied the prisoner's face for signs of his feelings at this excruciatingly tense and decisive moment. But though his very life hung in the balance, Jesse seemed as unnaturally indifferent as ever.

At precisely 10:10 P.M.—after less than five hours of deliberation—the jury filed back into the courtroom and took their places. The clerk then rose and, following the ritual formula, asked: "Gentlemen of the jury, have you agreed upon a verdict?"

"We have," came the reply.

"Who shall speak for you?"

"Our foreman."

"Well then, Mr. Foreman," the clerk continued, addressing Henry Linell, "is the prisoner at the bar guilty or not guilty?"

"Guilty of murder in the first degree," Linell replied with all the solemnity befitting the occasion.

Though rumor had already foretold this decision, Linell's words brought a gasp from the crowd. Jesse's mother buried her face in her hands and broke into wracking sobs. Jesse alone seemed utterly unaffected by the awful pronouncement, appearing so "careless and indifferent" that, according to one observer, "it was difficult to decide whether he really understood what the verdict was. He made not the slightest motion, showing either absolute stupidity or a hardness and stubbornness that was aggravating to witness."

Immediately after the verdict, Linnell handed a note to the clerk, who passed it along to Judge Gray. After scanning the paper, the judge announced that it was a recommendation from the jury. Though the verdict carried a mandatory death sentence, the twelve men urged that—because of his extreme youth—Jesse's punishment be commuted to imprisonment for life. Promising to transmit the recommendation to the governor, the judge adjourned the court after praising the jurors for their efforts.

The jury's divided feelings—between their outrage over Jesse's crimes and their reluctance to execute a fourteen-year-old boy (which Pomeroy himself had predicted)—foreshadowed the bitter controversy that would embroil the public for months to come. The trial was over and the verdict rendered. But in a very real sense, the battle over Jesse Pomeroy's fate had only just begun.

33

The interest in the trial of Jesse H. Pomeroy has not ceased with his conviction of murder in the first degree, and now continues in the speculation as to his sentence and as to whether the recommendation to mercy on the part of the jury will be considered.
—*The Boston Globe*, December 14, 1874

Like the teenage atrocities that have stunned our nation in recent years, the Pomeroy case struck many observers as a terrifying symptom of societal decay—of the evil that results from what we now call the breakdown of "family values." On December 12, 1874, for example—one day after Jesse's trial ended—the *Boston Globe* published an editorial that (allowing for its old-fashioned diction and dated details) could have been published in the wake of the so-called Jonesboro, Arkansas, massacre of 1998, or the 1997 slayings at West Paducah, Kentucky, where a fourteen-year-old high school student opened fire on eight of his classmates as they stood in a prayer circle.

Headlined "Keep Children from Crime," the editorial began by criticizing Jesse's parents for failing to provide those "restraining influences" that would have "counteracted the natural weaknesses of their son's moral character." "There can be little doubt," declared the writer, "that if there had been proper discipline exercised in his case, society would have been spared the horror of his crimes. . . . Jesse Pomeroy would probably have never developed a high moral character, but had he passed the period of youth under suitable discipline, his sense of the danger of indulging his cruel propensities would have saved his victims and society from atrocity."

Because his parents were separated, and his overworked mother was rarely at home, Jesse had been left to his own devices—free to indulge his taste for violent entertainment. Surely, the writer suggested, had Jesse been raised in a more settled household, his parents would never have permitted him to revel in the lurid thrills of dime novels. "Can there be a question," the editorialist wrote, "that instead of allowing him to gloat over the recital of Indian atrocities, which stimulated the worst tendencies of his nature, the best parental care would have ascertained and corrected these bloodthirsty characteristics?"

To be sure, the writer was sympathetic to Mrs. Pomeroy's situation. She was, after all, a hardworking, husbandless woman, struggling to make ends meet. But her son's case only highlighted the "danger to society" represented by "those who have no adequate care taken of them at home." In short, as portayed in this editorial, Jesse Pomeroy was the nineteenth-century equivalent of a type painfully familiar to our own day: the juvenile felon whose crimes are ascribed to his broken home, lack of parental supervision, and overexposure to violent entertainment.

According to the editorialist, moreover, Pomeroy's case—though clearly extreme—was by no means unique. On the contrary, it was evidence of a frightening social trend. Citing a recently published volume "by the National Prison Association of the United States upon the extent and causes of crime in this country," the writer was alarmed to note that "one-fifth of all our prisoners are mere boys, ranging from childhood to twenty years. Nearly half the convicts in one prison are young lads, another has nearly a third, and in another two-thirds of all the inmates are under thirty years of age." Though convicts in their early to late twenties hardly seem to qualify as "mere boys," the writer nevertheless concluded that this ostensible epidemic of juvenile criminality resulted directly from the absence of proper parental supervision (particularly among the poor) and urged that greater attention be paid to the care and education of neglected young children. By this means, he concluded, "the causes of crime may be largely removed, and the boys and girls who are growing up in ignorance and vice be made useful and happy citizens."

Other papers, too, weighed in with their opinions on the day after the verdict. Editorials in the *Boston Herald,* the *Boston Post,* the *Boston Daily Advertiser,* even the *New York Times,* all praised the Pomeroy jurors for their "discernment and courage" in "dis-

regarding the defense of insanity so earnestly urged by the prisoner's counsel." The jury's task had been made especially hard
by the extreme atrocity of Jesse's acts, which (as the *Post*'s writer
put it) "came nearer the borderland of insanity than most
crimes." But by exercising their common sense, the jurors had arrived at the proper decision, perceiving that—for all the "diabolical cruelty of his deeds"—Jesse had gone about them "with
deliberation, coolness, and method quite too remarkable to be
accounted for by any theory of mental derangement."

The papers were also in agreement that the jury's mixed verdict—guilty of murder in the first degree, with a recommendation that the punishment be imprisonment for life—was a
reasonable decision, given the natural reluctance of any civilized
man to condemn a fourteen-year-old child to the gallows.
Indeed, the editorial writers unanimously agreed that "the jury's
recommendation will most probably remit the death penalty."

Whatever the final outcome, however, the crucial point was
that "under no circumstances, now or hereafter, must the
Pomeroy boy go free, for there is no security against his repeating his horrible crimes." Ultimately, it would be for the governor
and the council to determine his fate. But as the *Herald* insisted,
"whether living or dying, society must be rid of the presence of
this strange being, whose career is one of the most remarkable in
the annals of crime."

34

I must save the life of that boy.
—Charles Robinson, Jr.

At first, it seemed as though, in predicting that Jesse would be spared from the gallows, the newspaper pundits had guessed wrong.

Firmly convinced that his client should have been acquitted, Jesse's attorney, Charles Robinson, Jr., filed exceptions that were argued before the Supreme Judicial Court on Monday, February 1, 1875. Robinson insisted that the boy was insane, as demonstrated by his "acts and declarations" not only *during* the commission of the crime but *after* it as well. The defense therefore had the right, within reasonable limits, to introduce evidence of his client's subsequent behavior. In the present case, however, the admission of such evidence had been treated not as "a matter of right," but as "a matter within the absolute discretion of the court." And the court, Robinson argued, had adopted limitations that were "too restrictive."

Robinson, for example, had wanted to call George B. Munroe, an officer of the county jail, to testify to Pomeroy's conduct while awaiting the start of the trial. The court, however, had "excluded this testimony, as relating to a time too long after the homicide to be material." Moreover, Robinson claimed that certain medical witnesses had not been allowed to be fully heard.

Attorney General Train's answer was, in substance, that no presumption of insanity could arise by proving *subsequent* insanity; that the defense alienists had arrived at their conclusions by examining the defendant more than three months *after* the crime, whereas the question submitted to the jury was whether the defendant was of sound mind *at the time* of the homicide; that the

203

"limitation of time within which the testimony was to be confined" was, in fact, "purely within the discretion of the court"; and that the defendant's counsel had acquiesced in the ruling of the court.

In the end, the court sided with the prosecution. Three weeks after Robinson argued his exceptions—on Saturday, February 20, 1875—Jesse Harding Pomeroy was sentenced to death.

Early that morning, Jesse was brought from the county jail to the Supreme Judicial Courthouse. At precisely 9:00 A.M., Chief Justice Horace Gray entered and took his seat upon the bench. Moments later, Attorney Train rose from his place and addressed the judge. After reviewing the salient facts—the grand jury's indictment, the prisoner's arraignment and plea, the "thorough and impartial" trial, the finding of the verdict and the overruling of the exceptions, Train moved that "the sentence of the law be imposed upon" the prisoner.

At Judge Gray's direction, the clerk then turned to Pomeroy and asked if he had anything to say before sentence was pronounced.

"No, sir," Jesse answered calmly.

Fixing Jesse with a somber look, Judge Gray then addressed the young prisoner directly. The verdict had been based, he declared, "upon the idea that the murder was committed, not with premeditated malice but under circumstances of extreme atrocity and cruelty." It was the jury's intention—and the judge's hope—that the punishment meted out to the prisoner "would serve as an example to all others who might thereafter be disposed to gratify a morbid love of cruelty."

Once the jury had rendered its verdict of murder in the first degree, Judge Gray explained, "the court had no discretion in imposing the sentence, which is fixed by statute." It was true that the jury had accompanied its verdict with a recommendation of mercy; but that recommendation, said the judge, "could have no effect upon the court." It would be forwarded to the governor, but "whether he would yield to its prayer was impossible to determine."

Folding his hands tightly before him, Chief Justice Gray declared that it was his duty to remind the prisoner "of the importance of turning your thoughts to an appeal to the Eternal Judge of all hearts, and a preparation for the doom which awaits you." Then, in the highly charged stillness of the courtroom, he cleared his throat and pronounced the grim sentence: that Jesse Harding

Pomeroy "be taken from this place and kept in close confinement in the County Prison until such day as the Excecutive Government shall by warrant appoint, thence to be taken to the place of execution and there be hanged by the neck until you are dead. And may God, of His infinite wisdom, have mercy on your soul."

Though the judge's voice did not falter as he spoke these words, he wore a look that struck several observers as deeply dismayed. Indeed, virtually everyone present—with the predictable exception of Jesse himself, who looked as unconcerned as always—seemed powerfully affected by the awful gravity of the occasion. The great and enlightened State of Massachusetts had just condemned a fourteen-year-old boy to the gallows.

35

Having read, with feelings of pain, of the visit of a number of persons, clad in the garments of womanhood, who waited upon you, praying that Your Excellency would *not* commute the sentence of the unfortunate being who bears the name of Jesse Pomeroy, I feel called upon, in the name of humanity, to make an effort in his behalf, scarcely daring to hope that my plea will be of avail; yet . . . I cannot remain silent and feel that my hands are free from the stain of bloodguiltiness.
—E. A. Robinson, Letter to Governor William Gaston, March 22, 1875

On the following Monday—February 22, 1875—the *Boston Globe* ran an editorial that conveyed the intense qualms many people felt about the sentence. Few would question that the "boy fiend" was "a most dangerous creature," said the paper, and that his sentence was "legally just." But "still fewer will applaud his execution," for "there is something revolting in the thought of the hanging of a mere boy, no matter what his crimes may have been." Perhaps the best solution would be to keep the boy "caged for life" with "some guaranty . . . that he would never be pardoned or released until death should release him." In the opinion of the paper, most Bostonians "would rejoice to see this disposition made of him."

Pomeroy's case, in short, presented a profound dilemma to the average citizen—a conflict between the dictates of the law and the promptings of Christian conscience. "Thoroughly bad, sane beyond a doubt, a cold, calculating, fiendish murderer of little boys and girls," the editorial concluded, "the law says hang him as a punishment for his crime and for the safety of the community. Humanity says anything save that."

The *Globe,* however, was only partially right about the humane sentiments of the public. To be sure, the revulsion against executing someone so young was shared by many Bostonians. But equally widespread was the desire to put Pomeroy to death, both as the proper revenge for his atrocities and as the surest way of protecting society. And the conflict between the representatives of those positions—between the people who were appalled at the thought of hanging "a mere boy" and the equally impassioned group that was determined to see the "boy fiend" done away with—began to rage in earnest as soon as the sentence was pronounced.

Within days of the sentencing, Jesse's lawyer, Charles Robinson—who was firmly convinced of his client's insanity—filed an appeal with the governor of Massachusetts, William Gaston. A hearing before Governor Gaston and his eight-man council was set for the last day of March, 1875.

In the weeks leading up to the hearing, Gaston's office was inundated with urgent telegrams and letters, half of them demanding Jesse's execution, the other half pleading for mercy. Some of these pleas came from highly imposing sources. No less an eminence than Dr. Oliver Wendell Holmes, for example, sent a personal note to Governor Gaston, appealing for young Pomeroy's life.

For the most part, however, the writers were ordinary citizens, moved by their passionate convictions. One Charlestown woman, Mrs. M. S. Wetmore, began her letter by posing a difficult ethical question: "By what authority can we as a community rob a fellow being of life?" Certainly, she argued, there was no *Scriptural* justification for such an action:

> *If we go to the Bible for authority, we find the Lord said, "Whosoever slayeth Cain, vengeance shall be taken on him sevenfold." "And the Lord set a mark on Cain, lest any man finding him should kill him." But in this nineteenth century, this age of supposed Christianity, when our land is filled with Churches where professed Christians worship and with penal institutions in which criminals can be confined and kept from committing murder, we take our unfortunates and deliberately choke the life out them, and then thank God that we are rid of them. God help us to see our wickedness, and to cultivate the God in us, till we behold God in every living creature, no matter how vile; and in-*

stead of taking from any the life they possess, may we use all the means at our power to cause such unfortunates to be placed where the spark of the Divine in them may become a living flame, illuming each poor darkened soul till it know something of "Peace on Earth and Good Will" ere it commence a higher life.

While some suppliants for mercy based their pleas solely on Jesse's age, the majority—like Mrs. Wetmore—made their appeals on religious grounds. Invoking the "name of Him who commanded the one who was without sin to cast the first stone," a writer named E. A. Robinson humbly petitioned the governor for mercy in the "earnest belief that to condemn any man to death was an offense against the higher law of 'Him who seeth not as man seeth.' " The potential for redemption existed in everyone, no matter "hardened in sin," Robinson declared, for "while a man liveth, he may mend." Signing himself as "the friend of the friendless," Robinson ended his letter with a little poem that conveyed his deepest convictions:

> Were *half* the *time* that's spent condemning sin,
> Were *half* the *money* spent for man's conviction,
> Given, freely given, the erring ones to win
> To virtue's path, by *kindness, benediction,*
>
> This hanging by the neck till you are dead,
> This cool, deliberate murder by judicial power,
> From sight of which sweet Mercy hides her head,
> This *licensed crime* could scarcely live an hour.
>
> The gallows tree would be a thing unknown,
> And prisons would be swept from earth ere long
> For lack of convicts; and the "Golden rule"
> Would be the burden of the nation's song.

To the opponents of commutation, however, people like Wetmore and Robinson were nothing more than bleeding hearts. "Let us have some Spartan justice," demanded a gentleman named Kittredge, "even if sentimentalists do look with horror on it and set up their imbecile cry." Another man, Hubert Radclyffe, concurred with this opinion, decrying the "persistent efforts of the sentimentalists who are petitioning for clemency. . . . If the young fiend POMEROY be allowed to live, he may get out of prison and exercise upon men and women his barbarous appetite to inflict torture. No, the Governor must in this case do what is best for the community, regardless of all sentimentality."

As for the argument that it was immoral to send a fourteen-year-old boy to the gallows, various writers scoffed at the notion. "Why recommend the Pomeroy boy to mercy?" asked one typically indignant citizen. "O, he is so young, is he? He is not so young, not of so tender years as the babes whom he brutalized and did to death. He was old enough to show that he knew he was doing wrong. Besides abundant evidence at the trial, the jury of the verdict shows that. For if not so, he should have been found not guilty. The verdict of guilty settles the question of responsibility." According to this writer, the jury—though correct in its verdict—had overstepped its legal bounds in making its recommendation:

Juries have no right, as such, to recommend to mercy. Our whole system of political government and of the dispensing of justice is constructed upon the principle of a division of duties and powers assigned to different departments. Each department should keep within its own lines. Juries are to find and truly say whether the criminal is guilty or not guilty, under the law as stated by the Court. Said the old form of administering the oath to jurors, "If you find him guilty you will say so, and say no more." The recommendation to mercy is an unwarranted assumption of power. It ought to be treated as, in law, it is—a nullity.

Some of the letters in support of Jesse's execution took on an actively threatening tone. "There is one thing and but one that will insure your reelection," a Boston man named A. C. Bradley wrote to Gaston, whose term had less than a year to run, "and that is the signing of the death warrant of young Pomeroy. The contest will be close and such action will turn wavering votes in sufficient number to insure your victory. Neglect action in regard to the young murderer and you are defeated."

Bostonians weren't the only ones to get caught up in the controversy. Indeed, letters poured into the governor's office from all over the country—a sign of the far-flung notoriety that the Pomeroy case had achieved. Some were appeals to the governor's conscience, like the brief but fervent note from James Lindsley of Nashville, Tennessee: "You cannot sign this death warrant with the New Testament before you and believing in Christianity. O, temper justice with mercy which endureth *all* things."

Others, like a letter from Dr. W. A. Mansfield of Winfield, Kansas, addressed the issue of Jesse's sanity:

> *I see by the papers that Jesse Pomeroy, the boy murderer, is found guilty and sentenced to be hanged. In view of the mental condition of the culprit, I trust the Governor of the great and enlightened state of Massachusetts will never lend himself to such an inhuman transaction, for the boy is clearly an irresponsible being. Every medical man who has paid attention to diseases of the brain and the history of this unfortunate as revealed in the papers cannot fail to see that he is subject to periodic attacks of monomania. In the name of everything that is good and great, save this mentally deranged boy from so horrible a death.*

And then there were those who—like their counterparts in Boston—cried out for Pomeroy's blood. From Maine, for example, came a letter denouncing opponents of the death sentence as dangerous "sentimentalists"—the same misguided "class of people" who had been responsible for Jesse's early parole from reform school. Through their "meddlesome interference," the "juvenile wretch was let loose upon the community and enabled to perpetrate all these atrocious crimes." Now, these same "sympathetic friends of the murderer" were out to "repeat their work" by securing Jesse's pardon. Speaking on behalf of the "friends of law and order," the writer urged the governor to heed the fears of the "wives and mothers of Boston" by ensuring that "the butcherer of little children never again be turned loose upon their little ones."

The efforts to influence Governor Gaston's decision weren't limited to letter-writing. For months, the governor's office was besieged by citizens from throughout Massachusetts, bearing dozens of petitions opposing or supporting the death sentence. Just a few days before the March meeting was to be held, for example, a delegation of women representing the "Mothers, Sisters, and Daughters of the Town and County of Nantucket" delivered a petition to Gaston, pleading for "executive clemency in the case of Jesse Pomeroy."

"We feel," read the petition, "that although the crime committed may seem to call loudly for the severest rigor of the law, yet the youth of the culprit and the humanitarian view of a future reform under the enlightened sanitary system of correction, prompt us to desire that his sentence may be commuted to imprisonment for life." At least a dozen similar documents—some containing as many as 900 signatures—were presented to the governor during the late winter and early spring of 1875.

A nearly identical number of petitions demanding Jesse's execution were circulated during the same period. These included petitions from the Ladies of Chelsea (153 signatures); Boston Citizens (45 signatures); Parents and Citizens of Boston (146 signatures); Citizens of East Boston (56 signatures); Wives, Mothers, and Daughters of East Boston (219 signatures); Parents and Citizens of South Boston (265 signatures); Citizens, Women, and Parents of South Boston (75 signatures); Ladies and Citizens of South Boston (856 signatures); Ladies and Parents of Chelsea (127 signatures); Citizens of Acton, Massachusetts (49 signatures); Parents and Citizens of Malden (150 signatures); and Citizens of Cambridge (528 signatures).

The bitter division in public sentiment—between the advocates of mercy and proponents of death—was mirrored in the governor's council chamber. Governor Gaston, a distinguished, fifty-five-year-old jurist who had served two terms as mayor of Boston, felt utterly appalled (like everyone else) at the enormity of Jesse's crimes. But—having determined that, in the entire history of New England, the youngest person ever hanged was an eighteen-year-old killer from Maine back in the 1830s—he was hesitant to send a fourteen-year-old boy to the gallows. (Partly as a result of the Pomeroy controversy, the law regarding condemned prisoners would ultimately be changed in Massachusetts, making it the responsibility of the Court to set the date of execution; in 1875, however, that responsibility still rested with the governor.)

Standing in adamant opposition to Gaston was his lieutenant governor, Horatio G. Knight, a vigorous supporter of the death penalty. The eight-man council was split directly in half, four of the members strongly in favor of commutation, the rest as staunchly opposed.

On March 31, 1875, the scheduled hearing was held before Governor Gaston and his council. Speaking on behalf of the prisoner, Charles Robinson urged that the death sentence be commuted to imprisonment for life on the grounds of Jesse's youth and irresponsibility. The prosecution, represented by Attorney General Train, vehemently argued against such action and called for the execution of Pomeroy in accordance with the law.

Averse to signing Jesse's death warrant—and faced with a hopelessly divided council—Gaston refrained from taking any definitive action. Instead, he called for a public hearing in two weeks' time, to allow the citizens of Massachusetts to vent their feelings on the matter before the governor, his councillors, and the world.

36

The force of the popular feeling in this case rests upon one of the strongest of our animal instincts: that which prompts to the defense of our offspring. The parent who finds the wolf waiting to ambush his little ones may slay the beast. Not so the parent who discovers a Pomeroy in like ambush. The majesty of the law must be invoked. . . . The law's penalty *must* be executed upon this the most dangerous criminal who ever drew breath within the bounds of our fair Commonwealth.

—Plea to the governor, April 13, 1875

The friends and foes of commutation turned out in force for the public hearing on Tuesday, April 13. Men and women from throughout New England flocked to the State House to hear their spokesmen plead for Jesse Pomeroy's life or urge his execution. At precisely 9:00 A.M.—with the spectator section of the Green Room filled to capacity—Governor Gaston, Lieutenant Governor Knight, and all eight members of the council filed into the chamber. A few moments later, the proceedings got underway.

The petitioners for commutation testified first, with Charles Robinson, Jr., making the opening address. Though he was there, he insisted, "not as a lawyer so much as a private citizen who knows more about young Pomeroy than anyone else," Robinson's hour-long speech was essentially a summary of the arguments he had set forth at the trial. He spoke of the "childhood disorders" that "had seriously affected Jesse's temperament." He described the "mania for cruelty" that had manifested itself by the time Jesse was four or five years old—the unnatural pleasure the little boy derived from "torturing small animals."

"In school," Robinson continued, Jesse had "shown a total lack of feeling, caring nothing about punishment and being not at all improved in any way thereby." Nor had he ever "displayed the least remorse" for the killings of Horace Millen and Katie Curran. All these facts—along with the sheer senselessness and atrocity of the murders (which Robinson reviewed in graphic detail)—proved beyond dispute that young Pomeroy was insane.

The two expert witnesses who had testified for the defense—Drs. John Tyler and Clement Walker—spoke next. They, too, gave an abridged version of the points they had made at the trial. Jesse, they agreed, was of "good mental ability" but "morally insane." This combination of sound intelligence and diseased morality made him a "very dangerous person to the community," which needed to protect itself from "any further acts of violence." Since young Pomeroy was not responsible for his acts, however, he should not be subjected to the death penalty. Rather, he ought to be imprisoned for life—"shut away forever," as Walker put it.

This view was supported by several other psychiatrists, including Dr. Theodore W. Fisher, the examining physician at the Boston Lunatic Asylum. According to Fisher, Jesse was "subject to what is called *impulsive insanity,* which rendered him at times wholly irresponsible." Indeed, Fisher "had not the slightest doubt" that, at the time of the murder, Jesse—in the grip of his mania—did not even know he was committing a crime. As a result, Fisher did "not consider him a case for capital punishment."

Judge Dwight Foster, one of several legal experts to appear at the hearing, concurred. Foster made it clear that he was not opposed to the death penalty *per se.* On the contrary, he thought the law "should be kept on the statute book." But for that very reason, he felt strongly that it had to be administered with the utmost caution. And to inflict "the extreme penalty of the law" upon Pomeroy was wrong.

There were several reasons for this belief, beginning with the jury's written recommendation of mercy. According to Foster, he had "never known a case, either in this country or in Europe, where such a recommendation has been disregarded." An even more important consideration was Jesse's innate and incurable "propensity to commit terrible acts." "The boy came into the world with these propensities, which he could not restrain," said Foster, "and when God permits such beings to be born, I do not believe the law ought to take their lives, unless the safety of society absolutely requires it—which is not the case in this instance."

Following an hour-long recess at noon, a colleague of

Foster's, Judge Edgar Thomas, added his voice to the chorus of speakers who favored commutation. Thomas declared that, after a careful examination of the evidence, he had come to believe, like Judge Foster, that "the jury would never have returned a guilty verdict had not the recommendation for mercy been appended." In his opinion, "the boy was wholly unaccountable and should be restrained for life, but not hanged."

Other jurists who spoke on behalf of clemency included the Honorable John A. Nowell and a young lawyer named H. A. Bowies, who addressed the widespread concern that, should the sentence be commuted to life imprisonment, Pomeroy would one day be set free to terrorize the city again. Consulting a sheet of paper containing the results of his extensive research, Bowies cited statistics showing that, while one hundred percent of imprisoned murderers were ultimately pardoned between 1800 and 1825, only forty-five percent were pardoned in the following twenty-five years. And since 1850, that figure had dropped to less than eighteen percent. Moreover, in *none* of these cases had a *"malicious murderer"* ever been pardoned. Indeed, Bowies argued, "the record of the Committee on Pardons conclusively shows that, in every instance, the circumstances of the murder were such that, if they were tried today, not one of the pardoned killers would have been convicted of murder in the first degree." Bowies concluded by urging that "true justice be meted out" and cautioned against those who would subject Pomeroy to the "extreme penalty of the law" on the basis of sheer emotion "or the logic of the heart."

The last—and most eloquent—witness to speak on behalf of commutation was the Reverend William H. H. Murray, who began by deploring the irrational dread—"unusual in the history of Massachusetts"—that had seized the community. "There is a fear in the minds of the mothers, and a cry of 'hang him,' lest, peradventure, he shall be pardoned out, and no mother's child be safe." After noting this dismaying state of affairs—akin, he suggested, to a mass hysteria—Wilson insisted that "the probability of this boy being again turned loose upon the community was too small to be considered." Barring the election of a "vicious" Executive—a contingency that seemed "impossible to conceive"—"society would be just as safe with Jesse Pomeroy in prison for life as with Jesse Pomeroy hanged."

Wilson took the opportunity to deliver an argument against

the death penalty, citing records from other states in America, as well as from Europe, to prove that an "increase in capital punishment did not cause a corresponding decrease in capital crimes." The law in Masachusetts, he continued, "was not based upon the principle of punishment but of *protection*—and the principle of the law would be as safe if the sentence were commuted as if it were carried out."

Wilson concluded with a heartfelt appeal to the feelings of the councillors; with a harsh rebuke to "the fear and lack of judgment of those women who had been induced, for the first time in the history of the state, to connect the holy name of *mother* with an appeal for blood"; and finally with a vivid evocation of "the woe of the one mother whose child's life" was in the governor's hands.

The opponents of commutation were allowed to speak next. They were represented by an attorney named Paul West, who made a powerful opening argument, urging the enforcement of the death penalty. West began by stressing the "weight that ought to be given to the petitions of the mothers of Boston," who would live in a continual state of anxiety should Pomeroy be spared from execution. Dismissing the defense psychiatrists as vague and unreliable—particularly in their claim that Jesse's crimes had been unmotivated—West declared that there was nothing at all mysterious about what drove the boy. The simple fact—as illustrated by the progressively savage nature of his assaults—was that Pomeroy had a "bloodthirsty disposition" and had deliberately set about "cultivating it." It was well-known, for example, that he enjoyed reading dime novels about frontier warfare and Indian torture—irrefutable proof of the extreme pleasure he took in indulging his violent propensities.

West took care to point out that Jesse had already received one commutation, when he was released from Reform School after less than eighteen months. That ill-advised action, West said gravely, "had cost two little children their lives." He concluded by urging that the death sentence not be commuted for two reasons: first, for the safety of the community, and second, for the sake of deterrence.

Another lawyer, Mr. Thomas Dudley, then read a petition in favor of the death sentence containing the signatures of over three hundred residents of Cambridge. Dudley was followed by the Reverend Mr. Toles of the Baldwin Place Home, who used the occasion to deliver an impassioned attack on the evils of "trashy" dime novels, whose celebration of frontier violence had ostensibly inspired several lads from his own orphanage to run off to the West and "shoot Indians."

The lengthiest—and in many ways most cogent—argument in favor of the death sentence came from ex-Representative H. W. Wilson of South Boston. In terms of *justice*, he declared, the "only question about the boy was the degree of murder of which he was guilty"—and that question had "been settled once and for all" by the jurors. Although they "had the alternative of bringing in a verdict of murder in the second degree—for which the punishment is imprisonment for life—they did not do this."

The present issue, therefore, had to do, not with justice, but with *mercy*. And on what possible basis, asked Wilson, should mercy be extended to Jesse Pomeroy, "the most atrocious criminal which the State has ever produced"? Was it his age? But the legal age of accountability in Massachusetts was fourteen. If Jesse's sentence were commuted because of his youth, Wilson argued, then the governor would be "undertaking to roll back the system of government and assume the legislative function."

Furthermore, Wilson declared, he "did not think it was the policy of the State of Massachusetts to say that it was a sufficient excuse for a criminal that he did not know why he did it." Taking issue with the Reverend Murray's position, West insisted that "law in Massachusetts recognized crime as crime—as something to be *punished*, and not as a disease to be restrained."

Following a closing plea by Charles Robinson—who pointedly asked whether, "in this century of our nation's life, we have come no farther than to take a boy, born with a blight inflicted by God, and string him up like a cat?"—Governor Gaston adjourned the hearing, thanking the participants and assuring them that he and his councillors would "take the subject under consideration."

37

When will the Governor and Council act upon this case? Is procrastination to prevail until the patience of the community is exhausted? Do men in such positions lose that power of reaching definite conclusions which characterizes them in private life?

—*The Boston Journal*, May 2, 1875

In newspapers and medical reviews, prestigious law journals and shoddy crime pamphlets, the issue of Jesse Pomeroy's death sentence continued to generate controversy throughout the spring of 1875.

Shortly after the April hearing, for example, the *Boston Globe* published a heated exchange of letters between representatives of the pro- and anti-commutation camps. One of the most eloquent correspondents was Mrs. M. S. Wetmore, the same woman who had written such a heartfelt plea to Governor Gaston several weeks earlier. Once again, Mrs. Wetmore's appeal was based on her deep-rooted religious convictions—her belief in the sanctity of every human life, in the possibility of spiritual rehabilitation, and in the miraculously redemptive power of true Christian love.

"There can be no greater consideration," she wrote, "now that the boy is under sentence of death and where he can harm no one, than that his life be spared; but not because it is of more account than any other life. It is the duty of society to protect the life of all its members, and just because this boy has committed such outrageous and fiendish crimes we have no right to deprive him of his life. I would not be understood as having sympathy alone for the boy, when there are those suffering so keenly from his seemingly fiendish nature, and I do not pretend that it is anything but fiendishness from beginning to end. But can the fiend not be exorcised? . . . I cannot help feeling that selfishness, which is itself unchristian, is manifested by those asking for his execution."

Mrs. Wetmore's solicitude for Pomeroy's life drew scornful responses from many of her fellow Bostonians, including a woman named Kathleen Phipps, who issued a challenge to Mrs. Wetmore: "Let her, especially if she has a family of little ones, give him the entrée of her house in true sisterly manner. Would she or any other mother expose her darlings so?"

Friends of Mrs. Wetmore immediately rallied to her defense. Among her supporters was an indignant ex-convict named John C. Fitzgerald who himself had been the beneficiary of her charity. In language that was shockingly blunt for Victorian Boston (however mild it seems in our own uncivil age), Fitzgerald attacked Mrs. Phipps for "inserting her ignorant proboscis into a matter which is evidently too far beyond the scope of her intelligence to ever be comprehended by her." There was absolutely no doubt in his mind, Fitzgerald insisted, that Mrs. Wetmore "*would* give Pomeroy a home beneath her roof, if he was so situated as to be permitted to avail himself of it, and if the nature of the case permitted such an action on her part. There are cases where she *has* made practical application of her theories. One young man, fresh from a convict cell where he had been confined for a long term of years, found with her a *home*, which he so much needed, and her *pure* and *ennobling* influences were the means of his salvation." That Mrs. Wetmore would readily extend the same sympathetic treatment to Jesse Pomeroy, Fitzgerald concluded, only underscored "the beautiful truth that 'Christ is yet with us/ And Love is still miraculous.' "

Christ's name was also invoked by other supporters of commutation. In a letter to the *Globe*, for example, a man named William H. Colcord addressed a question directly to the proponents of the death penalty: "What precept or example of Christ do you follow when you ask that Jesse Pomeroy be hanged by the neck until dead?"

Several days later, Colcord's challenge was answered by a writer named Thomas Kindersley, who began by citing Christ's words as recorded in Matthew, 5:17–18.

Think not that I am come to destroy the law, or the prophets: I am not come to destroy but to fulfill. For verily I say unto you,

Till heaven and earth pass, one jot or one tittle shall in no wise pass from the law, till all be fulfilled.

"Now, what was the law?" Kindersley continued. "It is to be found in Leviticus, 24:17—'He that killeth any man shall surely be put to death.' Or in our Saviour's own words, 'Put up again thy sword into his place; for all they that take the sword shall perish with the sword'—Matthew, 26:52."

Another of Colcord's respondents threw his question back in his face. "By what precept or example of Christ do *you* follow," demanded this writer, a man named Peter Pickart, "when you ask that Jesse Pomeroy be deprived of liberty and shut up in prison for the remainder of his natural life?" In Pickart's view, the self-professed "true Christians" like Colcord who rejected the death penalty on Scriptural grounds were being, at best, highly inconsistent, since their own position was equally unsup-ported by the Bible. If there was nothing in Christ's teachings to justify the death penalty, there was nothing in them to legitimize life imprisonment, either.

The daily newspapers weren't the only printed vehicles for the continuing debate over Jesse Pomeroy's sentence. In early May, a cheaply produced true-crime pamphlet appeared in the bookstalls of Boston and instantly became a popular seller. Though this book declared itself a straightforward biography of its subject (and did, in fact, offer a fairly reliable summary of the case, as gleaned from local papers), its obvious purpose—evident in everything from its lurid cover illustration to its overwrought language to its damning conclusion—was to inflame public feeling against Pomeroy.

Only thirty pages long, the booklet (published by the Taunton Publishing Company of Taunton, Massachusetts) was called *The Life of Jesse Pomeroy, the Boy Fiend*. A crude woodcut illustration—showing a neatly dressed boy viciously attacking a terrified little girl with a knife—was printed twice, first on the cover, then again on a separate page halfway through the book. The caption below this picture read: "With my knife I cut her throat."

Beginning with the birth of Pomeroy—a being "whose love for cruel deeds and inordinate thirst for human blood stand without precedent in history"—the anonymous writer went on to trace the early depredations of this "ghoul-like monster who seemed to be preying on human blood." Pomeroy, he wrote, "had all the cunning of a fiend and chose his time and place so well that he was never seen luring his victims to their destruction in some out of the way corner. . . . In some old rotten boat, or under some railroad bridge, the groans and cries of the little sufferers could not be heard, and the torturer gashed and whipped and chopped them as he pleased, regardless of their tears and writhings of agony, or only laughed at them in his devilish glee."

Though there was not the slightest shred of evidence to support the theory, the writer had no qualms about suggesting that Jesse's earliest crimes may not have been limited to beating and torture. "Whether he ever foully murdered any other weak little victim . . . will never be known, unless the chance discovery of some little bones in a retired nook may lead to the discovery of an unrecorded tale of bloodshed. During the time he was perpetrating his cruelties, more than one child left its home in the morning to play about the neighborhood and was never seen again. Its fate may be locked up in the heart of the boy monster, whom some are yet found to pity."

In his effort to stir up outrage at the "boy fiend," the anonymous author proved absolutely shameless. He acknowledged that the Millen murder had already been so extensively covered by the press that there was no need to repeat its "fearful details"; then he proceeded to offer an extended and highly graphic rehash of the "horrible deed." The remainder of the pamphlet consisted of an equally sensational account of the Curran killing; a brief review of the trial; a summation of the deliberations and verdict; and a discussion of the ongoing commutation controversy. As though there might be any doubt as to his own feelings on the subject, the writer ended with a bitter call for Jesse's execution: "The gallows is the proper doom of the wretched boy, who is as fit to roam at large or be confined in a weak cell as the tiger who has once tasted blood."

Jesse's death sentence was endorsed not only by the authors of tacky exploitation books but by contributors to far more distinguished publications as well. In its spring 1875 issue, for example, the editors of the *American Law Review* weighed in on the side of those who believed that Pomeroy should be executed.

The key issue, argued the editors, was the safety of the community. If "a sentence of imprisonment for life" were an absolute guarantee that Jesse would remain behind bars forever, "few would oppose this." But since "the average of life sentence in Massachusetts is seven years and a half, it would be difficult to imagine a case where the protection of the community more imperatively demands the infliction of the death penalty than this." Though its tone was far more measured, the editorial ended in the same way as the sensationalistic crime pamphlet, *i.e.*, by comparing Pomeroy to a wild beast that would remain an active threat to society so long as he was suffered to live:

> If the boy's impulse is under his control, there is surely no reason for sparing his life. If it is not, how does he differ from a wolf, except that he has the intelligence of a man, and is therefore more dangerous? If he is executed, the world is rid of one whose life is of no value to himself, and who is dangerous to the community. If he lives, no one can say how soon the mistaken clemency of some governor may turn him loose upon the public to commit new enormities like those for which he is now confined.

Calls for Jesse's death could be found in the pages of other professional journals as well. Dismissing as "trash" the notion that Jesse suffered from "delusional insanity," for example, the editor of the *Boston Medical and Surgical Journal* insisted that Pomeroy should be hanged. "We do not desire this consummation for the sake of punishment," declared the writer, "nor solely for the sake of example, but for the safety of the children of the Commonwealth. If he be condemned to imprisonment for life, some 'large-hearted philanthropist' will not fail, sooner or later, to procure his release. And then, as sure as the sun will rise, he will return to his amiable idiosyncrasies, and future parents will curse the 'humanity' which shall condemn their children now unborn to be killed in torments."

Several months later, an alienist named Charles Follon Folsom contributed an article to the same publication that also argued for Pomeroy's execution. After considering—and rejecting—a number of possible explanations for the boy's criminal behavior (ranging from "moral imbecility" to excessive masturbation), Folsom concluded that Pomeroy was "responsible for the crimes which he committed; not as fully responsible as you or I would be, but yet responsible before the law." Thus, he should be made to suffer the "extreme penalty of the law"—a punishment that would serve the three important objects: vengeance, justice, and, most vitally, "the protection of society."

"Is it fair to suppose that anything else than death will protect society from such a monster as Pomeroy," Folsom demanded (in language notably devoid of professional detachment), "when the chances of escape from prison are so many, and when we know that out of 266 men sentenced to imprisonment for life at Charlestown from 1828 to 1875, 135 have been pardoned? . . . Crimes of a horrible character have been fearfully frequent of late, especially in Italy and the United States, in both of which countries punishment for crime has become lamentably uncertain. I think that this terrible danger to society can be removed; but . . . in order to do it, it is necessary to hang some of these murderers."

Another prominent psychologist, however, Theodore W. Fisher (who had testified at the public hearing in April), held a very different opinion. Contrary to Folsom, Fisher—whose views were initially expressed in a speech before the Suffolk District Medical Society, then reprinted as an article in the *Proceedings* of that organization—believed not only that Jesse was insane but that his condition had "been induced by masturbation." While this explanation seems profoundly benighted (if not totally crackpot) from our own vantage point, it was perfectly plausible in an age that regarded "self-pollution" as the cause of everything from memory loss to mental retardation to physical emaciation and blindness.

Indeed, Fisher—who had met Jesse only once—claimed that a single glance was all he needed to see that the boy was addicted to the shameful indulgence. "The evidence of self-abuse," Fisher declared, "was plainly written on his countenance, as well as in his hands, which he kept concealed at first. On seeing that I observed them, he asked what was the matter with them. They were purple, cold, and clammy to a degree seldom seen except in cases of dementia with masturbation. He at first denied but afterward admitted the correctness of my inference. He also admitted that he had practiced the habit for years, and particularly at the periods when his crimes were committed."

Upon those who are in its thrall, Fisher explained, the insidious habit of self-abuse wreaks mental, emotional, and moral havoc. "The attention and memory are weakened and the judgment impaired. There is a state of vanity, conceit, and a love of notoriety, change, and adventure. . . . Sometimes great restlessness is observed, with a tendency to go from place to place without motive, to run away from home on some wild, impracticable errand in hopes of making a fortune or becoming famous, with inability or indisposition for continuous employment of any kind. The moral sense is blunted, and vicious courses new to the individual are entered upon."

These symptoms were unmistakably present in Jesse's case, which showed "many of the characteristics of mania from masturbation. Conceit and love of notoriety are especially prominent. . . . He twice ran away from home before the age of twelve, bought firearms, and took cars for the West to fight Indians. He was also known at an early age to be guilty of cruelty to animals."

Of course, masturbation alone was not enough to account for the singular depravity of Jesse's acts. After all, most boys who engaged in this vice ended up, not as multiple murderers, but merely as feebleminded cripples. In Jesse's case, however, there was another factor operating upon his mind: cheap, sensationalistic literature. As Fisher pointed out, Jesse was exceptionally "fond of reading stories of savage warfare. It is not improbable that impressions made in this way in his youth, under the stimulus of puberty and the excitement of constant self-abuse, with its accompanying impairment of willpower, developed into morbid, fixed ideas, and these idea passed uncontrolled into the horrible acts of torture and murder which have startled the community."

In short the deadly combination of masturbation and dime novels had turned Jesse into a homicidal maniac—a striking example of the way in which violent pop entertainment could plant poisonous seeds "in the congenial soil of a disordered and enfeebled brain" and "bring forth a ghastly harvest."

And so the debate raged on. In speech and in print, in telegrams and in petitions, in private discussions and in public exchanges, the citizens of Massachusetts continued to argue over

Jesse Pomeroy's fate. On each side of the issue, the weight of opinion was more or less the same.

And then, in the third week of May, something terrible happened—a crime that, though completely unrelated to the Pomeroy case, tipped the balance toward those who clamored for Jesse's execution.

38

Now if the POMEROY boy is hanged, it will be because PIPER has murdered little MABEL YOUNG.

—*The New York Times*, June 1, 1875

The victim was a five-year-old girl named Mabel H. Young. There are no extant photographs of little Mabel, but the newspapers invariably describe her as a radiant child—blond, blue-eyed, remarkably pretty. The atrocity that befell her, moreover, occurred not only on the Sabbath but within the sanctuary of a neighborhood church. This combination of circumstances—the angelic little victim, the hallowed setting, and the sheer, unspeakable savagery of the act—largely accounts for the extreme horror and outrage provoked by her death. In the view of the *Boston Herald*, the killing of Mabel Young was "perhaps the most shocking murder in the criminal annals of the Commonwealth, not excepting the slaying of the Joyce children and horrible deeds of Jesse Pomeroy."

Sunday school at the Warren Avenue Baptist Church was dismissed at around half past three that balmy afternoon, May 23, 1875. Emerging from the Reverend George F. Pentecost's classroom, little Mabel found her aunt—a woman named Hobbs—waiting to escort her home. After greeting her niece, Mrs. Hobbs turned back to the woman she'd been chatting with, the mother of one of Mabel's classmates. Their conversation lasted another ten minutes or so. When the two women were finished talking, Mrs. Hobbs glanced around the vestibule for her niece. But the little girl was nowhere to be seen.

After a quick, fruitless search of the premises, Mrs. Hobbs went outside, assuming that Mabel was waiting on the sidewalk, perhaps playing with some friends. A dozen or so people were milling on the sun-washed street. Her niece, however, wasn't among them.

Thinking that the little girl had grown impatient and started off without her, Mrs. Hobbs was about to head for home when a ghastly sound caused her heart to quail. It was the agonized cry of a child, emanating from the belfry of the church. Three male passersby, startled by the noise, dashed into the church, broke down a locked door leading to the tower, then quickly mounted the steep, narrow staircase. Arrived at the first landing, they immediately spotted a puddle of fresh blood and—poorly concealed under a loose floorboard—an object that proved to be a cricket bat, its wide, flat blade spattered with gore.

Proceeding up the long, ladderlike stairway that ascended to the next level of the tower, the men came to a heavy trapdoor. Grunting with the effort, the young man in the lead shoved it open and scrambled up into the belfry, followed by his companions. Dozens of pigeons, who made the belfry their roost, fluttered and cooed in an apparent state of agitation. On the floor lay a terrible sight—a grievously wounded little girl, emitting pitiful moans. One hand held tight to her Sabbath school books; the other was clutched to her cheek. The bridge of her nose was smashed flat, and the lower part of her face had turned a deep purple. Her yellow hair and white dress were drenched with blood. Her glassy eyes were open and unseeing.

As gently as possible, the men carried her down to the street. At the first sight of her niece, Mrs. Hobbs fainted. Bleeding and groaning, the child was carried to the nearby home of Mr. William Chesley, where she was promptly attended by a neighborhood doctor named Cotting. Palpating the scalp above her left ear, Dr. Cotting could feel the child's brains oozing through the shattered skull. There was clearly no hope for the little girl. As it happened, she clung to life longer than anyone expected, dying shortly after 8:00 P.M. on Monday, May 24, without ever having regained full consciousness.

By then, a suspect was already under arrest. Thomas W. Piper, the sexton of the church, was a reclusive young bachelor in his mid-twenties—a small, stoutly built man with wavy black hair, a curling moustache, and an unhealthy complexion. He had secured his position seventeen months earlier through the influence of his brother, Erastus, a pew-owner and regular attendant of the church. For the most part, Piper performed his duties reliably, keeping the premises nicely maintained and ringing the bell at the requisite hours. Still, his behavior had raised the eyebrows of more than one congregant. In recent months, he had been seen reading lurid novels during the Reverend Pentecost's sermons and engaging in inappropriate banter with some of the more nubile church members. According to rumor, he also had a fondness for the bottle. Had his respected older brother, Erastus, not vouched so emphatically for him, Piper might well have been fired long before the Mabel Young tragedy came to pass.

Certainly, the members of the Warren Avenue Baptist Church would have insisted on his dismissal had they known another fact about their sexton. In December, 1873—shortly before he was hired—Piper had been arrested as a suspect in the vicious murder of a servant girl named Bridget Landregan, whose skull had been crushed with a makeshift club during an attempted rape. Piper had ultimately been released for lack of evidence. But the Boston police had continued to keep him under scrutiny.

It was for this reason that—as soon as he heard about the attack on Mabel Young—Chief of Police Savage (who lived just a few blocks away from the church) ordered one of his men to take Piper into custody. Questioned at Police Station Five, the sexton stoutly denied his guilt and insisted that he did not even possess a key to the tower. When asked to empty his pockets, however, he produced a large bunch of keys—one of which turned out to fit the lock on the tower door. In the meantime, investigators conducted a search of his room. Besides several half-empty bottles of whiskey (at least one of which had been spiked with the opium-based nostrum, laudanum), they discovered a bloody handkerchief and collar stuffed inside a bureau drawer.

Over the course of the next few hours, Piper offered various, conflicting accounts of his whereabout at the time of the murder and seemed inordinately agitated for a man with nothing to hide. At one point in the interrogation, Savage asked him point-blank: "Piper, how could you find it in your heart to murder that innocent little child?" Piper made no reply. Suddenly, his lower lip began to tremble violently and he burst into tears.

Within twenty-four hours, the evidence against him continued to pile up. Several church members told police that they had noticed Piper unlocking the door to the tower shortly before the murder took place. Another highly reliable witness testified that—at around 3:45 P.M. on Sunday—he had seen a man resembling Piper leap from a window in the church tower, drop ten feet to the sidewalk, then dash along Warren Avenue and disappear into the sexton's house.

At least three little girls came forward to say that, during the past two weeks, Piper had tried to lure them into the belfry by offering to show them the pigeons. The murder weapon, moreover—a cricket bat used by the little boys of the congregation during church picnics—was routinely stored in the sexton's quarters.

Eventually, Piper would confess not only to the killings of Mabel Young and Bridget Landregan but to two other unsolved homicides as well: the December 1873 rape-murder of a young woman named Sullivan, who had been savagely bludgeoned with a club, and a nearly identical assault seven months later on a young prostitute named Mary Tynam.

From the moment it occurred, the Piper atrocity drew comparisons with the Pomeroy case. On the morning after the attack, for example, the *Boston Globe* described it as an example of what we now call "copycat" crime. The vicious assault on the five-year-old child, said the paper, "appears to be of an entirely Jesse Pomeroy character. It is a well-known fact in the history of crime that after the commission of a terrible deed, others of a similar character frequently follow, the actors in which appear to have no other motive actuating them than that of imitation, induced by a sort of maniacal impulse. To such a species of insanity the present crime might be attributed."

To many Bostonians, the murder of Mabel Young, coming so soon after the Pomeroy slayings, meant nothing less than that their city was in the midst of a "criminal epidemic" (as the *Globe* called it)—an outbreak of violence against children that could only be fought with the most Draconian measures. The public—roused to such a pitch of fury that there was open talk of lynching Piper—was in no mood for leniency. Within a week of Mabel Young's death, even people who were formerly opposed to Jesse Pomeroy's execution had done an abrupt about-face. the *New York Times*, in an editorial on the subject, took note of this shift:

Suddenly, the tone of public opinion has changed. It is said by one Boston paper, which undoubtedly reflects the general sentiment in the city, that "the feeling in favor of the execution of POMEROY has had an accession of intensity from the tragedy of a week ago that no one can fail to recognize." That is to say, people who were not before in favor of hanging the boy are now in favor of it because there has been another brutal child-murder. . . . A community, or at least a goodly portion of it, is shocked by a tragedy of uncommon wickedness, and it demands blood.

In the end, the editorial concluded, Pomeroy "may not be executed for the murder of HORACE MILLEN, though he was convicted of it, but for the killing of MABEL YOUNG, with which he had nothing to do."

And indeed, the outrage over the "Belfry Tragedy"—as the Piper case was quickly tagged—had an immediate impact on the Pomeroy debate. Within days of Mabel Young's death, letters like the following (from a gentleman named Ezra Farnsworth) began pouring into the governor's office: "The extreme necessity of executing justice in a case like that of the young fiend Pomeroy is made more clear, if possible, on account of the hideous murder perpetrated so recently upon the innocent little child, Mabel Young. Delay in the punishment of crime is one of the reasons—it may indeed be the most important one—for the increase of it. If there was more *certainty* that punishment would follow the commission of crime—and follow *speedily*—probably fewer crimes would be committed."

The drive for Jesse's execution also intensified within Governor Gaston's own circle. Lieutenant Governor Knight, who had been lobbying against clemency all along, became even more emphatic in his demands for Pomeroy's death. When Thomas Piper was ultimately convicted and sentenced to be hanged, Knight urged the governor to schedule Pomeroy's execution for the very same day.

The enormous pressure brought to bear on Gaston in the wake of the "Belfry Tragedy" finally forced him to take action. On the afternoon of Friday, July 2, 1875, he brought the

Executive Council together for a formal vote on the question of commutation. After a debate lasting more than four hours, the council members decided, by a vote of five to four, that Pomeroy's death sentence should stand.

Only one thing now stood between Jesse and the gallows: Governor William Gaston's signature on his death warrant.

39

Let us write good long letters to each other and so beguile our captivity.

—Jesse Pomeroy, letter to Willie Baxter

While the outrage over Mabel Young's murder swirled about him, Jesse continued to languish in the Suffolk County jail. Each of his days consisted of the same, unvarying routine. A guard would bang on his cell door at 6:00 A.M. and bring him a meager breakfast of coffee and bread. For the next few hours, Jesse would peruse the inspirational volumes supplied by an elderly spinster named Burnham, whose life was devoted to various charitable causes.

Dinner—the only substantial meal of the day—arrived at 11:30 A.M. Except for Thanksgiving and the Fourth of July, when his menu was varied slightly, Jesse was given the same food day after day: boiled meat and potatoes (along with an occasional treat delivered by his mother).

After a brief, postprandial nap, he would return to his reading and studying. At 4:30 P.M., a light supper was served. Like his breakfast, this meal consisted entirely of bread and coffee. Shortly afterward, the seventy-year-old chaplain, "Uncle" Cook, would make his daily visit, followed by the kindly Miss Burnham. An hour or so after sundown, Jesse settled back on his bunk and went to sleep.

Given the extreme tedium of this existence, it is no wonder that Jesse reacted so excitedly when a former playmate of his ended up in jail. It happened in the third week of June, not long after the "Belfry Tragedy" occurred. The boy's name was Willie Baxter. Arrested for petty thievery after pilfering a few bottles of whiskey from a railroad boxcar, he was placed in the cell directly adjacent to his notorious acquaintance. And his presence there over the next few weeks provided a welcome diversion for Pomeroy.

It is possible to document Jesse's feelings at this time thanks to a series of remarkable notes he exchanged with Willie Baxter during the latter's brief incarceration. For more than a century, these fading, fragile letters lay hidden in an old file box, and are reprinted here for the first time (with misspellings and punctuation errors intact). As absolutely direct, unvarnished expressions of the "boy fiend's" voice, they shed invaluable light not only on Jesse's general intelligence but—even more significantly—on his twisted inner life. Indeed—apart from the crimes themselves— they offer the most provocative clues we have to the nature, extent, and even ultimate source of his extreme psychopathology.

The letters were written with a stubby lead pencil on sheets of unlined paper ripped from a school notebook that had been given to Jesse by Miss Burnham. Jesse's script is perfectly legible, if strikingly inelegant—the handwriting of a schoolboy who has laboriously mastered the basic elements of cursive. (It is easy to imagine him composing his letters with the tip of his tongue protruding from a corner of his mouth.) His style of expression is also fairly rudimentary and even childish at times, though he was capable of turning a surprisingly sophisticated phrase. (The dime novels beloved by Jesse and his contemporaries might have been full of sensationalistic violence, but—in contrast to the high-tech pastimes of modern-day teens—they at least promoted literacy.)

It was Willie Baxter who initiated the correspondence. Unfortunately, his letters have not survived, though their general content can be inferred from Jesse's replies. Within a day or so of his arrest, Baxter had managed to pass his infamous jailmate a note, in which he identified himself by name and evidently asked if Jesse remembered him from the old neighborhood in Chelsea. He also included a few jokes.

Jesse promptly replied with a brief letter. He admitted that, though the name sounded familiar to him, he could not recall Baxter's face. "I should very much like to see you," he wrote, then suggested a way for Willie to show himself: "When the Man comes around and sweeps out your room tomorrow or the next day, step out on the corridor (that place in front of your cell). They will allow you too [sic]. Thanks for them jokes."

The next day, following Jesse's instructions, Willie positioned himself in a place where Pomeroy could see him. At the same time, he managed to slip another note to Jesse, which elicited an immediate response:

Friend Will,

I hasten to reply to your note. Of course I have seen you, did you not live on Ferrin St. when you knew me. I think you did. . . . I will send you all the paper I can. Let us write good long letters to each other and so beguile our captivity but don't make too much noise. I have only this lead pencil but will let you take it. Of course you know what I am here for and what I was sent up to the reform school for. Tell me what it is and what I did. Tell me all you have heard of me, everything bad and don't think I will be angry. Tell me what you thought when you heard of my doing in 1872. Tell me all you heard of and what the boys said. . . . There is one thing I wish to ask. Do you go to the Winthrop School. I have heard they flog the boys unmercifully there and that Willie Almeder got into a row with the Master and that the man whipt [sic] him till the blood ran down Almeders back and Almeder was almost killed. Is that story true. I don't ask out of curiosity but to find out the truth; and does Bert Pray or Frank Atwood get punished much. You will tare [sic] our notes up or do something with them so that the people here will not see them, and when you go out take care that they don't find it out or tell any of the boys what we write. You say you are 14. I am 15. I am quite tall. Willie I am sorry you are in trouble. What will they do with you. I am not going to preach you a sermon but I will say this. Willie if you love your friends and parents reform your ways. You know that if you persist in doing wrong you will come to a bad end. I ask you for and on the strength of former friendship take warning by example and while you and me are young let us turn back and do right. Answer all questions & write a long letter and believe me your friend,

Jesse H Pomroy [sic]

This letter introduces several motifs that would continue to inform Jesse's correspondence with Wille Baxter. First, there is Jesse's preoccupation with his own reputation ("Tell me all you have heard of me"), a common characteristic of psychopathic killers, who tend to derive great satisfaction from their own notoriety. Such beings have generally been filled from their earliest years with feelings of utter worthlessness and self-loathing, and their criminal celebrity allows them, for the first time in their lives, to feel like powerful and significant people—*some*bodies instead of absolute nobodies. That same perverse sense of egotism, of inflated self-importance, can also be seen in Jesse's closing exhortation, which rings with a kind of paternalistic superiority—with the desperate conceit that, though only one year older than Willie Baxter, Jesse is a person of infinitely greater wisdom and experience.

Most striking of all, however, is Jesse's avid interest in hearing every detail about the corporal punishment inflicted on other boys. Indeed, in his succeeding letters, this deeply prurient desire becomes the dominant theme.

> *Friend Willie,*
>
> *I received your note and wish you to reply to this when you can . . . Willie I remember you now. Have you not changed some during the last 2 or 3 years. Now you will please reply to the question I wrote in my last letter of last night. You are a good looking fellow and look as though you could not do wrong or ever get punished. Do you get a liking [sic] very often. I never used to much. Tell me if you do and tell me of the hardest whipping you ever got. Tell me all the particulars of it and I will tell you of the hardest flogging I ever got. Do not forget to tell me for if we are to be friends in here we ought to tell each other everything about ourselves. Will you tell me as I ask you about the hardest whipping you got, if it hurt much and how it was done to you and I will tell you about the hardest one I got. Also tell me all you have herd [sic] of about my doing to those boys on Powder hill and Railroad. Don't forget it. Write me a long letter.*
>
> *Jesse Pomroy [sic]*

The ardent, if not slavering way, in which Jesse hungers for stories about child-flogging is both deeply unsettling and highly revealing. Indeed, in reading this and Jesse's next few letters, it is hard to escape the conclusion that his perverse appetite for cruelty—thwarted by his long incarceration—sought vicarious gratification from the quasipornographic details that Baxter could provide: in short, that Jesse was using Baxter's graphic descriptions of juvenile corporal punishment as an aid to masturbation.

Such a conclusion is consistent not only with the profoundly sadistic nature of psychopathic killers in general but with Jesse's own admission to the alienist, Theodore W. Fisher, that he masturbated most frequently "at the periods when his crimes were committed." Fisher, of course—reflecting the skewed Victorian attitudes of his day—interpreted this to mean that "self-abuse" was at the root of Jesse's criminal behavior. But the more reasonable explanation is that, like other sadists, Jesse was driven to a high pitch of sexual excitation by torture.

In any event, Baxter complied with his jailmate's request by describing (if not quite as fully as Jesse had hoped) a particularly brutal whipping he had received from his father. Jesse's reply is arguably the most revealing letter in the series:

Dear Will,

Your note I have. I think you ought to write me longer letters but I suppose it tires you. Your account of the whipping is amusing. Tell me more about it. Did it hurt very much and was [sic] your clothes off at the time he did it. I will tell you about the hardest licking I got was about 3 or 4 years ago. I played truant and stole some money from mother. My father took me into the woodshed and I had to strip off my jacket & vest and two shirt so as to leave my back naked. Father took a whip and gave me a very hard whipping. It hurt me very much and every time I think of it I seem to be undergoing the flogging again. My father was sorry he had to whip & use so much severity but as I had played truant very much he thought I deserved it. You may just bet I never played truant again. Another severe flogging I got was . . . in July 1872. I ran away from home and got brought back again. My father gave me a lecture and ended by ordering me upstairs and take off the whole of my close [sic]. He took a strap and gave me a sound liking [sic]. It hurt me did yours.

The perverse, salacious tone of this note ("Your account of the whipping is amusing. Tell me more about it. Did it hurt very much . . .") is, of course, profoundly unnerving and speaks volumes about Jesse's alarmingly sadistic nature. Even more significant, however, is the light this letter sheds on one major *cause* of his pathology. Though information about Jesse's background is scarce, we do know that there was a history of wife-beating and child-abuse in his family. His paternal grandfather had been known in the community as a drunken brute who had driven his wife to divorce—a desperate expedient at the time. Jesse's mother had left her husband for the same reason. A violent alcoholic (who would ultimately die of cirrhosis of the liver), Thomas Pomeroy, Jesse's father, was always ready to mete out extreme physical punishment to his unruly younger boy. (Why Jesse received harsher treatment than his brother is an intriguing question, though his deeply unsettling appearance—repugnant even to his own father—seems to have been one of the reasons.)

Indeed Jesse's only recorded memories of his father involved beatings. In a published reminiscence, for example, he recalled the time he had attended a Sunday School picnic and returned home with his clothes so "covered with dust" that his mother seemed to despair of ever getting them clean. Thomas Pomeroy's solution—though presumably offered as a sort of jest—was nevertheless typical of the man. "Give him a good thrashing," he had growled, "that will make the dust come off."

While a brutalized upbringing might not be the sole cause of psychopathic lust-murder, it is certainly a key element. Criminological studies reveal that, almost without exception, serial killers have suffered extreme, often grotesque, forms of abuse—physical, emotional, sexual—during childhood. (Henry Lee Lucas, to cite just one of many examples, was forced to watch his prostitute-mother have sex with her tricks. She also made him dress in little girl's clothes, routinely beat him with a two-by-four, and took pleasure in torturing his pets.) As forensic psychiatrist Dr. Dorothy Lewis observes in her 1998 book, *Guilty by Reason of Insanity*, "murderers are made not born." Subjected to torturous punishment as children, such people grow up full of a murderous rage that is directed against all of humanity—a frenzied need to take vengeance on the world by inflicting as much pain and death as possible.

To be sure, other factors beside child-abuse are involved in the creation of a serial killer, and Jesse's next letter to Willie Baxter reveals another possible source of his pathology:

Friend Will,
I think you ought to tell me the answers to the questions I asked you in my letter last night. Don't be afraid of answering, for I only want to see if you know what I did to those boys on Powderhill [sic] and the railroad. Answer in full all you know

about it and I will tell you if you are right. Did you know of Will Almeder ever getting a whipping. I never did. Tell me some more of your floggings for want of something to talk about. Tell me it the same as I have told you of my two floggings, if it hurt and how your father did it. What do you think of me, my appearance. Do I look like a bad boy. Is my head large. You don't look as though you were 14 but as though you were only 10 or 12. I hope you do not do anything bad to yourself while you are in here. You understand what I mean don't you. I meant playing with yourself or abusing yourself. I am glad you prayed last night.

Yours truly
J. H. Pomroy [sic]

P.S. teare [sic] up my notes

Jesse's ostensible solicitude for Willie ("I hope you do not do anything bad to yourself while you are in here") clearly masks a keen, prurient interest in the younger boy's masturbatory habits. Perhaps the most significant aspect of the letter, however, is the part concerning Jesse's appearance.

At the core of most serial killers is a bottomless well of self-loathing. Their crimes are a way, not only of striking back at the world, but of boosting their egos. Torturing helpless victims becomes their perverse means of achieving a sense of power. The notoriety they receive also provides them with a twisted feeling of significance, affirming that they are people to be reckoned with.

The extreme sense of inadequacy that underlies their behavior derives from various sources. Foremost among these, of course, is growing up in a disturbed, pernicious household, where they are regularly beaten, belittled, and made to feel utterly worthless. But there may be other causes, too. In an intriguing 1994 article titled "The Role of Humiliation and Embarrassment in Serial Murder," sociologist Robert Hale argues that, in many instances of serial murder, the killer "is releasing a smoldering rage that is rooted in early embarrassment."

There is no question that, from his youngest days, Jesse Pomeroy had been made to suffer a great deal of embarrassment. With his exceptionally ill-favored looks—his milky eye, over-sized head, heavy jaw, and satchel mouth—he had been ridiculed all his life, not only by his peers but by his own inimical father as well. The "smoldering rage" he must have felt as the result of this constant humiliation was manifested most clearly, perhaps, in the way he mutilated the faces of several of his young victims. These acts can be seen as the pathological expression of his own sufferings, as if—having been unfairly disfigured by life—he was determined to make others share the same fate.

Given the horrendous nature of his crimes, it is clearly impossible to work up much pity for Jesse Pomeroy. Still, of everything he wrote, the plaintive questions he posed to Willie Baxter— "What do you think of me, my appearance. Do I look like a bad boy. Is my head large"—come closest to eliciting a certain amount of sympathy. They reflect the painful self-consciousness of an unsightly adolescent whose peculiar looks have brought him a lifetime of mortification.

Complying with Jesse's insistent demands—"Write and tell me what I did to those boys & the boy and girl. . . . Tell me all you have heard of me doing to those boys. . . . Don't forget to tell me about what you have heard of my doing on Powderhill & railroad"— Willie evidently replied to this letter by repeating what he knew about Pomeroy's crimes. Jesse's next two letters are extremely important. Written in the belief that their contents would remain confidential (he had advised the younger boy to destroy their correspondence and warned him not to "say anything to anyone of what we write for if we are found out we will be punished"), they constitute nothing less than signed, unequivocal confessions of his crimes. As such, they stand in marked contrast to his public statements, which would continue to hedge on the question of his guilt.

The first of these notes concerns Horace Millen and Katie Curran:

Friend Willie,

You asked me to tell you why I did those things and what I said to the boy and girl. The girl came in the store one morn and asked for paper. I told her there is a store down stairs. She went down, I killed her. Oh Willie you don't know how bad I feel for her and also the boy. What I said to the boy I have no reccollection [sic] but you know I killed him too. I feel very bad for him, and believe me I can't tell you the reason I did those things.

In the next letter, written later the same day, he spoke about the depredations he had committed in Chelsea and South Boston:

> *Dear Will,*
> *I met the boys and took them up on the hill and beat them but I do not remember sticking pins or knifs [sic] in them or putting salt water in their backs. I do not know why I did those things. I hope you will never do as I did, but hope you will and I also will be good boys here after don't you. Do you mean to be good or bad. Willie I hope you will be good. Give your heart to God. Are you a Christian.*

A few days later, Willie Baxter was taken to court and sentenced to a stint at Westborough. In his final letter to his friend, Jesse offered him the benefit of his own experience by telling him what to expect at reform school. Like his previous letters, this one contains a bizarre mix of elements—a preoccupation with corporal punishment, a markedly erotic interest in the younger boy, and a prim, paternalistic tone—that make it ineffably creepy:

> *Friend Willie,*
> *Each of the boys have a separate bed. They go in bathing every Saturday. The boys work at making chairs, washing clothes, making shoes, getting the dinner for the boys and officers, and working on the farm. I hope you will behave up there for if you do you will get out soon. If you don't you will get a good flogging every time you don't do right. . . . Don't do anything bad to yourself. You know what I mean don't you Willie. Don't mind the boys up there. They will plage [sic] you at first and ask you to do bad things but don't mind them. If you do you will get a whipping with a strap. Tell me about your being in Court. How do you feel to-day Willie. I am well. Did you undress & pray last night. I took off all my clothes except my shirt. I prayed too. Tell me all.*
>
>

> *Your friend forever*
> *Jesse H. Pomroy [sic]*
>

40

Human beings seem so many departures, more or less gross, from the line of beauty. For every success in nature's evident aim at perfection there are a thousand failures, and when the deviation from the type becomes extreme, we call it monstrous. What shall we do with it?
—Epigraph to the *Autobiography of Jesse H. Pomeroy* (1875)

Like certain infamous serial killers of our own era (most notably John Wayne Gacy, whose paintings of leering circus clowns and deranged-looking Disney characters are prized by collectors of macabre art), Jesse Pomeroy possessed something of a creative streak. His metier, however, was not visual art but the written word. Though the letters he composed to Willie Baxter display little, if any, literary potential, he clearly had a certain affinity for writing. Indeed, he would eventually turn himself into a jailhouse poet, contributing occasional verses to various publications and even issuing a slender volume of his collected works.

His first significant production, however, was a two-part memoir, initially published in the *Boston Times* on successive Sundays in July, 1875. Immediately following its newspaper appearance, this flagrantly self-serving life story would be reissued as a slender, fifteen-cent volume entitled the *Autobiography of Jesse H. Pomeroy, Written by him while imprisoned in the Suffolk County Jail and under sentence of death for the murder of H. H. Millen.*

There seems little doubt that this work is, by and large, the product of Jesse's own hand. True, it has clearly been treated to a certain amount of editorial polishing (as Jesse's letters indicate, he was an egregious speller, consistently miswriting even his own last name as *Pomroy*). And the syntax and punctuation have also been regularized for publication.

Even so, the memoir is a thoroughly amateurish piece of

work, rambling, repetitious, almost unreadably dull in places— precisely the sort of thing that a moderately literate fifteen-year- old would produce. Even Jesse was abashed by its shortcomings, describing it in a closing apology as "merely the disjointed ideas that are in my mind." Appended to the text, moreover, is an affa- davit by his mother—sworn before Justice of the Peace Russell H. Cornwell—in which she declares that "the composition of said autobiography is wholly and exclusively the work of the said Jesse H., and that the same was written by him without the assistance of any person." Almost without question, the docu- ment is authentic. As such—like Jesse's correspondence with Willie Baxter—it affords valuable insight into its author's men- tality.

There is one major difference, however, between his letters and the autobiography. Writing confidentially to his boyhood pal, Jesse readily (even eagerly) confesses the truth of his crimes. In address- ing the general reader, on the other hand, he insists on his inno- cence, going to great, often tortuous, lengths to deny all the charges against him. Indeed, one of the things this memoir reveals most clearly about Jesse is his genuine gift for hairsplitting, evasion, and casuistry. Had he not been a psychopathic killer of frightening pre- cocity, he might well have turned out to be a successful lawyer.

In an effort to dispel the widespread conception of himself as a "fiend"—a natural-born killer who had engaged in acts of cru- elty from the time he was a toddler—Jesse begins by depicting his early childhood as an era of idyllic pursuits. In describing this part of his life, he comes across as a kind of urban Huck Finn—a high-spirited lad who liked to play hooky from school so he could hang around the Navy Yard and "whittle a piece of wood." On Saturdays, he and his "chums" would go boating on the Mystic River or play baseball in a vacant lot.

To be sure, he occasionally got into trouble. He recounts the time that—after setting off some firecrackers in school—he was forced to stand in a corner "with a dumb bell in one hand and a stone on top of my head; [my teacher] told me if I dropped either of them or made any noise she would give me a thrashing, and I believe she would." Still, Jesse hastens to add, "you must not think I was always bad at school; I gave my teacher trouble enough I am sure; but as a general thing I was what is commonly called a good boy." Indeed, he describes himself as an inveterate reader not only of adventure novels but of "good solid books that will be to my advantage in the future." He also "went to Sunday School every Sunday."

While most of these recollections are presented in entirely general terms, he does take time to recount two incidents in specific detail. Both of these passages represent heavy-handed attempts to address a recurrent charge against Jesse—*i.e.*, that his glaring lack of remorse was the sign of his cruel, unnatural temperament. To counter this allegation (made by virtually everyone who had observed him, from policemen to reporters to psychologists), he describes a time when he and his brother were fishing side-by-side on Chelsea Bridge. As Charlie went to cast his line into the river, the hook "struck and caught" Jesse's face just below his left eye, burying "itself deep right near the bone." The two boys rushed to the home of the neighborhood physician, Dr. Bickford, who extracted the hook from Jesse's cheek.

Jesse's reason for mentioning this incident, he writes, "is this—that though the pain was great and hurt very much, I did not show any feeling at all, either when it was in there or when the doctor was taking it out; and now what strikes me as curious at this time is that it might furnish a clue as to why I do not show any feeling now in regard to this case. Though I did not at this time show any feeling, it was no sign I had none, and now if I do not show any in regard to these cases, it is not to be supposed that I have none."

The second incident he relates is meant to reinforce this very point. Several years earlier (according to Jesse), he and his Sunday School class were returning by train from a picnic at Walden Pond when the locomotive struck a deaf man who was strolling on the tracks and did not hear the warning shriek of the engineer's whistle. "When the train was stopped," Jesse writes, "the men of the engine picked him up dead. Poor man! To be cut off so suddenly, almost without warning, it was too bad. I know it made me feel bad the rest of the night, and I could not help thinking about it for a long time after; the rest of our company felt very bad, for some of them cried, particularly the girls; but then as they are the weaker sex I suppose that was all right." Like the tale of the embedded fishing hook, this anedote is clearly meant to demonstrate that—far from being a callous brute—Jesse is a person of deep feeling ("Poor man! . . . it was too bad") who is simply not given to open displays of emotion, partly because of his natural disposition and partly because (as his remark about the "weaker sex" suggests) he regards it as girlish to do so.

Having covered (in less than three pages) the highlights of his life between 1859 and 1871, Jesse then cuts to "the time my troubles came"—the period when (as he tells it) he was unjustly accused of crimes that he never committed. According to his version of events, he was strolling home from school on the afternoon of September 21, 1872, when—"out of mere curiosity"—he stopped to take a perfectly innocent look inside Police Station Six. A few moments later, as he continued on his way home, he was accosted by an officer who grabbed him by the arm and led him back into the station house. Protesting that he had "done nothing," Jesse "commenced to cry, I was so frightened." Inside the station, several "of those boys that had been so maltreated by another came and said that I was the boy that did it to them, and the only way they identified me was because I had a spot on the right eye."

Terrified and confused, Jesse was "locked up in a cell, not allowed to see my parents or friends. Here that night I was kept in torture. . . . I could not give an iota of the way I was treated by the men and officers of that station. They used nasty language to me, called me all sorts of names, and I venture to say that never was a boy of my age placed before in such a condition. All this time, bear in mind, I . . . did not have hardly an idea of what I was arrested for."

After suffering this brutal mistreatment for hours, Jesse was finally allowed to get some sleep—only to be awakened in the middle of the night by an officer who threatened that, if Jesse did not confess, "they will send you to prison for a hunded years." Unable to bear the pressure any longer, poor Jesse broke down and told the policeman what he wanted to hear. "What wonder is it that I confessed? I was half awake, and nearly dead with fear, and hardly knew what I was saying."

Having been coerced into making this false confession, Jesse was then brought to the Tombs and confronted with a number of his supposed victims, all of whom positively identified him as their assailant. As far as Jesse is concerned, however, all seven of the little boys were mistaken:

Now is it not singular that those boys [could] not identify me except on account of my eye. Not one of them did or could tell what dress I wore or how my voice sounded—in fact, failed to notice everything that a sharp boy would, and fell back on the untenable ground of identifying me by my eye. And how, you will say, untenable? For this reason: it is utterly impossible for me to believe that these boys could be taken on the street and done as they said they were used, and not see some other points of this boy; they would be most likely to see what kind of clothes this boy wore, if he had a black, white, or blue suit on, and in fact all about his personal appreareance. And again, their position of identifying me solely on the ground of my eye is untenable for the reason that there are other boys with eyes like mine.

The trial that followed was—from Jesse's point of view—an utter miscarriage of justice. "The complaints were read to me, and I understood them about as much as I would Greek or Latin . . . no one was allowed to speak for me; I was not allowed to speak for myself." In the end, he was unfairly convicted on the "untenable" testimony of the seven untrustworthy boys, and sentenced by a judge "who would not (or didn't know enough to) weigh the testimony against me; who allowed himself to judge in a partial manner." "No," Jesse protests with all the indignation he can muster, "I did not have justice, have not had it, and what I am the law has made me."

After describing at some length his stint in reform school—during which he was "never punished in any way, shape, or manner" and was universally regarded as "a good, behaved boy"—Jesse arrives at the crux of the work: his convoluted and flagrantly specious attempt to prove himself, if not absolutely innocent of the two murders, then at least not morally responsible for them.

Shortly after his return from Westborough, he informs us, "a small boy was murdered on the South Boston marsh." For some inexplicable reason, the police immediately assumed that Jesse might have a connection to the crime. "Somehow—I have never been able to find a reason—suspicion fell on me," he declares in a perfectly disingenuous tone, "and at ten o'clock that night, just as I was going to bed, two gentlemen came to see me . . . and told me that they wanted to know where I had been during the day."

At this point in the memoir, Jesse launches into an amazingly detailed, virtually minute-by-minute account of his supposed whereabouts on the day of the Millen murder. Needless to say, he was nowhere near the crime scene. Nevertheless, he was dragged down to the police station, stripped of most of his clothes, and subjected to hours of grueling interrogation. "All this time," he avers, "I had not the slightest idea of what I was arrested for."

It was not until the following morning that Chief Savage informed him that he had been "arrested for the murder of that boy on the marsh." According to Jesse, this disclosure came as such an unexpected shock that—when his interrogators persisted in grilling him—he finally blurted out, "I might have done it." This statement, however, was merely the desperate recourse of a stunned and terrified boy. "I was so frightened and resolved to say it so as to get rid of them," he insists. "I did not know hardly what I was saying."

As for his confession to Detective Wood following the viewing of Horace Millen's corpse at Waterman's undertaking parlor, Jesse indignantly denies having made it. "His story of my confessing is a lie from beginning to end, and he knows it," Jesse proclaims. "Or at least, if I did say so, I have no recollection of it, and I do not believe I said I did do it." Wood's behavior, according to Jesse, was typical of the deplorable tactics of the police. "They get every fact they can from the accused, and somehow or other they twist it and turn it against [him]."

Indeed, throughout his autobiography, Jesse presents himself as the persecuted young victim not only of the police but of the public and the news media as well. "The moment suspicion falls on anyone, whether justly or unjustly," he complains, "the people, led on by the press, raise such a hue and cry against this one or that one that a candid person cannot, for the life of him, tell whether the one is guilty or not."

At this point in the memoir, Jesse provides his own, novel version of the Katie Curran affair. Once again, he professes shock and indignation that he was accused of the crime. After all— aside from the fact that he was already in custody for child-murder and that the little girl's decomposed corpse was found in the cellar of his family's store—there was no reason in the world to suspect him. By arresting his mother and brother, moreover, the police were guilty once again of resorting to coercive tactics. Full of concern for his loved ones, Jesse "resolved to do all I could to get them out, so I kept in mind that proverb, 'One may as well be hanged for stealing a sheep as for stealing a lamb,' altering it to suit my case, 'One may as well be hanged for killing one as two, etc.' " By the following morning, he had concocted an extremely convincing but (as he now reveals) completely phony confession.

After denouncing the inquest into the Curran murder as yet another travesty ("Strip the case of all its glitter, and we find the evidence consists only of finding the body in the cellar. . . . Do you see justice? No! Injustice!"), Jesse goes on to dissect, at significant length, the testimony offered at his trial. He begins by deriding the witnesses who claim to have seen him with Horace Millen. He is scathing toward Mrs. Eleanor Fosdick, for example, who testified that she had noticed his white eye from a distance of forty or fifty feet. "How foolish for her to say so," he sneers, "when she knows she did not nor cannot. If she did, she ought to hire out to Barnum."

As for the evidence presented by the prosecution, it was—he declares—"not sufficient. They produced none to show that I led the boy from the street, that I sent him to buy the cake, that I took him along the track, or that I went along the wharf. They produce none to show that anyone saw me go off from the marsh, or that I got any blood on my clothes, or that anyone saw anything strange in my behavior, and in fact they produce not a particle of evidence to show what became of me during the rest of the day."

Ultimately, Jesse takes as many straws as he can grasp and weaves them into an argument of breathtaking illogicality. Summed up in a sentence, his conclusion is that the evidence positively shows that he did not murder Horace Millen; but if he *did*, he must have been insane. His exact argument, however, is such a dizzying example of harebrained reasoning that it is worth quoting at length:

These are the reasons why I THINK THAT IF I DID THOSE THINGS I WAS INSANE, or that I could not help doing it. Considering:

That I was found at the age of five years cutting a kitten with a knife.

That I was subject to a peculiar feeling in the head at times.

That those acts to those boys indicate a diseased mind on the subject of those acts; they were insane because no one but an insane person would do so. . . .

Because of making a boy go on his knees and repeat the Lord's Prayer, and then swear.

Because of the sticking of a boy with a knife, and holding it up so that the blood could drop down, and laughing at the time, and then repeating it.

Because it is the blood that seems to be that which excites me, as shown by the story of the snake; also, of sticking the knife into the boy and the holding it up and letting it drop off; and that two doctors, who had each of them been to see me six times, pronounce me insane; I think, therefore, that if I did those things I was insane.

But, notwithstanding all that, as I have said, I DO NOT THINK I DID THOSE THINGS, for these reasons:

That I was not at the age of five seen on the street cutting a cat.

That the Government failed to prove me guilty of those first cases.

Because my confession was given through fear and under promise. . . .

Because the evidence was not sufficient to show that I was the boy who did those things.

Because all the evidence came from the boys who were injured, and they were prejudiced against me. . . .

Because the judge did not weigh the evidence impartially.

Because the sentence was unjust.

And because I know that I did not do it to those boys, I conclude that I was not guilty of the acts.

Following his wholesale attack on the witnesses, the judge, the prosecution, and the jury, Jesse goes after the petitioners who are clamoring for his death. A total of 2,300 signatories, he says, have demanded his execution. But "does 2,300 names represent a total population of 300,000 people? No, it does not, and the fact . . . proves that Boston people do not want me executed." Moreover, he insists, the "ones that signed those petitions are nearly all women . . . and their demand is so extraordinary that it shows that WOMEN KNOW NOTHING OF LAW OR HUMANITY, or at least those who petitioned didn't. No. I do not believe that they proved by presenting petitions from women that people wished me executed." Like other criminals of his ilk, Jesse possessed a monstrous egotism that made him oblivious to anything beyond his own desires, and that often led him to make statements that were astonishingly tactless and ill-advised. Here—even while attempting to win the sympathy of the public—he manages to insult the entire female population of Boston.

That same self-defeating arrogance is evident at the close of the memoir, where Jesse makes what is arguably the most outrageous statement in the entire work. Proffering a final "word about our jury system," Jesse actually raises a valid concern, one that continues to be a knotty issue in our age of saturation news coverage. The rise of modern mass communication, he argues— railways, telegraphs, and especially newspapers—has made it difficult for certain highly notorious criminals (like himself) to receive fair and impartial trials. "A murder is committed," he writes, "there is great excitement, the papers are full of it, and men read about it. The case is to be tried by twelve of the men of the county in which the murder was committed, and . . . the men can't help forming an opinion of the case, or help hearing of it."

So far, Jesse's point is perfectly reasonable, even astute. He immediately undercuts himself, however, by delivering a brazenly offensive remark that is clearly aimed at the jurors in his own case. "The result," he says, "is that the twelve men who have formed their opinion, but are willing to change it if the evidence warrants it, are turned away, and their place is filled with a set of human donkeys. . . . Ten to one they say he is not guilty when he is, and say he is guilty when he isn't."

Having thus reviled the jurors as "human donkeys (or, as he elsewhere puts it, "twelve jackasses . . . good and true"), Jesse then goes on to make an even more outlandish statement, one that crosses the line separating the merely insulting from the actively disturbing. In both the newspaper and pamphlet versions, it is printed in capital letters for added emphasis: "IT IS A QUESTION IN MY MIND," he declares, "WHETHER THE JURY ARE NOT FITTER TO DIE THAN THE PRISONER."

That Jesse would conclude his memoir by suggesting that the

men who convicted him ought to be taken out and killed seems, at best, highly impolitic—certainly not the smartest way of convincing the public of his harmless good nature. But then, rational and prudent judgment was not Jesse Pomeroy's long suit—as the world would be forcibly reminded before his full confession was even published.

41

I ain't going to be shut up here all my life.
—Jesse Pomeroy

Written communications were forbidden among prisoners at the county jail, as Jesse was perfectly aware. As a result, he and Willie Baxter had taken pains to conceal their correspondence, passing their messages back and forth as surreptitiously as possible. Willie had also been instructed to destroy Jesse's notes after reading them and to keep their letter-writing a secret from the other inmates.

In spite of these precautions, the turnkey, Mr. Bradley, had somehow gotten wind of the exchange. And so, on Tuesday, July 20—just two days after the first installment of Jesse's autobiography appeared in the *Boston Times*—Bradley decided to pay an unexpected visit to Pomeroy's cell, hoping to catch him in the act of writing one of the forbidden letters to his friend.

Since his conviction, Jesse had been incarcerated in cell No. 19, located on the second tier of the south wing of the jail about midway between the rotunda and the barber shop. The cell—normally used for the detainment of debtors—was relatively spacious and equipped with an iron-framed cot, a wooden chair, two slop buckets, and a wash basin. Besides these meager furnishings, it contained Jesse's books and papers, an iron spoon, and some miscellaneous articles—including various tins of prepared food—supplied by his mother.

It was just before noon when Bradley unlocked the wooden door of cell nineteen and entered without warning. Contrary to his expectation, he did not find its occupant seated on his cot, composing a letter to Willie Baxter. Instead, Jesse was casually leaning against the front wall, right beside the barred window.

His arms were folded carelessly over his chest, his features arranged into a look of extreme nonchalance. There was something so exaggerated about the boy's pose that Bradley immediately grew suspicious. As he glanced around the cell, his attention was suddenly caught by a bewildering sight—several bricks lying on the floor beneath the cot.

Hurrying over to Jesse, Bradley ordered him to step aside. For a moment, the boy simply glowered at the turnkey. Then, with a little snort of contempt, he did as he was told—revealing several sheets of paper stuck to the wall directly below the bottom edge of the window. Frowning deeply, Bradley tore away the paper—then made an incredulous sound.

Underneath the paper, there was a gaping hole in the wall where three bricks had been removed. A quick examination of the space revealed that the mortar around four adjoining bricks had also been dug out. It was clear at a glance that—had Jesse succeeded in extracting those remaining bricks and prying out a single bar of the window—he would have created a hole large enough to wiggle through.

Bradley immediately summoned Sheriff Clark, who—along with the turnkey—proceeded to conduct a thorough search of Jesse's cell. They quickly turned up the makeshift tools that Jesse had used in his attempted jailbreak: a length of stout wire pried from the outer rim of his washbasin; his iron spoon (which had become severely bent out of shape); a rung from his chair; and the sharpened lid of a sardine tin (one of the treats sent by Jesse's mother). To conceal his handiwork, he had used a bar of soap to paste together several blank sheets of paper and affix them to the wall. Sitting on the window ledge—concealing the bottom of the iron bar he'd already begun loosening with his implements— was a large world atlas that had been given to him by the charitable Miss Burnham. Suddenly, Jesse's observation in his just-published memoir—that he had been supplied with "good solid books . . . [that] will be to my advantage in the future"—assumed a new and deeply ironic meaning.

At first, Jesse sullenly refused to talk. Before long, however, his egotism got the best of him, and—unable to resist the chance to flaunt his ingenuity—he told his captors everything.

His plan—which he had hoped to put into effect sometime during the coming week—was to wait until midnight, when the officer who kept watch over the inmates retired for the night. With five unattended hours before the morning guard came on duty, Jesse would finish sawing off the outermost bar of the window, squeeze outside his cell, and lower himself to the ground floor of the rotunda by means of a long, knotted rope he had fashioned from the cords that supported his mattress. Though he expected to meet no resistance, he was prepared (as he told his interrogators) to "knock over"—and, if necessary, to kill—"anyone who opposed him." Once he had cleared the jail building and scaled the outer wall, he intended to make his way to Canada, traveling by night, and "become a citizen of that country."

How Pomeroy planned to saw off the iron window bar was made clear in a letter that Sheriff Clark discovered inside the boy's coat pocket. Addressed to his mother, this letter described Jesse's jailbreak scheme in lengthy detail, and urged her to bring him a file when she came for her next semiweekly visit. The file, he suggested, could be hidden inside "a banana, as fruit can be passed to a prisoner without examination."

Following his interrogation, Jesse was placed in a different cell, this one on the lower tier of the north wing. One of the most impregnable in the jailhouse, its walls were constructed of solid granite blocks "which no one could cut through in a year," as Sheriff Clark assured the public. Taking no chances, Clark also posted a twenty-four-hour watch in front of the cell.

Just before locking him inside, turnkey Bradley asked Jesse "why he did it."

"I ain't going to be shut up here all my life," Pomeroy growled in reply. "I was going to make a trial for liberty."

News of Jesse's "latest exploit" (as the *Boston Post* called it) caused a sensation. By Thursday morning, every paper in the city had run a major story about the "boy fiend's" attempted escape. "An Ingenious and Daring Plan!" proclaimed a headline in the *Boston Globe.* "One of the Most Remarkable Attempts of Jail-Breaking on Record!" declared the *Herald.* According to the *Boston Journal,* Pomeroy had diplayed "The Cunning of an Old Jail Bird" in concocting the scheme.

Needless to say, whatever sympathy Jesse may have generated with his just-published memoir was completely undone by the discovery of his planned escape. His brazen bid for freedom confirmed the worst fears of those who believed that no prison would ever hold the "boy fiend"; while those who scoffed at his claims of insanity felt bitterly vindicated by this proof of his obvious cunning.

"For an insane person, as the professional philantropists claim him to be," the *Globe* commented dryly, "he certainly displays a remarkably clear head when any planning is to be done." In a similarly sardonic vein, the *Herald* observed that "If Jesse Harding Pomeroy . . . is an insane person, as was claimed at his trial, the malady has developed itself in a form heretofore unknown to the profession who have made insanity a study. For a boy of his age, he has recently shown himself to be a genius in cunning, and has within a week made for himself a reputation for faculties rarely found in one of his years, and which are proof positive that he is not only in full possession of his senses, but has an extraordinary adaptability for conceiving bold and desperate schemes and plans for defeating justice, and the nerve to attempt their execution."

While the the rest of the world may have perceived Jesse as a prodigy of evil and a "genius in cunning," his mother and brother remained stubbornly convinced of his innocence. At one point in mid-April, for example, they had been visited by a man named James Ingalls, who identified himself as a prison guard at Randall's Island in New York City. According to Ingalls, one of his inmates, a teenaged boy named Coe who was in the last stages of tuberculosis, had confessed to the murders of Horace Millen and Katie Curran and wished to make a dying statement directly to a member of the Pomeroy family.

Mrs. Pomeroy—convinced that her faith was about to be rewarded and Jesse fully exonerated—gave Charlie thirty dollars for travel expenses and sent him off with Ingalls. Over the next few days, she waited impatiently to hear from her older son— but the anticipated telegram never arrived. Finally, nearly a week after his depature, Charlie showed up with nothing to relate but a tale of petty and malicious trickery.

Ingalls, it turned out, was an imposter. After decoying Charlie to New York, he had contrived to finagle all thirty dollars from the boy and left him stranded penniless in the city. Somehow, Charlie had managed to scrape enough money together to make his way home.

As for Ruth Pomeroy, her feelings about her younger boy were expressed in a lengthy letter she sent to a San Francisco woman who had written to ask for a lock of Jesse's hair. (Like many notorious sociopaths, Pomeroy attracted the fascinated attention of various—mostly female—correspondents, the sort of morbid admirers we now refer to as serial-killer groupies.) Somehow, the press got hold of Mrs. Pomeroy's letter, which was widely reprinted in papers throughout the country, including the *New York Times*. The full text ran as follows:

DEAR FRIEND

For such I deem you by your writing me in this, my hour of trouble—I feel it my duty to answer you immediately. Although I may differ with you in regard to this case, you have written to me expressing sympathy with me, and I feel deeply grateful for your kindness, although a stranger to me; yet by your letter it shows that there is one woman who does not feel disgraced by writing to a poor, heartbroken mother. I cannot write you that Jesse is guilty of those terrible crimes, although he has been convicted—yet not proved—by law. You will no doubt be surprised, yet I mean just what I say, there is no justice in Massachusetts for a poor boy. Had he been the son of some rich person, the case would have had a more thorough investigation. That is my view of the subject.

Jesse's confession was given after the girl was found in the cellar of the store occupied by three or four different parties, having to go there every day after coal, within three feet of where the body lay. If three policemen searched the cellar, looked in the very spot where it was found, and found nothing—if it was there, then I don't see why there was no smell, it being about six weeks after the girl disappeared. When found it was only partially covered with ashes, workmen having worked there nine days without smelling anything. I said his confession was made after the girl was found—or the bones—for there was nothing to recognize her by except shreds of clothing, I was told.

I and my son were dragged to prison, and for what? Just to satisfy the public. I had done nothing, nor did I dream of such a thing as that body being there: nor do I believe, today, that it was. I was taken from my home bareheaded to the station from my work, thinking all the while that everything was coming out right, and I could afford the stings and scorn of people that were cast upon us, when the last blow fell upon me, crushing my heart to atoms. Ah! I never can tell you what we have suffered. No pen can describe, no tongue can tell the deep agony of that hour. From the first I believed the body was placed there after we moved from the store, and that nerved me up to more strength to bear; and I determined to rise above it, believing yet, till at last the terrible news came that Jesse confessed that he had done the deed.

For a while I was almost wild, but when I came to reason the case, I began to doubt, not believing it possible that it could have been done and we not knowing anything about it. They told me Jesse would tell me all about it, but when I asked to see him they refused my request; they kept me five weeks and my oldest boy six, and after I had been home five or six weeks they allowed me an interview. I knew Jesse thought the world of me, and I knew it would nearly set him crazy to have me and Charlie in jail. My suspicions were correct, for when I got the papers I saw by the Chief's testimony that Jesse had confessed to save his mother and brother. I was not surprised—I knew Jesse better than anyone, and I knew his generous heart; and today he would rather suffer death than have any harm come to us. I do not doubt that he is insane—driven insane by the treatment that was heaped upon us. Jesse is no ordinary boy, but I do believe he is no criminal. If I could see and talk with you, and tell you all the mysterious circumstances surrounding the mysterious affair, I think you would agree with me that there is some terrible mystery about the whole affair that has not been brought to light. Jesse never was of a cruel disposition; there never was a more kindhearted boy. Is it not a little strange that his mother never saw a thing in the boy that would lead me to suppose him capable of committing such crimes? It is entirely different from his disposition—and the people have been blinded by passion, and shut their eyes to the real facts, and been blinded by the horrible crimes recently committed in our midst; and as I write you this last blow has fallen. They tell me that my boy is to die, and for what? Why, to satisfy the mothers of Massachusetts. Yes—mothers. But I do here declare that the time will come when this great injustice will be known. It may be too late to save the life of my boy, yet it must come, sooner or later. Mark what I say, Massachusetts will yet bow in shame for murdering my boy, for murder it will surely be. I have no fear for my boy; God will take care of him. Remember, "Vengeance is mine; I will repay, saith the Lord."

Did you see anything in the lock of hair to make you believe Jesse capable of committing such crimes? I do not know as I can get your kind letter to Jesse, as they will not allow it to be given to him.

Again, I thank you for your kindness in writing to a broken-hearted mother.

Deeply grateful,
Mrs. R. A. POMEROY

However impassioned, Mrs. Pomeroy's letter served no other purpose than to impress Bostonians with the deeply deluded nature of blind mother-love. The startling news of Jesse's aborted escape inspired a fresh burst of calls for his execution. In spite of this pressure, Governor Gaston remained staunchly opposed to signing Jesse's death warrant. This principled but highly unpopular stance effectively cost Gaston any chance of reelection. In August, 1875, the Democrats nominated the Honorable Charles Francis Adams to run for governor in the fall elections.

As soon as the campaign got underway, a committee of the city's most influential women sent a small delegation to sound out Adams's opponent, Alexander H. Rice, on the subject of Pomeroy. Rice assured them that, if elected, he would promptly set a date for Pomeroy's execution. Partly as a result of this promise, he handily won the election.

Contrary to his pledge, however, Rice—who was, in truth, no more eager than Gaston to send a teenaged boy to the gallows—found ways of stalling his decision. And by the summer of 1876, the situation had undergone a significant change. Nearly two years had passed since Jesse's trial, and—though feelings against Pomeroy still ran high among a certain segment of the public—most Bostonians had put the matter out of mind. Moreover, on May 26, 1876, Thomas Piper—"the Monster of the Belfry"—had gone to the gallows, and his death seemed to have slaked, at least to a degree, the public's thirst for vengeance. Even Lieutenant Governor Knight—the most vociferous supporter of the death sentence on the Executive Council—had done an about-face by then and no longer demanded Jesse's execution.

The final disposition of the case occurred on the afternoon of

August 31, 1876, when—during a brief, closed-door meeting—
the council reversed its previous position and, by a six-to-three
vote, decided to commute Jesse's death sentence. From all reports, the councillors were deeply influenced by the impassioned pleas for mercy submitted by some of the most eminent
members of the Suffolk bar, including Judges George Tyler
Bigelow, Benjamin F. Thomas, and Dwight Foster, all ex-justices
of the Supreme Court of Massachusetts. Recognizing, however,
that the public would not be placated unless Pomeroy were subjected to something more extreme than mere imprisonment,
Governor Rice sentenced the boy to "solitary confinement for
the remainder of his life."

The news of the governor's decision created only a minor stir
among the populace. True, there were those who felt that, in
sparing Jesse's life, Rice had commited political suicide. "The
Pomeroy business killed Gaston last year," one Boston man commented bitterly, "and it will send Mr. Rice back to private life."
For the most part, however, the public appeared to respect the
decision, viewing it (in the words of the *Boston Herald*) as "the
honest conviction of those upon whom the great responsibility
of this trying duty has devolved."

For Ruth Pomeroy, news of the commutation came as a joyous
surprise, and she received it, according to the *Globe*, "with tears
of gratitude." Jesse's reaction, on the other hand, was considerably more subdued. By that time, he was nearly seventeen years
old. Though no longer the barely pubescent "boy fiend" of the
popular imagination, he was still appallingly young to be facing
the awful prospect of a lifetime in solitary. From his vantage
point, the governor's decision was no cause for celebration. Jesse
had concluded his published autobiography by remarking that
the prospects he faced were equally grim. "If they say I must die,
I am dead," he had written. "If they send me to prison for life, I
am dead too." Now, the second of these two ghastly fates had
come to pass. Jesse Pomeroy had been saved from the gallows—
but condemned to a living entombment.

PART 5

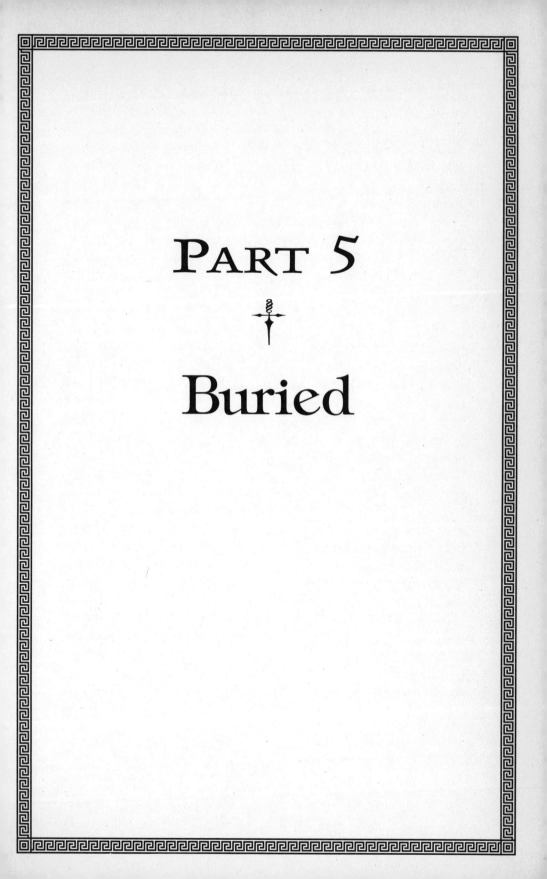

Buried

42

Whoso diggeth a pit shall fall therein.
—Proverbs 26:27

On September 7, 1876—a bleak, drizzly Wednesday, less
than three months before he turned seventeen—Jesse Harding
Pomeroy entered the Massachusetts State Prison at Charlestown.
Except for a brief interval during the early 1880s—when he,
along with the other inmates, were temporarily transferred to another institution while Charlestown underwent renovations—he
would remain immured within its grim, granite walls until 1929:
a period of fifty-three years, extending from the time of "Custer's
Last Stand" to the start of the Great Depression. And of that half
century of internment, he would spend forty-one years in solitary confinement—the second-longest such stretch in U.S. penal
history (surpassed only by the forty-two years in "deep lock" en-
dured by Robert F. Stroud, the so-called "Birdman of Alcatraz").

Though he would eventually be transferred to a somewhat
larger space, Jesse passed the first decade of his sentence in what
was little more than a sealed, granite vault—a seven-by-nine-
foot cell with a few narrow loopholes high in the walls to provide a modicum of light and ventilation. His only furnishings
were a little table, a narrow bunk, a metal wash pail, and a
wooden slop bucket. The inner, solid iron door weighed more
than five hundred pounds; the outer door of heavy wood
shielded him from the sight of any other living being.

His endless, crushingly dreary days were all the same. He
would rise at around 8:00 A.M., when the daylight leaking into
his cell had grown strong enough to see by. At the height of summer, his cell was as stifling as a coke oven; but in the winter, it
was so frigid that the water in his wash pail would freeze

overnight. After breaking the top crust of ice, he would perform his morning ablutions—assuming that the rats hadn't made off with his soap chips and tooth powder.

Three times a day, a guard would slide his tasteless meals through a slot in the wrought-iron door. The food was always the same: beans, brown bread, hash, rice, molasses, and a thin, flavorless soup with a few limp cabbage leaves or slivers of onion floating in it. His only beverage was a weak, barely palatable coffee-substitute, made of burned rye steeped in boiling water.

Any infraction of the rules, no matter how small, was met with brutal punishment. According to the statute books, prisoners in solitary were forbidden any form of communication with fellow inmates. Sometimes, however, in his desperation for human intercourse, a man might try to contact his neighbor by tapping out a message on the stone wall dividing their cells. Anyone caught committing this offense, however, was liable to be subjected to a swift, savage beating—often meted out with a brass-handled cane.

Though Jesse, in his lifelong intransigence, often refused to do any work whatsoever, he was expected to perform "hard labor" during his sentence. For the first few years of his incarceration, his main task consisted of making scrubbing brushes. He would sit at his little table for hours at a stretch, affixing the stiff bristles to the wooden handles while reading sporadically from a book propped open on his lap.

Even at the height of summer, dusk would begin to gather in the unlighted cell by mid-afternoon. By 5:00 or 5:30 P.M. (earlier in winter), night had fallen for Jesse Pomeroy.

Retreating to his bunk, he would lie there listening to the pandemoniac sounds that issued from the neighboring cells and filtered into his own: shouts, catcalls, curses, whoops, shrieks—a crazed, infernal racket that would last throughout the night.

There was virtually no relief from this unbearable existence. Once every three months, as permitted by prison regulations, his mother came to see him, a ritual that continued until her death in 1915. On a handful of occasions, he received visits from various notables. In 1910, for example, during a Christmas Day tour of the prison, the wife of Governor Eugene Foss chatted with him briefly about his reading. Four years later, Foss's successor, Governor David I. Walsh, held a brief conversation with Jesse through the bars of his cell. Otherwise—beside prison officials, an occasional clergymen, and a lawyer or two—Jesse had no direct contact with other human beings for forty-one years.

By condemning Jesse Pomeroy to life under such harrowing conditions, the state of Massachusetts had, in effect, taken a man that the courts had found sane and condemned him to an existence almost guaranteed to drive him crazy.

Both anecdotal evidence and scientific research have shown that, for many men, even a few days of solitary can be a shattering experience. At the time of Jesse's incarceration, every newly admitted prisoner to Charlestown was forced to serve the first twenty-four hours of his sentence in isolation—partly as a brusque initiation into life in the "big house," and partly as a foretaste of the punishment meted out to anyone who violated its rules. Many first-time convicts found this experience—as one former inmate testified—"the most terrifying twenty-four hours in life." Condemned to longer stretches, even the toughest men might crack. Writing in the *Boston Globe* of his experiences in Charlestown, an ex-prisoner named Waldrop recalled that, when faced with the prospect of a month's stint in a solitary cell, a jailmate of his named Romano—an unregenerate hardcase doing time for manslaughter—hanged himself.

Clinical studies have proven that prisoners subjected to even relatively short periods in solitary confinement commonly begin to show severe psychopathological symptoms, ranging from hallucinations to panic attacks to paranoid delusions. More protracted stints can drive a man to madness. In December 1949, after three years in Alcatraz's notorious "dungeon," a small-time hood named Henri Young stabbed a fellow inmate to death. At his trial, his lawyers successfully argued that Young's prolonged isolation was a form of cruel and inhuman punishment that had made him insane. Even the administrators of Devil's Island—the infamous penal colony off the coast of French Guiana—put a two-year limit on the time a man could spend in solitary.

That Jesse Pomeroy survived forty-one years of this treatment has made him—in the eyes of certain devotees of American penal lore—something of a folk-hero, a man who refused to be subjugated by the brutal conditions of the "pen," who never caved in to authority or surrendered to the system. Even some people with very little love for Jesse Pomeroy have expressed a grudging admiration for his fierce, unbending willpower. In October 1930, for example, James R. Wood—the onetime Boston police detective who had played such a key role in Jesse's arrest a half century earlier—published an article on the case in a pulp magazine called *The Master Detective.* ("At last!" screamed the headline. "The real truth about America's most notorious lifer—this ogre in human form who, as a boy, took his place among the most infamous arch-fiends of modern times!") Though Wood was no fan of Pomeroy's, he could not keep a certain respectful tone from his voice when describing Jesse's prison existence. "But there was one thing they could not break," wrote Wood, referring to the Charlestown officials. "That was Pomeroy's indomitable spirit."

Other historians of crime, however, have seen Jesse's experience in a very different light. According to these writers, Jesse never lost his sanity during his decades in solitary for the simple reason that he had none to lose—*i.e.,* that he was criminally insane to begin with. These experts view Pomeroy's unremitting struggles against his captors, not as a sign of his heroic willpower, but as the symptom of his monstrously warped, hopelessly incorrigible nature. In a *Boston Globe* article that appeared in 1932, for example, a writer named Louis Lyons described Pomeroy as "the meanest prisoner" in the history of Charlestown:

> He could not be trusted a minute. He would steal from other prisoners. A moral degenerate, a pervert, a sadist, his traits persisted through the years. Even at the State Farm, young lads had to be kept away from him. . . . He never responded to kindness, was always suspicious of everyone, and never showed any interest even in his mother, who martyred herself to seek his freedom through forty years. He never would talk to her about anything except his case and her efforts toward his release. . . .
>
> Obsessed with his importance, he was forever demanding hearings, pardons, commutations, forever complaining, forever seeking publicity by any means, never ceasing to insist on his martyrdom.

However one views Pomeroy—as a resolute, unyielding freedom-seeker (a kind of homegrown Papillon) or a sociopathic monster forever contriving diabolical ways to break out of his cage (a sort of real-life Hannibal Lecter)—one fact is incontrovertible. From virtually the moment that he entered the grim fortress of Charlestown until the day, fifty three-years later, that he was finally transferred to the State Farm at Bridgewater, Jesse Pomeroy was a persistent, rankling, irredeemable source of trouble for his captors.

The "punishment books" from the years of Jesse Pomeroy's confinement in Charlestown can be found today in the vaults of the Massachusetts State Archives in Boston. These enormous ledgers—fourteen in all—record the transgressions of each prisoner, along with the sanctions meted out (typically, a day or more locked up in the "strong room," a lightless isolation cell in the basement).

These bare-bones entries offer a revealing glimpse of the exceptionally strict discipline enforced at the penitentiary—of the harsh penalties imposed for even the most trivial reasons. Indeed, for the most part, the infractions noted in the books seem no more heinous than the misdemeanors of unruly highschoolers. In any given year, the average inmate might have committed one or two offenses, the most common of which were "disobeying orders," "insolence to officer," "refusing to work," "bad conduct in hall," "smoking in cell," "talking in cell," "singing in cell," "talking on line," "fooling in corridor," and "fighting in shop."

Jesse Pomeroy's record, however, is of a strikingly different order. A typical yearly entry for a prisoner in Charlestown, for example, reads as follows:

JOHN LOFTUS

DATE	OFFENSE
Jan 26, 1886	Disobedience
Mar 8	Laziness
May 5	Profanity
Oct 26	Not doing his work
Dec 1	Refusing to go to shop

By contrast, Jesse Pomeroy's entries from November 9, 1877, through 1912 are as follows:

<u>Date</u>	<u>Offense</u>
1877	
Nov 9	Trying to escape, digging through cement
Apr 18	Cutting bars in cell
1880	
Nov 2	Cutting iron work of cell
1887	
Sept. 4	Attempt to escape, cutting bars of cell door
Nov. 10	Causing gas to explode in cell
Dec. 26	Tampering with cell door
1888	
Jan 10	Digging in his room
May 29	Cutting cell door, having tools in his room
1891	
May 25	Cutting cell door
Aug 17	Attempting to escape, cutting bars in cell window
1892	
Aug 14	Cutting cell door
Aug 25	Cutting cell door
Oct 17	Attempting to escape
1894	
Jan 26	Digging bricks out of the wall of his cell
1895	
March 9	Cutting bar in cell window
July 25	Digging around cell window
1897	
Jan 6	Attempting to escape
Feb 8	Digging a hole in the floor of cell
1898	
Sept 6	Cutting cell door

_1899_
Feb 3   Cutting cell door
June 26   Cutting cell door

_1900_
Oct 26   Cutting iron work in cell; attempting to escape

_1904_
Aug 7   Digging around the water pipe in his cell

_1912_
Dec 30   Cutting bars in cell door

Cut-and-dried as they are, these notations serve as an eloquent testimony to one of Jesse Pomeroy's most remarkable qualities— the trait that kept him in the public spotlight throughout his lifetime, and that has earned him a special place in American penal history. For fifty years—with a persistence that was either insane or undaunted (depending on your point of view)—Pomeroy never gave up his efforts to dig, cut, detonate, or bore his way out of his cell. Even the _Boston Globe_—a paper that never failed to portray him in the most fiendish light imaginable—seemed perversely proud of the fact that, in the person of Jesse Pomeroy, New England had produced "the most ingenious . . . and utterly tireless worker for freedom who ever occupied a cell."

According to prison records, the first of Jesse's more than two-dozen jailbreak attempts occured in November 1877, slightly more than a year after he was first locked up in Charlestown. Patrolling the arch of the west wing—the section of the prison where Jesse was initially housed—a guard heard a faint scraping sound emanating from Pomeroy's cell. Throwing open the door, he found the prisoner kneeling by a wall, working away at one of the stones with a little digging tool made from a bit of wire. Apparently, Jesse had been engaged in this enterprise for months. When the guard took a closer look, he discovered that—by painstakingly removing the surrounding mortar, a grain at a time—Jesse had actually managed to loosen the stone.

Five months later, Jesse was caught sawing at the iron bars of his cell door with a piece of sharpened tin. For this attempt, he was shut up in the dark, nearly airless "strong room" for a week. But nothing—no amount of time locked in a dungeon, no beatings administered with a brass-tipped cane, no efforts at reinforcing his cell—discouraged Jesse for long. When plates of boiler-iron were bolted to his walls to keep him from digging at the stones, he set to work prying loose the bolts. When the walls were painted with a white preparation that would make even a pin-scratch conspicuous, he turned his attention to the floor, cutting loose one of the heavy boards, then digging at the ground underneath.

The singleminded tenacity Jesse displayed as a jailbreaker was matched by his mechanical ingenuity. Over the course of fifty years, virtually everything that fell into his hands became a potential implement of escape: eating utensils, drinking cups, writing implements, slop pails, bits of tin, wire, and string. When he was finally permitted a few hours of solitary exercise every week in a small, enclosed yard, he would scour the ground for anything useable—a rusty nail, a metal scrap, a piece of wood. With these and other objects (including the occasional knife blade or steel spike smuggled to him by a sympathetic fellow prisoner) he managed, over the decades, to fashion an amazing assortment of tools: awls, chisels, saws, drills, files, pry bars.

One of his most spectacular escape attempts occurred in November 1887, just two months after he was caught in an attempt to saw through the iron bars of his cell window. At around 1:00 P.M. on Thursday, November 10, an enormous explosion rocked the west wing of the prison. Revolvers drawn, guards rushed to the scene. Outside Jesse's cell, the corridor was thick with smoke, plaster dust, and the smell of escaping gas. Throwing open the door, they found Pomeroy crumpled in a corner, his face badly singed. A huge block of granite, dislodged from the ceiling, lay in the center of the floor—vivid testimony to the power of the blast.

Transported to the prison hospital, Pomeroy remained unconscious for nearly an hour until the physician, Dr. Charles Sawin, managed to revive him. Jesse's eyebows and eyelashes were entirely burned off and his lids badly swollen. Early reports declared that he had been "totally blinded," though he soon recovered the full use of his one good eye. Eventually, he supplied his captors with the full details of his latest and most audacious plan.

By that point in his sentence, Jesse was allowed to leave his cell for forty-five minutes of exercise three times a week. Always vigilant for anything he might turn to his advantage, he had noted that the dim gas-lights in the corridor were fed by a pipe that ran along the upper wall just outside his cell. Day by day for the next several months—working with nothing but a sharpened scrap of tin and infinite patience—he had dug a little opening through the mortar in his cell wall, concealing each day's progress with a paste made of soap. Eventually, he had broken through to the other side at a spot directly beside the gas pipe. Then, with a piece of wire sharpened to a fine point, he had bored a little hole in the pipe, releasing the gas through the opening in the wall and into his cell. Working quickly, he had taken a makeshift length of tubing, constructed of water-soaked newspapers mixed with bread, and piped the gas to another portion of the cell, where he had loosened several blocks after months of painstaking toil. His idea was to feed the gas through the crevices he had created in the stonework and blast a hole in the wall.

In the end, this elaborate—if wildly ill-conceived—scheme had no other effect than to injure Jesse, damage the floor of the prison hospital (located directly above his cell), and trigger a fresh burst of public outrage. Jesse's jailbreak attempt—his second in as many months—was reported in newspapers throughout the country, though it created the greatest sensation, of course, in Massachusetts. One Boston man voiced a common sentiment when, in a letter to the *Herald*, he expressed his "regret that the 'boy fiend' didn't get his body through the wall so that the keeper might have had an excuse to shoot him and forever rid the world of him."

This letter is striking for several reasons. It reveals not only the deep, abiding antipathy toward Pomeroy among the citizenry of Boston, but also the extent to which he had achieved a kind of mythic status. In the perception of the public, Jesse Pomeroy was still—and would remain for many years—the monstrous "boy fiend." (Indeed, several generations of New England children would grow up hearing bedtime spook-stories about this legendary, juvenile bogeyman.)

In reality, of course, Pomeroy was far from a boy. In November 1887, when this letter was written, he had been locked in solitary confinement for more than a decade and was already twenty-eight years old.

43

There can be no doubt that the most interesting convict in the Commonwealth of Massachusetts, if not the whole country, is JESSE HARDING POMEROY. He is the only convict in the United States who is absolutely consigned to a cage, and who is looked upon by the community as a veritable fiend.
—E. Luscomb Haskell, *The Life of Jesse Harding Pomeroy* (1892)

By 1892—following the renovation of Charlestown—Jesse was inhabiting a larger (if equally cheerless) cell in a section of the prison known as "Cherry Hill." He was no longer engaged in making scrub brushes—or in any other task, for that matter. All such menial labor, he claimed, was injurious to his health and therefore a violation of his constitutional rights. Since Jesse was in the habit of squirreling away little bits and pieces of his work material and using them in his endless escape attempts, the prison officials had no objection to relieving him of his duties.

With nothing but time on his hands, he devoted himself to other activities. With supplies provided by the chaplain, he tried his hand at painting, producing mawkish watercolor landscapes that he regarded as significant works of art, though at least one observer found them "hardly worth admiring." Always mechanically inclined, he conceived of a hollow, self-sharpening lead pencil, but his efforts to construct a workable prototype came to nothing. Most of all, he spent his time reading. Since sensationalistic novels were in short supply in the prison library, he was forced to make do with more uplifting material—books on science, mathematics, language, chemistry, and religion. According to various sources, by the time he left prison, Jesse had gone through all four thousand books in the library, along with an indeterminate number of volumes supplied by the chaplain.

Though reports of his intellectual accomplishments would be greatly exaggerated (for years, stories would circulate that Jesse had proved to be a jailhouse genius, who achieved proficiency in Hebrew, Greek, and Latin, taught himself geometry, algebra, and calculus, and became an expert on classical literature), he did, in fact, pick up a smattering of knowledge in several fields and gained enough mastery of several languages, particularly German, to be able to read them with a fair degree of fluency. (He was never able to speak them, since—deprived of virtually all human communication—he had no way of learning the correct pronunciation.)

He also put in a good deal of time studying law books.

As far back as 1876, when he composed his autobiography while languishing in the Suffolk County jail, Jesse had shown a certain knack for legalistic argument. Now, after immersing himself in every law book he could get his hands on, he acquired just enough knowledge of the subject to turn himself into a source of endless annoyance—an incorrigible gadfly. Next to his improvised drills, saws, and chisels, Jesse's pen became his primary tool for making life as difficult as possible for his keepers.

For fully half a century, he generated hundreds of letters, writing to everyone from district attorneys to members of the prison board to justices of the United States Supreme Court (including Oliver Wendell Holmes). Jesse's term in Charlestown would span the administrations of no less than twenty-two Massachusetts governors—and every one of them was bombarded with correspondence from Pomeroy. Many of these letters registered various complaints. Like other psychopaths—who tend to be full of self-pity, however incapable they are of feeling bad for their victims—Jesse constantly felt ill-treated by his jailers. In letter after letter, he griped about everything from the poor light in his cell to his lack of holiday privileges to the deplorable condition of his toothbrush.

Other letters were, in effect, fairly sophisticated legal briefs. In 1888, for example, while poring over some old law books, he discovered (as the *New York Times* reported) "an old statute which provided that no person should be sentenced to solitary confinement in a prison for a period of more than twenty days." Jesse immediately began petitioning for his release from solitary. Dozens of these letters still exist in various archives. The following, dated October 14, 1888, is a typical example. Addressed to Henry B. Pierce, Secretary of State of Massachusetts, it was written on lined, monogrammed notepaper and penned in the neat, even elegant handwriting that Jesse had by then developed:

Sir,

Certain laws, records, etc., necessary to my right of self-defense, and necessary to properly present the same are on file in your office, and I understand that the law permits me copies of them.

Within is an expression of my wants and I declare that I believe them to be necessary to me as above stated. I ask of your courtesy such a fulfillment, certified under your seal as the laws permit.

I ask,

1. A copy of the revised statutes of this state in force in 1874.

2. A copy of the acts and resolves of the Legislature in 1874.

3. Literal copies of all the laws passed by our Legislature at any time, which regulate the punishment of close or solitary imprisonment or confinement, provided it is a punishment for crime.

4. If this request is too vague and causes too much trouble, please give me only what was the law on the subject in 1806. 1845. 1855. 1874.

5. Literal copies from the record of the Governors Council of all entries therein showing executive action in any way upon my case, from March 1875 to Sept. 1st, 1876.

Please observe, I want records of executive action only: nothing about trials, indictments, etc.

6. Literal copies from the records of the Council from 1780 to 1875 inclusive, showing commutations to the penalty of solitary or close imprisonment or confinement with—or without— hard labor: and pardons or commutations of those penalties.

I declare these last two requests to be absolutely necessary to me to be granted, and I ask that all papers embraced in the 6th request be certified under seal, because I intend to lay them before the Supreme Court.

I can assure you, Mr. Secretary, that my need is great and is my only excuse for so much asked for.

> *Very respectfully,*
> *Jesse H. Pomeroy*

Thanks to this and scores of similar letters, Jesse eventually earned a reputation not only as a scholar of classical languages, literature, and mathematical knowledge but also as a self-educated lawyer—a man who (as the *Boston Globe* put it) "had developed legal qualifications not possessed by some applicants for admission to the bar."

Between his jailbreak attempts and legal maneuverings, Jesse managed to maintain his notoriety as the century drew to a close. In 1892, a full-length true-crime book—E. Luscomb Haskell's *The Life of Jesse Harding Pomeroy*—became a popular seller, confirming the public's ongoing fascination with the case. Two years later, when a writer for the *Boston Globe* managed to interview Jesse, the story created a sensation.

Exactly how he finagled the interview isn't clear, but on the afternoon of Thursday, June 2, 1892, the unnamed reporter— who was visiting Charlestown on unrelated business—talked his way into Pomeroy's cell, where he held a thirty-minute talk with the "world's criminal of criminals" under the watchful eye of a guard. At that time, Jesse was forty-two years old: a compact, square-shouldered man of medium height, dressed in the usual convict garb—trousers, shirt, and jacket, all of coarse gray wool. His hair was receding, he wore a walrus moustache, and his deformed right eye—whose pale, filmy surface looked to the reporter "like a white cloud in a bleared window"—had lost none of its deeply unsettling power.

Jesse—who hadn't spoken to a stranger in thirty-six years— seemed extremely ill at ease at first. Perched on the edge of his table, he chewed on a corner of his droopy moustache and refused to say a word. Finally—when the reporter asked whether he had any complaints—Pomeroy twisted his mouth into a snarl and replied, "I don't complain. It does no good." Then, shooting a murderous look at the hovering guard, he added: "They don't make my life any too pleasant to bear, and to tell anyone about it only makes it worse."

In spite of this remark, however, Jesse's comments to the reporter consisted largely of complaints. He grumbled about the poor light in his cell, which made it hard for him to read; about the confiscation of the Christmas "goodies" sent by his mother; about the lack of sufficient exercise. When the reporter asked about food, Jesse barked a laugh. It didn't seem right to complain, he replied, since he had gotten "fat as a pig" in prison (indeed, as the journalist noted, the former "boy murderer" had grown into a distinctly paunchy adult). Still, though he was given "plenty of food to eat," its flavor and variety left a lot to be desired—though he supposed that the unappetizing sameness of his meals was "part of the punishment."

When the guard signaled an end to the interview, the reporter rose from his chair and asked Jesse if he had anything more to say. At first, Pomeroy merely shook his head. Then—fixing the reporter a look of "fierce" determination—he declared that he still planned to get out of prison someday. By one means or another.

Following the interview, the reporter spoke to several of the officers, gleaning additional facts about the prisoner. He discovered that—though Jesse had read many of the books in the library, some more than once—the Bible wasn't among his favorites. Indeed, on one occasion, a guard heard such uproarious laughter coming from Jesse's cell that he went to the door to see what so funny. He found Pomeroy reading the Bible with a broad, jeering grin, "as much as to say, 'I don't believe a word of it.'" Even the prison chaplain—a man of such sweet disposition that he was beloved by virtually all the inmates—had become so put off by Jesse's flagrant disdain of religion that he seldom visited Pomeroy's cell anymore.

The reporter also learned that, at one point, Jesse had taken up the "mouth-harp." Unfortunately, the only song he had learned was "Home, Sweet Home," a tune he played so often that the guards were nearly driven crazy. Finally, they decided to confiscate the instrument. When they entered his cell, however, they discovered that Jesse had already taken the harmonica apart and made one of the metal pieces into a little saw.

As for his escape attempts, the guards didn't take them very seriously, regarding them as little more than Jesse's way of causing "deviltry." He would never make it out of the prison. Even if he managed to break out of his cell, he wouldn't get far—"for the orders are that he shall be shot without hesitation if he once gets into the yard."

44

Jesse Pomeroy, the boy-murderer of 20 years ago, the fiend whose crimes were even more revolting than those of Jack the Ripper, and whose name has always brought to mind all that is repulsive, blood-curdling, and inhuman, has evidently not given up hope that some day he may escape from the Charlestown State Prison.

—*The Boston Globe*, September 29, 1893

Until the day he finally reemerged, Lazarus-like, from his vault, Pomeroy continued to make so many attempts at breaking free that only the most spectacular were reported in the press.

On January 8, 1897, for example, the *Boston Globe* ran a front-page story headlined "JESSE POMEROY AGAIN TRIES TO ES-CAPE. Only 24 Inches Between the Prisoner and His Freedom." The previous Wednesday, a prison guard named Eugene Allen—peering into Pomeroy's cell through the little slot in the outer door—had seen him pacing nervously around the floor. There was something so odd about Jesse's overwrought manner that Allen immediately ordered him out of the cell, removed its bare-bones furnishings, and began to conduct an inch-by-inch search.

After satisfying himself that the white-coated walls had not been tampered with, Allen turned his attention to the floor. Armed with a case knife, he inspected every crack in the wooden boards, beginning at the threshold and working his way back across the cell. He was about two feet away from the rear wall when the blade of his knife suddenly slipped through an appar-ent joint in the flooring. Frowning, Allen took a closer look—then let out a little grunt of surprise. What he'd taken for two boards connected by a joint was actually a single board that had somehow been cut in half.

Using his knife blade, he pried the two sections from the floor and immediately discovered that several adjacent boards had been cut in an identical manner. By the time he'd removed all the loosened pieces, there was a substantial hole in the floor. Fetching a candle, Allen peered down into the cavity, and—to his astonishment—discovered that Jesse had actually managed to cut through a joist that ran beneath the floorboards and re-move a half-dozen bricks from the outer wall of the cell by chip-ping away the mortar.

Interrogated by Warden Bridges, Jesse freely—even proudly—revealed the details of his latest scheme. For more than six months, he had "worked like a mole." Every night, he would re-move the loosened boards, and—reaching one arm down into the hole—peck away at the joist with an awl he had fashioned from a stout piece of wire pried from the rim of his water pail. Laboring with what the *Globe* described as "almost inconceivable pa-tience," he had finally managed to remove a section of the joist, then excavate the bricks until he had made a ten-by-twelve-inch opening in the outer wall . "To get through," reported the *Globe*, "was only a question of time. Had he been allowed to dig for 24 inches further, he would have breathed the air of . . . freedom."

The discovery of this audacious plan created an uproar. The night guard in charge of "Cherry Hill" was immediately sus-pended by the outraged warden, who told reporters that "he did not see how a convict could have worked for so many months without being detected. The boring and the scratching ought to have been easily heard." Jesse himself, Bridges declared, had been treated with entirely too much leniency. He had been shown "every consideration" by his keepers and displayed nothing but "traits of ingratitude" in return.

"Hereafter," the warden vowed, "he will be placed under the closest surveillance, and his treatment will be of the most rigid sort."

Still, no one seriously expected Pomeroy to abandon his des-perate bids for freedom. As the *Globe* predicted, "It is safe to say that he will proceed to make another attempt as earnestly and with as great a will as he has in the past."

In the following years, that prediction was fulfilled again and again. Shortly after midnight on Sunday, August 7, 1904, for ex-ample, a night officer named Charles Jorandorf heard a suspi-cious sound emanating from Pomeroy's cell. Throwing open the door, he found Jesse crouched in a corner, chipping at the wall with a knife blade. Five years later, in October 1909, another officer, L. F. Burk—suspecting that Jesse was up to more mischief—summoned a colleague named Wood. As the two men entered Jesse's cell, the startled prisoner popped something in his mouth and made for the toilet bowl. Before he could reach it, Burk and Wood wrestled him to the ground, forced his jaws apart, and extracted a small, chisel-shaped implement from his mouth. Another homemade tool turned up in August 1911, when an officer named Willard Davis—having reason to believe that Pomeroy was in possession of contraband material—frisked the prisoner and discovered a crude, eight-and-a-half-inch steel drill concealed inside his coat sleeve.

Except for the gas explosion episode of 1887, none of these escape attempts amounted to much. In 1912, however, Jesse actually managed to make it out of his cell.

It happened on the last day of the year. At around 2:30 A.M. on Monday, December 31, a guard named Thomas Brassil was patrolling the solitary wing. Aside from the usual sounds of sleeping men—a cough, snore, an occasional moan—there were no noises issuing from the cells. So eerily silent was the corridor that Brassil's footsteps echoed audibly as he made his early-morning rounds.

A wooden armchair, used by the guards, stood at one end of the corridor. As Brassil passed it, he saw the prison mascot—a yellow cat named Buster—curled up on the seat. Brassil continued on his rounds. He was about to turn the corner and pass into the adjacent wing, when Buster—tail bristling, paws scrabbling on the concrete—came racing past him and vanished into the shadows ahead. Something had evidently startled the cat awake.

Puzzled, Brassil retraced his steps—then froze in surprise. Someone was crouched against the wall beside the chair. Though the man's face was obscured by shadow, Brassil could see that he was dressed in the coarse garb of a convict. Drawing his revolver, the guard ordered the prisoner to "throw up his hands" and come out into the light. After a momentary pause, the man slowly rose to his feet, hands raised, and took a step forward. To his amazement, Brassil saw that it was Jesse Pomeroy. He immediately spotted something else, too—a large screwdriver clutched in Pomeroy's right hand.

"Drop it," Brassil barked, motioning his pistol at the implement. When Jesse hesitated, Brassil sprang forward, shoved the barrel of his gun into Pomeroy's belly, and tried wresting the tool from his grasp. A brief tussle ensued, during which the guard sustained a few scratches on his left hand. In the end, however, he managed to secure the screwdriver. Then he marched Jesse into a holding cell and summoned the warden.

At first, Jesse sullenly refused to explain how he'd escaped from his seemingly impregnable cell. Eventually, however, the full story emerged. Using an improvised saw, he had managed to remove three bars from the bottom of his steel door. It had taken him three solid years of stealthy, nocturnal labor to get the job done. Worming his way through the hole, he had opened the outer wooden door by sticking his arm through the food slot and using the saw to work the iron bolt from its socket.

To fool any guard who peered into his cell, Jesse had resorted to the time-honored ruse of the prison escapee, creating a dummy out of an old carton and a bunch of newspapers, then arranging the bedclothes over it to make it appear as if he were sleeping peacefully on his cot.

His plan, once he broke out of his cell, was a little hazy. He apparently intended to sabotage the electric box controlling the lights in the solitary wing, plunging "Cherry Hill" into utter darkness and permitting him to escape in the confusion. In any event, his plan had come to nothing—thanks largely (as the newspapers told it) to the heroic vigilance of Buster, who gained instant celebrity as "The Cat Who Foiled Jesse Pomeroy."

Following this latest failure, Jesse seemed genuinely deflated. He told Warden Bridges that he "had given up the idea of making any more attempts to escape," and vowed to become "a model prisoner." Besides, Jesse added, even if he *did* get out of prison," he "would not know what to do or where to go." He had known freedom for only thirteen years of his life. And on December 31, 1912—the day Buster the cat became a local hero—Jesse Pomeroy had just turned fifty-two.

45

The great state which gave the lyceum its birth and its first real purpose, the state which wept over the sins of black slavery in the South, the state which morally gagged every time the word "bondage" was mentioned, has for forty years maintained a worse form of slavery than ever existed in South Carolina.

—Fred High, *Prison Problems*

On June 28, 1914—just a few months before the thirty-eighth anniversary of Jesse's incarceration in Charlestown—a bullet fired by a young Serbian nationalist set off a conflagration that would engulf the world and create unimaginable desolation and suffering. From all available evidence, however, it appears that the start of the Great War made little or no impact on Jesse's awareness. Not one of the many letters he wrote during the following year contains even a single reference to it. For him, the world was a nine-by-sixteen-foot cell, and the only suffering that mattered was his own.

Though he stuck to his pledge to forego any further escape attempts, he continued to churn out a steady stream of petitions, appeals, and complaints. On September 5, 1914, for example, he sent a letter to Frank L. Randall, chairman of the Massacusetts Prison Commission. As a mere boy of fourteen, Jesse wrote, he had been condemned to a sentence of "unmeasured inhumanity—'Solitary imprisonment at hard labor for life'—and in these almost 40 yrs. since, nothing has been done to uplift this life, to hold before me any incentive, inducement, or privilege which might tend to bring me upon the road of reformation, to be a law-abiding citizen. I have been left to my own devices, and you will not find another 14 yr. old boy in that condition."

Far from seeking to rehabilitate him, Jesse charged, the state had engaged in an active campaign to demonize him as a way of justifying the "unheard-of sentence." "If half the effort which is made to distort the truth about me should be made to do something in my behalf," he averred, "a great change and improvement would follow." Urging the chairman to help him "in my effort to be something more than a degenerate (which I am not)," Jesse concluded by praying that "there may be for this friendless prisoner something beyond perpetual hard labor in solitary, pointing out that there are limits to human endurance, even if I have been outside the pale of human sympathy to this date."

In point of fact, Jesse was not completely "beyond the pale of human sympathy." By 1914, his situation had attracted the attention of various individuals, who agreed that—by condemning him to a lifetime in solitary—the Commonwealth of Massachusetts had committed an act of "unmeasured inhumanity."

Besides his mother, Jesse's most ardent supporter was a Chicago man named Fred High, publisher of a magazine called *The Platform*. In 1913, High brought out a volume called *Prison Problems*, an anthology of essays and poems whose high-minded purpose, as expressed in its preface, was to rouse public sentiment against the "barbarism of the present penal system . . . so that our penitentiaries shall cease to be criminal factories and become reform institutions." High saw himself as a stalwart Christian reformer, one of the "soldiers of the common good" who were doing "our little mite towards bringing about a better day . . . for our fellows who have stumbled on the rough journey and have stepped aside from the straight and narrow path."

As it happened, he was also a deep-dyed bigot and anti-Semite. In an April 1914 letter to the chairman of the Massacusetts Prison Commission, High compared Pomeroy's situation to that of Leo Frank—the Jewish factory superintendent wrongfully accused of the murder of a thirteen-year-old girl named Mary Phagan in Atlanta, Georgia, in 1913. Frank's conviction was widely denounced as a flagrant case of homegrown anti-Semitism—"the American counterpart of the Dreyfus affair" (as the *Baltimore Sun* put it). To High, however, Frank's defenders were nothing but a "great army of Jews trying to save the neck of a Jew." By contrast, he insisted, poor, friendless Jesse Pomeroy remained locked up in prison simply because he "does not happen to be Jewish, Irish, Geman, or any other nation that sticks up for their own."

High's most impassioned defense of Pomeroy appeared in the volume *Prison Problems.* The essay (the only one in the anthology written by High himself) begins with a bitter denunciation of the state of Massachusetts and, more specifically, of the Charlestown penitentiary. "The New Orleans slave market which stirred the soul of Abraham Lincoln to righteous wrath," wrote High, "was an altar of justice as compared to the den of gloom where this human being, made in the image of his Creator, has been confined for forty long years. To me, Simon Legree was a merciful benefactor as compared to Warden Russell, who for twenty-one years has carried out the blind verdict of a jury, perhaps long since dead."

The crux of High's argument was that there was no defensible reason for subjecting Pomeroy to such punishment. "There are only two conclusions that a thinking mind can arrive at," High declared. "First, this man, Jesse Pomeroy, is a degenerate, unsound of reason, with defective mental and moral faculties. If this is true, he should have had medical treatment, he should have been in a hospital, had fresh air, God's sunshine, a mother's love in more constant potions. . . . Shame on the state! Thrice shame on the officials if Jesse Pomeroy is as described!"

The second possibility was that Jesse "is sane, fully equipped, mentally." But "if so," then hadn't he "suffered enough for the crimes he is supposed to have committed forty years ago? Why shouldn't he have at least the freedom of the penitentiary the same as an ordinary criminal? Why is he even denied the privilege of attending the concerts? Even the religious services . . . are for the others but not for him. Surely he has suffered enough to merit his release."

To stir the indignation of his readers, High reprinted a long, piteous letter sent to him by Jesse's mother. By then, Ruth Pomeroy was a feeble, ailing woman in her early seventies who had spent the better part of her life in an unavailing effort to persuade the world of her son's innocence. The past forty years had done nothing to change her feelings about Jesse. "I have never believed my son guilty of these crimes, NEVER!," she proclaimed. Her son, she insisted, had been a "happy and bright boy" who was railroaded for a murder he did not commit because the South Boston police were under intense pressure to make an arrest in the Millen case, and Jesse—having just been released from reform school and being a "stranger in the neighborhood"—made a convenient scapegoat.

"Jesse was only a boy of a little over fifteen years when he went to Charlestown State Prison," Mrs. Pomeroy continued. "In his solitude he put himself down to study and has succeeded in educating himself. . . . He is a learned man and could do a great deal of good if out. He has already served a lifetime and ought to come home, but you see the people do not know the real 'Jesse Pomeroy.' No one gets to see him and he is friendless with the exception of his mother. I can do but little; I am old, over seventy, and I feel my time is short here, but through all these years I have cherished the hope that before I passed away I might have my son with me once more. . . . Thank you for your kindness and hope and pray you may be able to do something for my son."

High concluded his essay with a heartfelt appeal (plus a dash of racist rhetoric). After leveling a few final insults at the state of Massachusetts (which had "tried for forty years to crush, torture, and brutalize Jesse H. Pomeroy"), Warden Russell of Charlestown ("this Simon Legree of cultured Boston"), and Governor Eugene Foss (a political "turncoat" and "flip-flopper" who was no better than Pontius Pilate), High urged his readers to do all they could "to prevent this disgrace from becoming a greater monstrosity and travesty of justice":

> Why can't we try kindness, love, and patience, abolish brutality and barbarity, and see if Jesse H. Pomeroy is not a man who will respond to humane appeals? Who knows but that he may even yet take his place in the world of usefulness to comfort and cheer his faithful old mother who has stood by him through all these years, faithful and true; watching, waiting, working, and hoping against hope that her boy will yet be given back to her. . . . Do the guards, officials, and whatnots of the Massachusetts penitentiary and the yellow journals know the same Jesse Pomeroy that the faithful mother describes? How can they? You might as well hand the score of a symphony orchestra to a band of Hottentots and ask them to bring forth the same soul vibrations that were born in the brain of Mendelssohn.

As 1914 progressed, Jesse's written appeals began to fall on more receptive ears. In March of that year, for example, he was finally permitted to file a formal petition with the governor and executive council, requesting a "pardon of my said offense and a release from further imprisonment on said sentence, either absolute or upon such conditions and under such limitations as the Governor deems proper."

Jesse's petition was based on the same highly dubious argument he had been making since 1876—namely, that his conviction of "murder in the first degree on the ground of atrocity" was illegal, since the prosecution had failed to prove that there was anything truly atrocious about the Millen murder. In light of the cruelties inflicted on the four-year-old boy—whose throat had been slashed, right eyeball punctured, and scrotum torn open—this assertion seems outrageous at best. Jesse's reasoning—which reveals a great deal about his complete inability to comprehend the enormity of his crimes, even after a span of forty years—was that the victim was already unconscious (and possibly dead) by the time he had been gashed, sliced, and nearly castrated. "Hence," Pomeroy concluded, "no torture, no aggravating circumstances."

Needless to say, this argument didn't carry much weight with Governor Foss and his councillors. Far more compelling was Jesse's assertion that, after thirty-eight years of solitary confinement, "the ends of justice have been obtained." Indeed, the sheer, inhuman length of Jesse's immurement had become the most politically charged and controversial aspect of his case. Even those who recalled, with undiminished horror, the "boy fiend's" reign of terror felt that it was time "to give Pomeroy a little freedom—a little of God's pure air and sunshine" (as one petitioner, a man named Levi Parker, urged the governor).

In the spring of 1914, responding to growing public pressure, Governor Foss appointed a commission of four medical experts to examine Pomeroy and ascertain whether, in their opinion, "the severity of his solitary condition" might be eased. Their final report, issued on July 14, 1914, constitutes the most complete description of Pomeroy's psychology on record and is therefore worth quoting at length.

The report begins with a survey of Jesse's criminal history and childhood background, then continues with a brief but telling summary of his prison experiences:

Although living in solitary confinement all these years, Pomeroy has been far from idle. From the first he has been a constant reader and student and claims to have taught himself to read books in several foreign languages including Arabic. He has also spent much of his time in tireless and incessant efforts to make his escape from prison, beginning shortly after his commitment. Besides making ten or twelve determined attempts to break out which were thwarted as he was putting them into execution, tools and other cleverly devised implements have been repeatedly found in his possession. . . . A fellow prisoner reports that he seems to have a mania for anything that will cut or bore. This has been the extent of his manual labor for he has repeatedly refused to take up any of the various kinds of prison work or even to exercise regularly in the prison yard. . . .

His main employment is his determined and unremitting effort to prove that he was illegally sentenced, in order to secure pardon or discharge from custody. This is his aim in life. He has made a study of his case with the aid of law books furnished him. . . . He has written many hundreds of pages setting forth his defense which has been sent to various courts (including the United States Supreme Court), to the Secretary of State, and to His Excellency the Governor and numerous lawyers. His applications have been invariably denied and he has received no encouragement from legal sources whatever. Nevertheless, he persists in his appeals . . . and will not deny that he intends to urge his claims until he obtains his freedom.

Throughout his prison life he has been uniformly insensible to personal interest taken in him by others. . . . He takes kindnesses as a matter of course, is highly egotistical and inclined to dictate to prison authorities. His only interest in his mother is the aid she can give him in securing his release. He shows no pleasure at seeing her but begins on his case as soon as she comes and talks of nothing else. He is very unreliable on account of his untruthfulness. He thinks everyone is against him and apparently never loses his suspicions for a moment.

Turning to Pomeroy's mental condition, the physicians agreed that the prisoner was an "extreme example" of "a moral degenerate." Possessed of "sharp wits," a "good memory," and

"a desire to improve his mind," Jesse had "no delusions whatever, the nearest approach to one being his fixed obsession that
he was illegally convicted, a common one with long-sentence
convicts." He possessed a "knowledge of right and wrong in the
abstract," had acquired an impressive "knowledge of criminal
law," and had "shown indefatigable energy and considerable
ability to utilize legal points." In short, in terms of his reasoning
abilities and "intellectual capacity," Pomeroy seemed perfectly
normal, even above-average.

"On the other hand," the experts cautioned, he was "unquestionably defective on the moral side to a degree which . . . was
plainly extreme and much more pronounced than in the ordinary criminal. The unusual, atrocious, and cruel nature of his
criminal acts, his pursuit of crime for crime's sake only, . . . his
utter insensibility to suffering, and his gratification in torturing
his victims 'for the same reason that a cat does a mouse before
killing it' . . . are typical of the moral defective, and when taken
as a whole are far different from the motives and conduct of the
ordinary malefactor." Jesse, in short, was a classic case of what
later criminologists would call a sociopath: a terrifyingly depraved individual whose superior cunning and rationality were
linked to—and deployed in the service of—an utterly remorse-
less, sadistic, and bloodthirsty nature.

In the final section of the report—labeled "Prognosis"—the
authors made it clear that the vicious propensities of "moral de-
generates" like Pomeroy could never be fully controlled, let
alone eliminated. Once past a certain age, such beings were
utterly immune to rehabilitaton. "To properly safeguard the
community," they declared, "close and continual custody is absolutely necessary." There was no doubt in their minds that "if at
large, [Pomeroy] would still be a menace to society in spite of his
thirty-seven and a half years of solitary confinement." That Jesse
had not committed any atrocities since 1874 was a result of only
one factor—"lack of opportunity."

The doctors concluded with a cautious, carefully hedged recommendation that indicated just how dangerous they still considered the fifty-five-year-old prisoner to be. "We are of the
opinion," they wrote, "that some amelioration of the prisoner's
solitary confinement would be advantageous and that he might
be allowed certain of the privileges that are enjoyed by other life-

prisoners *provided absolutely effective measures be taken to prevent his escape.* If he could be induced to take up regular employment and if his yard-privileges could be extended—always under adequate supervision—life would be less irksome to him and possibly his mind might be diverted from his obsession with escaping and from continual legal contention about his rights. We should regard it, however, as a hazardous experiment in view of the fact that this besetting determination of his, which has been growing in strength ever since his commitment, has become a habit of mind and calls for the exercise of the utmost precaution."

46

I am glad of this opportunity to show the world that I can behave myself because it may lead to further consideration and possibly a pardon. I know people think I am some sort of an animal thirsting for blood. I know that they think I will pounce on the first living thing I see, human or animal, and try to kill it. I have a normal mind. I am not deranged. I will prove it to you all.

—Jesse Pomeroy, January 24, 1917

Ruth Pomeroy's feeling that—as she wrote to Fred High—"my time is short here" was not so much a premonition as an accurate appraisal of her condition. Always a tough and hard-working woman, she had been the proprietress of a lunchroom at 489 Neposet Avenue, near the terminal of the Bay State and Boston Elevated car lines, for many years. But a severe bout of double pneumonia in 1909 had shattered her health and forced her to close her business. Since that time, she had been residing in the home of her married granddaughter, Mrs. Walter Giddens, at 47 Pearl Street in the town of North Weymouth, Massachusetts.

By the late fall of 1914, Ruth had become so weak that—for the first time in nearly forty years—she was unable to make her monthly visit to Jesse. A few months later, during the first week of January, she was again stricken with pneumonia. "Aged and weakened with sorrow," as the *Boston Globe* would report, "she could not fight the disease."

On the afternoon of January 10, 1915, Ruth Pomeroy died in her sleep, without having realized her most "cherished hope"—that "before I passed away I might have my son with me once more."

Even with his most ardent champion gone, the pressure to alleviate Jesse's condition became more intense as 1916 approached. September 7 of that year would mark the fortieth anniversary of his incarceration in Charlestown—a grim milestone not only for Pomeroy but for the Commonwealth of Massachusetts as well. Never before in U.S. penal history had a human being been subjected to such a torturous stretch of solitary confinement.

True, there were some people who continued to protest any mitigation of his sentence. Interviewed by the *Boston Post,* James Bragdon—the former police officer who, in 1872, had collared Jesse for the series of child-assaults that had terrorized South Boston—declared that he would be "sorry to see" Pomeroy given any sort of liberty. "The mania which caused him to cut little children will never leave him," said Bragdon, now a frail and wizened seventy-year-old, "and he will not be safe, even in a jail ward with men. No one will ever convince me that he will ever be normal or safe, and I think he should be kept in solitary confinement to the end of his days."

For the most part, however, there was a growing clamor throughout the country for a commutation of Jesse's sentence. In California, for example, an editorialist in the *Los Angeles Times*— noting with horror that Pomeroy was about to observe his fortieth year in solitary confinement ("in other words, his fortieth year spent in hell")—exclaimed: "It does not seem possible that this is true. It appalls the soul to think of it. And in Massachusetts, above all places. Massachusetts, with its boasted intellectuality, its schools, its churches, its learnings, and the sacred codfish whirling in the winds of heaven on the spire of the old State House in Boston!"

The Literary Digest, in its February 19, 1916, issue, equated Jesse's forty-year immurement with the "barbarity [of] the Dark Ages" and reprinted an editorial from the *Kansas City Star* that vividly evoked Jesse's appalling isolation from the world of the living:

> Ever since the year of the Centennial Exhibition in Philadelphia, Pomeroy has lived within those stone walls, never walking out into the sunshine, never speaking to any one, never seeing a person from the outside world, except his mother, who has faithfully visited him once every two months. Within one hunded yards of

his cell, the human tide of the great city of Boston has ebbed and flowed for nearly half a century, but he has never heard even a footfall of it. Mule-cars have given way to trolleys and the underground tubes; the telephone has come into general use, but he has never seen one.

The judge who tried him, the attorney general and district attorney who prosecuted him, the lawyer who defended him, the governor who spared his life and gave him a living death instead, all died years ago; he has survived nearly all who knew him. His keepers say he has read every one of the eight thousand books in the prison library, that he reads French, German, Greek, Latin, Spanish, Italian, and Arabic, and that he is a superior mathematician, having educated himself, but that in all the forty years his face has never been seen to lighten with a smile.

Responding to this growing outcry, Governor Samuel McCall appointed a three-man committee to interview Pomeroy at Charlestown. Their visit took place on December 8, 1916. Arriving at the prison at around 2:45 P.M., they found Jesse enjoying his daily, fifty-minute walk in the prison yard under the scrutiny of an armed guard. He was escorted to an office in the Cherry Hill section, where the committee members—Councillors Richard F. Andrews and Timothy J. Buckley of Boston and Henry C. Mulligan of Natick—conferred with him for more than two hours.

Though Jesse's attorney, Edwin J. Weiscopf, was also present at the meeting, it was Pomeroy himself who did most of the talking. Pleading with "all the eloquence of an able lawyer" (as one newspaper reported), he asked that he be granted, if not a full pardon, then at the very least "equal privileges with other inmates of the institution." He requested that the "solitary features of his sentence be eliminated"; that a window be cut into the rear wall of his cell so that he could "get just a few more stray beams of God's sunshine"; that the heavy oaken door that shielded him from view be removed; that he be allowed to participate in religious services and holiday entertainments, play ball, and mingle with the other men in the yard during exercise. He made it clear, however, that—though he wished to be treated like the rest of the prisoners in all other ways—he drew the line at work. After so many years of idleness, he explained, he did not care to be employed in the prison shops. Instead, he "preferred to devote his time to reading and studying."

To demonstrate that he had put his long incarceration to good use, Jesse gave a display of his shorthand technique (another skill he had mastered during his endless hours of solitary) and demonstrated his linguistic abilities. At the end of the meeting, he was informed that—though they "could hold out absolutely no hope for his pardon"—the councillors would "report favorably on his request for greater liberties."

The following month, on January 17, 1917, while speaking before the Elms Hill Council, Knights of Columbus, in the Columbus Club of Dorchester, District Attorney Joseph C. Pelletier declared that—though he was against any form of pardon for Pomeroy—he supported "such commutation as would take him out of solitary."

Exactly one week later, on the afternoon of Wednesday, January 24, the Governor's special committee made a formal recommendation of clemency. That same evening, Governor McCall—acting "with the advice and consent of the Council"—signed an official order, commuting Jesse's sentence from life in solitary to straight life imprisonment.

As one observer noted, Jesse's four decades of "almost unbroken solitude" had been a punishment of epical proportions, "surpassing by several months the forty-year period during which the children of Israel were condemned to wander in the wilderness." If a full pardon represented Jesse's Promised Land, then—like Moses—he would never achieve his goal. Still, the fifty-seven-year-old prisoner had at least been granted a certain measure of freedom.

The commutation made headlines throughout New England and beyond. Every paper in Boston ran a front-page story on McCall's action: "FREES JESSE POMEROY FROM SOLITARY CELL AT THE STATE PRISON" (the *Herald*); "POMEROY'S LONG TERM OF SOLITARY ENDED" (the *Post*); "POMEROY GRANTED GREATER FREEDOM" (the *Globe*). Even the *New York Times* took note of the story, running a piece headlined: "BAY STATE SOFTENS POMEROY'S PUNISHMENT. Removes

Famous Prisoner After 40 Years From Solitary Confinement to Ordinary Cell."

Public reaction to the commutation was decidedly mixed. In the days immediately following McCall's decision, his office was flooded with letters and telegrams, some of which roundly condemned him. One writer accused him of exposing the general prison population to a "bloodthirsty animal" who was likely to "tear his fellow prisoners to pieces"; while another, with heavy-handed sarcasm, suggested that—since the governor and council were so intent on coddling Pomeroy—they might as well give him "a cradle and a nursing bottle."

Most correspondents, however, praised the governor. His action (in the words of one South Boston man) had effaced a "terrible blot on the fair name of Massachusetts." Indeed, a number of people urged McCall to go even further and set Pomeroy free. In a gesture that was widely reported in the press, one prominent Back Bay woman made it known that—should Jesse be granted a full pardon—she was prepared to employ him as her servant.

McCall himself had little to say about his decision, telling reporters that he "would rather have the act speak for itself." Other officials were only slightly more forthcoming. "Pomeroy's was a terrible crime," declared Prison Commissioner Cyrus Adams, "but his has also been a terrible punishment. In view of his age and feebleness and his punishment of nearly forty-one years in solitary confinement, it seemed to me wise, just, and humane to recommend commutation of his sentence." Warden Adams of Charlestown made it clear, however, that Jesse's new liberties were entirely contingent on his good behavior and could be revoked at any time. "It is up to Pomeroy himself how long he enjoys the new privileges," he told a group of reporters. "Should he fail to make good, it will be his fault alone. We will do the best we can for him."

At first, Jesse seemed delighted with the news. The morning after the governor's announcement, a mob of newsmen descended on the prison and were granted permission to interview Pomeroy, who expressed his gratitude "to the Governor, his special committee, my attorney, Edwin I. Weiscopf, and others for this consideration." Speaking in a voice that sounded weirdly shrill and unnatural, as though rusty from years of disuse, Jesse declared his "ambition to live honest and law-abiding and so deserve the added privileges now granted me. I can see that this opportunity to associate with fellow prisoners may lead to further favorable action. I will demonstrate that it is not dangerous for me to mingle with other men.

"God is good," he continued. "I only wish my dear mother were alive to know that one further step has been granted toward my freedom. She hoped to see that day, but she is gone."

Asked if he would pose for some photographs, Jesse responded with an enthusiastic, "Sure!" Throughout the shoot, he appeared to be in a buoyant mood. At one point, two of the cameramen asked him to turn in their direction. "Take it easy, boys," Jesse cheerfully replied, "I can't look both ways at once."

The following day, every daily in Boston featured at least one front-page photo of the "world-famous lifer." In some of these shots, Jesse stands stiffly in a corner of the yard. Wearing his lumpy three-piece suit, a loosely knotted tie, and a round, small-brimmed cap, he looks less like a hardened criminal than an old-time railroad conductor—a holdover (as indeed he was) from the era of Jesse James and the Dalton Gang. In other pictures, he poses awkardly at a roll-top desk. With a pen clutched in his hand and his jacket lapel adorned with an American flag pin, he looks like the world's shabbiest bank manager. Still other pictures are close-ups of his profoundly unappealing face: the disconcerting eyes, the massive jaw, the bristling moustache, and the frowning, lipless mouth. In none of the photos does he look a day younger than sixty-five.

By the time these pictures appeared, however—less than two days after his long-coveted commutation was granted—Jesse's attitude had undergone a confounding shift. When Warden Nathan Allen and a pair of guards showed up at his cell on Friday morning to escort him to his new quarters, they expected to find him waiting impatiently for the transfer, his belongings bundled up and ready to be moved. Instead, Pomeroy was seated at his table, composing a letter on a sheet of lined stationery. Everything in the cell—his books, papers, toilet articles, etc.—was still in its customary place.

"What's going on, Jesse?" asked Allen.

Ignoring the question, Pomeroy continued with his writing. Several moments passed before he set down his pen. Only then did he look up at the warden and say: "I'm staying here."

"What do you mean?" Allen snapped.

"If I can't have a pardon, then I don't want any change in my sentence," Jesse answered. Reaching for the stationery, he handed it to Allen. The warden's eyes narrowed slightly as he read.

It was a letter to Governor McCall, respectfully declining the commutation and repeating Jesse's demand for a full pardon.

"You can't do this, Jesse," Allen said sternly. "The order's been signed."

"I didn't ask for a commutation," Jesse said, "and I don't want it." As far as he was concerned, being released from solitary only made his situation worse. Dismal as it was, his old cell had certain amenities that the newer ones lacked, including running water, its own heating control, and enough space for his personal library. Besides, he had no interest in doing menial chores like the other inmates. "The state has made me a scholar," he grandly proclaimed. His dream, he told Allen, was to get out of prison and become a schoolteacher. Until the governor released him, he intended to stay right where he was.

Allen tried arguing with him, but Pomeroy wouldn't budge. By refusing to obey the governor's edict, Jesse was living up to his legend as Charlestown's most persevering troublemaker, and the press made the most of the story. "POMEROY SPURNS COMMUTATION," the *Post* trumpeted. "REFUSES TO WORK, DEMANDS FULL PARDON, AND WANTS TO TEACH THE YOUNG." As the weekend progressed, the papers ran regular, front-page updates on the battle-of-wills between Jesse and his jailers. Bostonians learned all about Jesse's refusal to march to meals with the other inmates, leave his cell for exercise, perform light work, or attend chapel services on Sunday.

As for Warden Allen, though he was "not disposed to be harsh with the aged prisoner" (as the *Boston Globe* put it), he was compelled "to enforce the rules if he hoped to preserve discipline." On Sunday evening, he presented Pomeroy with an ultimatum. If Jesse was not ready to accept his new sentence by the following day, he would receive the same punishment as any other insubordinate prisoner—*i.e,* he would be placed in a "detention cell" with no light, a wooden plank to sleep on, and a diet of bread and water.

At around 8:30 the next morning—Monday, January 29—Allen and his deputy, William Hendry, arrived at Jesse's cell and found him seated on the edge of his bunk.

After bidding Pomeroy good morning, the warden asked if he had "thought over the matter we discussed last night?"

"Yes," Jesse answered.

"And have you made up your mind to obey the orders of the governor and the rules and regulations of the prison?"

"No," Jesse said calmly.

The old man's cool obstinacy made Allen's temper flare. "I order you now," he commanded, "to go into the yard this morning with the other men. Will you go?"

"No, sir," Pomeroy said. "I won't."

"Then you do not propose to obey the rules under the new sentence?" Allen said.

"No."

Tightening his lips, Allen turned and nodded to Deputy Warden Hendry, who immediately stepped to the bunk, grabbed Pomeroy by one arm, pulled him to his feet, and marched him to the Fort Russell section of the prison, where Jesse was shut up in a punishment cell.

As it happened, he remained there for only twenty-four hours. On Monday afternoon, Warden Allen traveled to the State House to consult with the governor and other officials. In the end, they agreed that there was no sense in punishing Jesse. The whole point of the governor's commutation was to defuse the accusations that the state's treatment of Pomeroy was horribly inhumane. To keep him in prolonged detention would only make the Massachusetts prison system seem even more brutal than before. By 8:30 the following morning, Jesse was back in Cherry Hill.

"Pomeroy Wins Out in Strike," reported the *Boston Globe*. Still, his triumph wasn't entirely without its costs. On Tuesday morning, Warden Allen announced that there would "be no more special bulletins from the prison about Pomeroy." Jesse may have won the right to remain in his old cell, but he had lost something vitally important to him—the publicity that not only fed his pathological egotism but generated support for his still-hoped-for pardon.

At some point, he clearly recognized that he had won a Pyrrhic victory. Jesse's name would not appear in the newspapers for another few months. And when it finally did, it would be in an article headlined: "JESSE POMEROY GOES TO WORK. Notorious 'Lifer' Decides to Accept Commutation of Solitary Confinement."

According to the story, on the evening of Saturday, April 30, 1917—exactly three months after he had been released from detention and allowed to return to his old cell—Jesse suddenly announced that he was prepared to accept the change in his sentence. At 10:30 the following morning, he attended chapel with the other men. Later that afternoon (as the paper reported), "for the first time in more than 40 years [he] mingled with his fellow convicts in the main yard of the state prison" and "listened to the strains of the prison band."

Jesse, the story went on to say, would "be assigned the task of spading up soil in the prison yard, where a potato patch will be started." Prison officials, however, did not expect the old man to be especially productive, since "his muscles, practically atrophied after years of solitary confinement, will be of little use on the planting line."

47

I'm thinking of you,
  Yes, I'm thinking,
As New Year's comes along—
  Two score, nineteen hundred—
Let's heed its happy song;
While golden Hope may spread
  A rainbow o'er the ways;
I'm thinking of you,
  Ever thinking,
  As in those early Days.
              —Jesse Pomeroy, "I Am Thinking of You"

In his celebrated history of the 1920s, *Only Yesterday*, Frederick Lewis Allen characterizes that colorful decade as the "Ballyhoo Years"—an era when "millions of men and women turned their attention, their talk, and their emotional interest upon a series of tremendous trifles," from flagpole-sitting to the mahjong craze to the death of Rudolph Valentino. Sporadically throughout the twenties, news items about Jesse Pomeroy would appear in the press—and, in keeping with the giddy spirit of the times, they tended to deal with the most frivolous subjects.

On Tuesday, February 3, 1920, for example, newspapers around the country carried stories about Pomeroy's triumphant appearance in Charlestown's second annual minstrel show. The show had taken place the previous evening in the prison chapel before a wildly enthusiastic crowd of inmates and visitors (whose number included some of the city's most prominent men). The chapel had been decked out for the occasion with red-and-blue bunting, American flags, and a brilliant display of yellow-and-white artificial chrysanthemums. Beginning at 7:00 P.M., the audience—which filled every seat on the chapel floor, the auditorium, and the balcony—was treated to two and half hours of music, comedy, and dance by a cast of nearly fifty cons in checkered coats, white trousers, red neckties, and blackface. Highlights included Jack Mulhall's toe-tapping rendition of "I Used to Call Her Baby," Edward Washington's juggling act, Walter Furness's harmonica playing, Sylvester Parham and Harry Thornton's performance of the "Darktown Strutter's Ball," and a "plantation breakdown" by Jack McGuffin.

The greatest applause, however, was reserved for Jesse Pomeroy, who recited, wholly from memory, an original, thirteen-stanza poem entitled "Then and Now in Charlestown." Dressed in a Prince Albert coat, white duck trousers, white gloves, and black shoes, Jesse—his face blackened with burnt cork—appeared nervous as a schoolboy as he began his recitation:

> "Good friends, to you would we recite
> A fascinating lay tonight.
> 'Tis of a place of great reknown
> At Prison Point, in Charlestown.
> Its walls of gray and ramparts high
> Look quite exclusive to the eye:
> But that's a case where looks deceive,
> You can get in, but never leave."

Before long, however, he became fully relaxed. By the time he reached the end of his hundred-line poem, he was declaiming with all the vivacity of a practiced public orator:

> "Kind Friends, the palm is but your due,
> For sympathy, with kindness true;
> For all you've done to ease the load
> Our gratitude this eve has showed.
> To all who make our life so bright
> May Heaven bless you—and good night."

So wildly did the audience respond to his perfomance that Jesse was obliged to return to the footlights for a curtain call. At first, their cheers seemed to render him speechless. He quickly regained his composure, however, and—after waiting for the

noise to subside—said: "I wish to thank you for your apprecia-
tion of my efforts to entertain you. This is the first time in sixty
years I have received public applause. I want to thank the administration heads for their kindness and courtesy to me."

Then, with a little bow to his fans, he exited the stage.

Jesse had, in fact, been churning out poetry for years. Since
1915, he had been a frequent contributor to *The Mentor,* a monthly
literary magazine produced by the inmates of Charlestown and
devoted (in the words of its credo) "to the interest of that great
body of men who, while in prison, are earnestly seeking for a
way out into the light of Reason, up the Path of Courage, to
Success." Like his thirteen-stanza ode to Charlestown—recited to
such acclaim at the minstrel show—his pieces for *The Mentor*
were characterized by formal clumsiness, mawkish sentimentality, banal language, and utterly vapid subject matter.

Nevertheless, Jesse took a deep pride in his writing abilities.
At the time of the minstrel show, he was already sixty years old, a
half-blind old man who answered to the nickname of "Grandpa"
and had been behind bars for nearly half a century. His insipid
verse and equally trite little essays (on subjects like "How I
Learned Spanish" and "Some Momentous Events in History")
served an important function in his appallingly barren existence.
They allowed him to believe that his life hadn't been utterly
wasted, that he had accomplished something worthwhile—"a
good education by my own effort" (as he put it). When one of his
compositions, a hundred-word essay titled "How to Make Good
in Prison," won a Christmas competition sponsored by a publication called *The Volunteers' Gazette,* he proudly trumpeted the
news to his fellow inmates. (He was especially gratified by
the monetary part of the prize—$1.00 in cash—describing it as
"the first money earned by any of my writings.") Completely de-
tached from reality, he regarded himself as a man of substantial
intellectual achievement and real artistic talent.

In January 1920, he collected his finest literary efforts and—
reportedly with the financial assistance of "old friends from his
boyhood days"—arranged for their private publication. Entitled
*Selections from the Writings of Jesse Harding Pomeroy, Life Prisoner
since 1874,* the resulting volume featured a formal frontispiece
portrait of the author and thirty-one compositions in both poetry

and prose on such stimulating subjects as "Mother's Day," "The Reading of Books," and "My First Movie Show." A characteristic piece of verse (it is impossible to reprint the best of the bunch, since they are all more-or-less equally inept) is "An Industrial Muse," a rapturous ode to the products manufactured in the prison shops. A typical stanza runs as follows:

> And Hosiery, both short and long,
> With underwear, so neat and strong;
> Our Brushes too
> Of all sorts view;
> And Mattresses for modest sum,
> With wares shaped from Aluminum.

Jesse's book elicited the kind of reaction that Samuel Johnson famously ascribed to the sight of a dog walking on its hind legs ("It is not done well, but you are surprised to find it done at all"). Because of the author's notoriety, the book attracted a certain amount of fascinated attention. A popular monthly magazine of the time, *The Survey*, described it as "a book of almost unique interest"—but only because it had been written by the most infamous life-prisoner in U.S. history. As for the writings themselves, the reviewer's judgment was brutal (if accurate). Pomeroy's poetry and prose only served to prove that he "could not acquire, even in the concentration of his cell, any real mental ability; there is nothing in his book of intrinsic merit."

Jesse's writing—or at any rate, a vague approximation of it— made the news again the following year, when *The Boston Telegram* advertised its forthcoming serial publication of "Pomeroy's own story," *Buried Alive*. The front-page, two-column announcement, which ran on June 27, 1921, resounded with the portentous tones of a Gothic melodrama:

> Out of the grim dungeon that is Cell 25, Cherry Hill, Charlestown State Prison, comes the tale of the man who is known all over the country, whose name is a by-word, whose fate has been held up as a warning to evil-doers for 46 years.

> Jesse Pomeroy tells his own story of a lifetime within stone walls.
>
> It is such a story as has never been written before. It is such a story as will never be written again, unless the world reverts to barbarism.
>
> The story of his life, ground out by the "lifer" in his cell after he had made himself a master of English by years of study, is an arraignment of the penal methods of civilization so bitter as to appear incredible at first glance.

Not content with merely piquing the reader's interest with the promise of a sensational exposé, the announcement went on to compare Jesse to François Villon, Victor Hugo, Charles Dickens, Oscar Wilde, and other "masters of diction [who] have attempted to paint the horrors of prison life for the world to read."

The first installment of *Buried Alive* appeared on page one of the June 28 edition of the *Telegram*. Though far from masterful, the piece was written in a style conspicuously more polished than Jesse's clumsy contributions to *The Mentor*. Indeed, anyone familiar with Jesse's jailhouse publications would have had good reason to be suspicious of the absolute originality of the supposed autobiography. Unsurprisingly, by the time the third installment appeared, its ostensible author had issued a statement that he had "never written such a story or authorized its publication."

Buried Alive turned out to be a fraud, perpetrated by a journalist named Walter C. Mahan, who had assembled it out of various newspaper accounts dating back to the 1870s. Far from being a shocking new exposé, it was nothing but a cobbled-together rehash. It did, however, demonstrate something significant about Jesse Pomeroy—that in 1921, forty-seven years after his arrest, he was still famous enough to be front-page news.

Intermittently throughout the remainder of the decade, stories about Jesse continued to pop up in the nation's press. One of the papers that covered his case most diligently was the *New York Times*. In November 1923, the *Times*—along with various Boston dailies—reported that, like millions of his fellow countrymen in those high-flying days, Pomeroy was playing the stock market. With a bit of money inherited from his mother's estate,

Jesse had purchased shares in a company called Moon Motors through a State Street brokerage house.

"Naturally, he has no stock ticker in his cell," Warden William Hendry hastened to assure reporters. "Neither does he telephone his orders. It is all done by mail between Jesse and the brokerage house." According to the warden, Jesse was "ahead of the game," having earned dividends of more than $60 on his $300 investment.

Five months later—in April 1924—Jesse reached his fiftieth consecutive year behind bars, an event that was widely noted in the national press and that provoked yet another round of impassioned calls for his pardon. No less a figure than Clarence Darrow—who had defended the most notorious juvenile thrill-killers of his own era, Leopold and Loeb—publicly denounced the State of Massachusetts for having kept Pomeroy in prison for a half century. "It is an outrage," Darrow declared. "I have often thought of leading a rescue party into Massachusetts and attempting to free the man."

On the opposite side were those like Boston socialite Alice Stone Blackwell, who continued to regard the shambling, half-blind sixty-five-year-old prisoner as a potential menace to society. In a letter to the *Boston Herald*, published in March, 1925, Miss Blackwell insisted that "It would be mistaken kindness to pardon Jesse Pomeroy. Many of your readers are too young to remember the crimes for which he was sentenced to life imprisonment. He deliberately tortured several children to death. The case was much worse than that of Leopold and Loeb. He would have been put to death but for his youth—he was 17 at the time, if I remember correctly—and but for a belief that he had an abnormal mental makeup for which he was not responsible. It is this latter fact that makes it unfitting to release him.

"It is reported that after he had been for some years in prison, he was allowed the companionship of a kitten in his cell. He skinned the kitten alive."

Miss Blackwell's claim about the kitten (one of several widely circulated, though wholly apocryphal, legends that had sprung up around Pomeroy and reflected his status as a semimythical fiend) drew a furious response from Jesse. He immediately retained a lawyer named Ira Dudley Farquhar who—claiming that his client's "reputation had been damaged"—filed a $5,000 libel suit against the elderly socialite. The case eventually came to trial in January 1928, and ended in a moral victory for the plaintiff, who was awarded a verdict of one dollar in damages. From his cell, Jesse let it be known that the money meant nothing to him. "The pleasure of winning the verdict in my suit," he declared in a statement to the press, "is satisfaction enough."

A fascinating glimpse of Jesse during the decade of the twenties was provided by an unusually literate ex-convict named Victor Nelson. Unlike Pomeroy, Nelson really did possess a flair for writing and eventually produced a book called *Prison Days and Nights,* published to widespread acclaim by the Boston house of Little, Brown, and Company.

Born to Swedish immigrant parents in 1898, Nelson—a brilliant but deeply troubled young man—landed in reform school at the age of fifteen. In October 1920, he was arrested in Roxbury on a charge of armed robbery and sentenced to three to five years in the Massachusetts State Prison. The following May, he made a spectacular escape and remained at large for the next four months. After attending a lecture by Thomas Mott Osborne—former warden of Sing Sing and an ardent champion of prison reform—Nelson made himself known to the older man, who persuaded the young fugitive to surrender. Nelson was returned to the Massachusetts State Prison, where he spent the next two years. It was during his term in Charlestown that he became intimately acquainted with the "world-famous lifer."

On his very first afternoon in Charlestown, Nelson—after receiving his shabby gray uniform—wandered out into the icy yard, where he was immediately accosted by "a short, thickset man with one blind eye and a scraggly moustache."

"Hello, lad," said the old man. "I'm Jesse Pomeroy. They call me 'Grandpa.' "

Nelson was struck by the self-important air of the old-timer, who looked (as he later wrote) "as proud of himself and his sordid fame as if he were a prince of men."

Born and raised in Boston, Nelson had been hearing tales about the infamous "boy fiend" all his life. "Sure," he said. "I know all about you."

At this remark, Jesse "straightened his shoulders and beamed with delight." The "way in which he responded to my recognition of his notoriety—or fame, as he regarded his prominence in the world—astounded me," wrote Nelson. "I was aghast at the lack of shame or consciousness of guilt the old man showed."

As Nelson quickly learned, this way of introducing himself to new arrivals was habitual with Pomeroy. As the years progressed, however, the awed reactions Jesse was accustomed to receiving began to fade. Nelson vividly recalled one of his final glimpses of Pomeroy. It occurred on a raw December afternoon in 1923. A pair of young newcomers, recently sentenced to Charlestown for rolling drunks, were lounging in the prison yard when—"in accordance with his habit"—Jesse "approached them and introduced himself" as he had to Nelson.

"To Pomeroy's chagrin and amazement," Nelson later recalled, the young men were profoundly unimpressed.

"Oh yeah?" snorted one, "Who the hell is Jesse Pomeroy and what's your racket? We never heard of you."

This sneering rebuff was a devastating blow to Jesse's vanity. "It was pitiful to see the crestfallen face of the old aristocrat whose claim to stardom in his own domain had been so ruthlessly belittled," Nelson wrote.

Mortified and deflated, Jesse "lowered his head, turned on his heels, and slunk away—a dethroned monarch among the minnows."

48

I am going to keep trying for my freedom. Only death will stop me.
—Jesse Pomeroy, August 3, 1929

Though Jesse Pomeroy's name no longer inspired fear (or even recognition) in the younger generation of criminals, the world at large had not forgotten him. That fact was made strikingly clear in the summer of 1929, when stories about the "most remarkable convict in the world" appeared in countless newspapers throughout the country. The occasion was his transfer to the prison farm at Bridgewater. After more than half a century inside the grim fortress of Charlestown, Jesse Pomeroy was about to get his first glimpse of the modern world.

Though he had been struggling to get out of Charlestown for decades, the transfer was not his idea. On the contrary, he vigorously protested the move. And there were some who sympathized with Jesse's desire to stay put. "Old people cling tenaciously to their homes, to every article of furniture, every valueless knick-knack, every creaking floorboard," observed a writer for the *Worcester Telegram* in a widely reprinted editorial. "Thus they maintain their identity in a world that has forgotten them. Transplant them and they wither and die. Jesse Pomeroy's original crime is probably to him no more than the half-remembered dream of some former existence. But his Charlestown cell is his life, vivid to him through a hundred little habits of the daily round. One need not descend to pathos to wish that he might be permitted to die where he has lived—and where all of us want to die—at home."

But cell space was at a premium at Charlestown, and Jesse had become what one official described as a "drone." Old, infirm, with an enormous inguinal hernia and failing eyesight, he was perceived by officials as little more than deadwood. By placing him in the airier, far more pleasant surroundings of Bridgewater, they could presumably perform a humanitarian act, while freeing up his cell for more practical uses—for criminals who represented a far more serious threat than a half-blind, increasingly disabled seventy-one-year-old.

And so on August 1, 1929, Jesse was compelled to pack up his belongings and leave his barred and cloistered home. Physically, he was a radically different figure from the smooth-shaven adolescent he had been when he first entered Charlestown: a shambling, hollow-cheeked, balding old man. But his temperament hadn't undergone much of a change. According to one reporter who had known him for more than thirty years, the younger Pomeroy had been "an unlikable, harsh, sullen fellow. He was stubborn and unruly from the first. And when he left prison today, he was just about the same singular figure."

When Warden Hogsett came by to wish him good luck, Jesse refused to say a word or shake the warden's hand. Dressed in a rumpled business suit, his face half-hidden by a floppy, checkered golf cap, he shuffled out into the yard, stepped inside a waiting automobile, and was whisked through the gates of the prison, while spectators gawked, newsmen scribbled notes, and a horde of cameramen snapped photos.

His one-hour-and-forty-three-minute ride was tracked by a caravan of reporters. The following day, newspapers from Maine to California ran major stories on Jesse's "remarkable journey"— "probably among the most unusual ever taken by man," as one newsman proclaimed. Headline after headline trumpeted his supposedly wonderstruck reaction to a world that had "changed more in the last 50 years than in the preceding 500." "POMEROY HELD ALMOST SPEECHLESS AS HE SEES FOR FIRST TIME TWENTIETH-CENTURY INVENTIONS." "POMEROY AWED BY WONDERS SEEN ON RIDE TO PRISON FARM." "POMEROY MARVELS AT MODERN PROGRESS." "POMEROY AMAZED AT MODERN WORLD."

According to all these accounts, every sight Jesse glimpsed had filled him with rapt fascination—an airplane, a steam roller, an elevated train, a string of high-tension power lines. "Where have all the horses gone?" he plaintively asked at one point. At another, his car stopped at Randolph, where one of his guards ran into a drugstore and bought Jesse a bottle of ginger ale and a vanilla ice cream cone—the first time the old man had ever tasted such treats. The portrait that emerges from almost every one of these newspaper stories is of a man almost stupefied by awe—"struck dumb, eyes bulging from his head, mouth agape."

In truth, there was no real way of knowing how Jesse reacted to his trip, since—apart from his question about the horses and a favorable word about the ginger ale—he said almost nothing during the drive. Nor (in spite of the colorful descriptions of his bulging eyes and gaping mouth) did his expression betray much excitement. Only one journalist, a writer for the *Waterbury American*, acknowledged this fact, offering a perspective that— though considerably less dramatic than the countless stories comparing Jesse to a "modern Rip Van Winkle"—was probably closer to the truth:

> The story of the automobile ride of the famous "lifer," Jesse H. Pomeroy . . . is not a story of the real impressions upon the mind of Pomeroy but of the imagination of writers.
>
> This prison inmate who began his life sentence at 17 years of age and spent 41 years of his prison life in solitary confinement, is a deadened creature gazing with lusterless eyes upon a world that means nothing to him. He does not show the quick, excited reaction to an amazingly progressing world that an alert boy would evidence. It is notable that the newspaper reports do not quote any animated conversation from him with comments upon automobiles, high tension wires, aeroplanes, and all the other things of the modern world upon which his eyes were gazing for the first time.
>
> Immediately the reporter thinks, as the reader thinks, "I wonder how this new world would appear to me if I were suddenly to gaze upon it for the first time after being removed from it for 50 years?" The answer to that speculation does not give the correct answer to what the effect would be upon a mind like Pomeroy. . . . Pomeroy is not a normal human being. That he should look upon whatever the world had to show with dullness of

perception is to be expected. What the world has been doing has meant nothing to him, even though he might have read about it. Why should he be stirred at reading that radios had been invented or that motor cars capable of speeding a man along paved highways at 50 miles an hour had supplanted horses? He could not use them. Nor is he to be able to enjoy them even now that he has gazed upon them in this change in his status. He is still a prisoner. And if he were to be released, he would not know what to do with life. Death would probably come to him all the more quickly, as it usually does to those who have been released after years of prison life.

For the first few days after his arrival at the prison farm, Jesse—still deeply resentful over his forced removal from Charlestown—maintained an obstinate silence. When reporters interviewed Bridgewater's superintendent, Henry G. Strann—who had been introduced to Pomeroy several years earlier during a visit to the state prison—Strann remarked: "He was surly, reticent, and unsmiling then, and he is surly, reticent, and unsmiling now. As far as I know he has told no one whether he likes this place or not. He only answers when he feels like it."

Gradually, Jesse seemed to adjust to his new circumstances. One year later, however, in June, 1930, he was back in the headlines after a guard discovered a cache of getaway tools—a hand drill, a crude saw, several pieces of heavy wire, a screwdriver, and a short length of bent iron—stashed in his room. Not that Superintendent Strann or anyone else at Bridgewater seriously believed that the incapacitated seventy-one-year-old man was capable of escaping.

"He would have collapsed after hobbling for half a mile," a prison doctor told reporters.

"He just didn't want Lindbergh hogging all the news," said Strann. "You know, Jesse hasn't had much publicity since he was compelled to leave the state prison, and he doesn't like an environment that keeps him out of the newspapers."

Two years later, on September 29, 1932—exactly two months shy of his seventy-third birthday—Jesse Harding

Pomeroy died of coronary heart disease at the Bridgewater prison farm.

His passing was universally unlamented. "If one were to seek for the most friendless man in the world," the *Springfield Republican* noted, "Jesse Pomeroy would have been the man finally designated."

"He was a psychopath," the *New York Times* said flatly.

Perhaps the bitterest obituary notice appeared in the October 2, 1932, edition of the *Boston Sunday Globe*. Written by a reporter named Louis Lyons, the piece was an outpouring of unmitigated bile, denouncing Pomeroy as a "mean, scheming criminal with an inflated idea of his own importance" and heaping scorn on the "bleeding hearts" who had expended years of misplaced sympathy on him. "His was the greatest case of miscarriage of sentiment in the annals of American crime. . . . There was nothing in his personality to commend him to the sympathy that was slobbered over him in lugubrious gobs of maudlin sentiment year after year."

In accordance with Jesse's final wishes, his body was cremated. Having already been entombed for what must have seemed like an eternity, he had no desire to be buried again.

Fifty-eight years after he was first jailed for the most heinous crimes ever committed by a juvenile, Jesse Harding Pomeroy was free at last.